The Sensory-Sensitive Child

III

Karen A. Smith, Ph.D.

Karen R. Gouze, Ph.D.

The Sensory-Sensitive Child

Practical Solutions for

Out-of-Bounds Behavior

Collins

An Imprint of HarperCollinsPublishers

Designed by JoAnne Metsch

The Library of Congress has catalogued the hardcover edition as follows:

Library of Congress Cataloging-in-Publication Data

Smith, Karen A. (Karen Ann), 1957–
    The sensory-sensitive child : practical solutions for out-of-bounds behavior / Karen A. Smith and Karen R. Gouze.
        p. cm.
    ISBN 0-06-052717-X (hc)
    1. Behavior disorders in children—Treatment.   2. Problem children—Psychology.
I. Gouze, Karen R.   II. Title.

RJ506.B44S64 2004
618.92'8914—dc22

                                                            2003056767

ISBN: 0-06-052718-8 (pbk.)

07 08 09 ❖/RRD 10 9 8

For our children

Acknowledgments

IIIIIIIIIIIIIIIIIIIIIIIIIIIIIIIIIIIIIIIIIIIIIIIIIIIIIIIIIIIIIIIIIIIIIIIIIIIIIIIIIIII

MANY PEOPLE have helped us make this book happen. We owe the greatest thanks to the children and parents who have been willing to share their stories in these pages. Their determination and resilience in the face of misunderstanding are the heart of this book. We would also like to thank our agent, Carole Mann, who understood this project from the beginning and made it possible for this story to be told. Our editor, Toni Sciarra, guided us along an unfamiliar path through the world of publishing with infinite patience and good humor. She achieved the perfect balance between leading us and letting us find our own way. Our readers—Molly Efland, Ann Kohler, Anita Lumpkin-Barnett, and Frank Zelko, Ph.D.—read portions of the manuscript. Crystal DeVito, Ph.D., Mimi Elliott-Gower, Joyce Hopkins, Ph.D., John Lavigne, Ph.D., Rose Mary Martin, OTR, Kris Razma, OTR, and Lizanne Thomas read every word, asked questions, made suggestions, and kept us moving in the right direction. Without their thoughtfulness and expertise we would have written a less accurate, less helpful, and certainly less interesting book. Many friends, colleagues, and family members learned exactly how often and in what tone of voice to ask about our progress. Their enthusiastic encouragement supported us every step of the way.

KAREN S. WRITES:

At the beginning of the idea for this book, when I first knew I had a story I wanted to tell, Pat Priest, Amy and Allen Flurry, and Richard Simon helped me get started. *Thank you! Because you believed in me as a writer, I have become one.* And thanks to Katherine and Bertis, who gave me a place of my own for as long as I needed it. *Your shelter extends far beyond the walls of that room.*

To my parents, Harold and Sarah Smith, who have been pleasantly surprised by me for years, thank you for inspiring me to always try a bit harder. As Evan likes to say, "Without you, there would be no me." *This story is yours, as well.*

To my husband, John, who listened carefully, waited patiently, cheered wholeheartedly, and stood in for me without complaint for a very long while, sufficient thanks cannot be spoken. *You have given me my dream.*

To my children—Evan, who truly is my hero, and Gemma, whose spirit is my guide—thank you for the joy, the love, and the grace you shower down on me every day. *I'm yours.*

KAREN G. WRITES:

To my parents, Robert and Grace Gouze, who have provided a lifetime of unconditional love and unwavering support . . . who have always known when to talk and when to listen, *thank you.*

To my children—

Sarah—who welcomed me into her world as a little girl and who is the best big sister a kid could have. *Your simple grace and sparkling enthusiasm made motherhood irresistible.*

Ben—without whom there would be no book. *Your generosity of time and spirit, your honesty, and your unwavering desire to tell this story have kept me going. You are an amazing young man.*

Kate—the real writer in the family. *Your love, your support, and your beautiful voice have been like a steady light throughout this process. You have been my biggest fan.*

To my husband, Norman, without whom this book would be very different. *For twenty years you have talked with me about life and love, our parents and our children, my joys and my struggles. Your love has been constant and complete. There are no words to thank you.*

Contents

///////////////////////

Why We Wrote This Book

||||||||||||||||||||||||||||||||||||||||||||||||||||||||||||

THIS BOOK is the story of children whose senses have failed them. These children do things that baffle their teachers, try the patience of their parents, and disappoint themselves. They refuse to cooperate with the simplest requests. They come across as different, awkward, or preoccupied. They may appear frustrated, anxious, or just out of sorts. This is the story of children who are in trouble despite their best intentions.

It is a story we stumbled upon. As two mothers, friends, therapists, and professors of clinical psychology, we had been working with children and their families for almost two decades. However, it was our own sons—Ben, now 15, and Evan, now 9—who caused us to reexamine our core beliefs about the problems that parents of young children had been describing to us for years. We thought we knew how to manage difficult behavior until we found ourselves living with two boys who didn't fit the models from which we had been operating. They caught us by surprise. We were not prepared for what they had to teach us. They laid markers along a path that required us to look beyond the traditional teachings of our discipline to a broader view of the underlying causes of problematic behavior in children.

Through our experiences with Ben and Evan and many other children in our practices, we became convinced that the standard diagnostic labels historically attached to children who are difficult to get along with do not always capture the complexity and nuance of their perplexing behavior. Teachers, psychologists, and parents frequently blame the problem on the child, labeling him as stubborn, hyperactive, or just downright ornery. Others are more benevolent, joking that he is a "horse of a different color." Over time, it becomes hard for him not to think of himself as a troublemaker or an oddball.

We believe that most uncooperative children don't want to cause trouble. They want to please their parents. They want to succeed, but for reasons little understood by them or by the adults around them, they frequently fail. We believe that a significant number of these children are in trouble because they are having difficulty processing sensory information. They avoid and resist seemingly simple everyday tasks because they cannot manage the smells, tastes, sounds, textures, and motion of their everyday lives. This book is about how we came to understand these difficulties in our sons and in many of the children who are brought to our offices by parents in need of help.

We offer readers sensory solutions to behavior that might best be described as out-of-bounds or poorly regulated. This approach is based on sensory integration theory, the life work of the late occupational therapist and educational psychologist Jean Ayres. According to Ayres, dysfunctional sensory processing can contribute to a wide range of behavioral, academic, and emotional problems. Although her theory has not yet been validated from a scientific point of view, it is compatible with and complementary to several well-established bodies of psychological research on child development, brain-behavior relationships, and emotion regulation.

We have come to see that a sensory-based approach to out-of-bounds behavior can be helpful to children who have been given a variety of diagnoses, including oppositional defiant disorder, attention deficit hyperactivity disorder, pervasive developmental disorder, and some anxiety disorders. It also offers promise for many children without a specific psychiatric diagnosis. It is a nonblaming approach based on the belief that children—especially young children—want approval. To say that they want to misbehave or that they enjoy negative attention is misguided. They do not want to be in trouble. In *The Explosive Child*, author Ross Greene says it clearly: *Children do well if they can.* It sounds self-evident to us now, but we didn't always believe this. It was our own sons who guided us to the realization that kids don't say *no* for no reason.

We wrote this book wearing an assortment of hats. As mothers, we have shared our personal thoughts, feelings, and experiences. We cannot tell our own stories objectively; however, we have tried to tell them accurately and honestly so that other parents may recognize themselves and their children in our examples. Many parents express feelings of great relief when they hear us describe experiences that they assumed were uniquely theirs. For this reason, it is our hope that authenticity is worth the sacrifice of objectivity in our personal narratives.

As psychologists, we have written this book from both a clinical and a scholarly perspective. Scientific knowledge advances through a dynamic exchange between research and practice. Clinical observations almost always come first: teachers, therapists, physicians, and parents notice an unusual behavior and begin experimenting with different responses to it. Over time, a body of anecdotal or observational data begins to accumulate. At some point, this information is organized into a theory or a proposed explanation for the phenomenon. The theory is then tested through rigorous scientific research, and the results of these studies are used to modify and refine the theory. Thus, what we know is always changing.

Ayres's ideas about sensory integration grew out of her clinical work with brain-damaged children. By all descriptions, she was a brilliant clinician, and she used her clinical experiences to formulate ideas about the neurobiological foundation of the relationship between sensory processing and behavior. She developed her theory long before the Decade of the Brain (the 1990s), but she intuitively made a lot of good guesses. She expected that the theory of sensory integration would change over time. In 1979, she wrote: "Lacking a universally accepted conceptual framework of how the brain works as a whole, this theory has been constructed to provide a unifying concept for heuristic purposes. It is a provisional theory with continued modifications anticipated as research and clinical knowledge help it to evolve."

We are writing this book more than twenty years later. Ideas about brain-behavior relationships are being rapidly reformulated and there is a consensus among researchers that child development research must begin to incorporate knowledge from many disciplines, including biology, neurology, psychology, and education. In light of what is being discovered about the brain and its workings, the time seems ideal for the careful reconsideration of Ayres's ideas about the contribution of the senses to behavior. We see many exciting connections between her theory and scientifically solid areas of investigation in the fields of child development and developmental psychopathology.

As therapists, we have many stories to share about children with a wide range of problems who have been helped by a sensory-based treatment approach. Rarely is sensory dysregulation the only problem a child is experiencing—it is usually part of a bigger picture. In fact, it may be a missing link in the successful treatment of many unhappy, out-of-bounds children. Understanding a child's sensory processing limitations can lead to dramatic changes in the quality of his school and family life. It is often the mismatch between a child's sensory processing abilities and the sensory demands of his immediate environment that is the key to understanding his behavior. When parents learn to recognize the problems associated with sensory dysregulation, they are able to make sense of behavior that once seemed incomprehensible. They can then analyze a problematic situation from a sensory perspective and arrange the environment accordingly so that the child's sensory needs are respected and accommodated. This makes for a happier child, a more harmonious family, and a more cooperative classroom!

In this book, we offer an in-depth look at how one family discovered a child's sensory sensitivities, a thorough discussion of how sensory processing affects behavior in general, and a guide to how you and your child can cope with his specific sensory-based difficulties.

The Prologue and Epilogue tell the personal story of Karen S. and her son, Evan, with a final note from Karen G.'s son, Ben. In Part One, we discuss sensory integration theory and its relationship to a range of problematic behaviors. Chapters One and Two describe the processes of sensory integration and explain how sensory processing problems can interfere with your child's daily functioning. Chapter Three is a discussion of the possible connections between sensory processing problems and psychiatric diagnoses. In Chapter Four, we explain step-by-step how to analyze your child's behavior by viewing it through a sensory lens.

In Part Two we discuss specific issues related to living with a child with inefficient sensory processing. In Chapter Five, we address the relationship between your child's nervous system and his sensory integration difficulties. Chapters Six through Nine illustrate how viewing your child through the sensory lens can help him succeed at home, at school, and in his friendships. Our commentary in these chapters is enlivened by Karen G.'s son, Ben, who offers a teenager's perspective on the challenges of living with sensory sensitivities. Finally, Chapter Ten summarizes the current state of scientific knowledge about sensory integration and tells readers what they can and cannot reasonably expect from a sensory-based approach to out-of-bounds behavior.

We believe that many children can be helped by the approach described in this book. By highlighting the role of the senses in everyday behavior, we illustrate how behavioral and emotional problems may be related to poorly regulated sensory processing. This way of thinking requires that we move away from diagnostic oversimplification toward a more complex understanding of why some children behave as they do. It requires that we move beyond punitive parenting practices to a more empathic, respectful approach to child rearing based on the belief that children do well if they can. When this happens—when adults change their core beliefs about children's intentions—then it becomes possible to understand and respond differently to the problems children are experiencing.

It is our hope that after you read this book you will see your child's behavior through a sensory lens. This new understanding and the changes it will bring to your family will launch your child on a happier, more successful course in life.

—*K. S. & K. G.*

||||||||||||||||||||||||||||||||||||||||||||||||||||||||||||||||||||||||||||||||||||

Coming to Our Senses:
One Mother's Story

*You're walking . . . and you don't always realize it, but you're
always falling. With each step . . . you fall. You fall forward a
short way and then catch yourself. Over and over . . . you
keep falling and catching yourself falling. And this is how
you are walking and falling at the same time.*

— LAURIE ANDERSON
United States Live

WHEN DID I first realize that we were in trouble, Evan
and I? It's hard to say. There were clues, but I didn't
see them. More to the point, I didn't recognize them,
even though I stared hard at them on a few occasions. Looking back, I
can see the clues that I missed. For several years they drifted in and out
of my consciousness like fragments of a melody, not quite a song that
could be named or sung.

But when did I know—really know for sure—that something was
wrong?

It could have been the time I had to wrestle Evan to the ground to
get him off the swings at the end of his preschool picnic. I was the only
mother scuffling with her child on the playground that pleasant spring
evening, the only parent who couldn't persuade her 3-year-old that it
was time to go home. As I struggled to take charge of the situation, to
control my temper, to move him toward the car, I tried not to think
about how we must have looked. I tried to convince myself that there
was no reason for me, the psychologist who had trained the preschool

staff in behavior management techniques, to be embarrassed about being caught in a clinch with my son.

Get over it, I told myself. *Every parent has these moments. Tonight it's your turn to look foolish; next time it will be someone else's.* I tried to believe that this was an experience that every parent has. Never mind that it felt different somehow.

Maybe it was the day in the grocery store when I heard a tired mother nagging her child incessantly, telling him what to do and what not to do up and down every aisle. *Don't touch that. Stay with me. No, you can't have Cocoa Puffs. If you don't follow directions, you'll have to ride in the cart. Stop running. Give that to me. Come back here.*

The voice was mine, and I couldn't stand listening to it. I sounded as demoralized as the parents I saw in my practice. I looked around self-consciously and hoped no one I knew was within earshot. What was going on? Why couldn't I ease up? Right there in the cereal aisle I resolved to be less critical, more patient, less controlling, more relaxed. *What kind of child psychologist can't get her own child to behave?* I asked myself. *Of all people, I should be able to do this.* Why was it so hard?

The enlightening moment might have been the next fall at Evan's first preschool conference. After a few preliminary remarks, his teacher announced that Evan was the 4-year-old in her class she was most concerned about. According to her, he was always testing the limits, pushing against her, defying the rules of the group and the structure of the classroom.

I knew this about Evan. I flashed on a memory of a visit I'd made to his last preschool. It was the winter holiday party and the teacher was reading a story to the children, who were all seated in a circle around her. All except Evan, that is. I looked around the crowded room and found him sitting by the Christmas tree eating Cheerios off of one of the ornaments the children had made. I told him to join the group. He refused. I told him he was missing the story. He kept crunching and ignored me. *Oh well,* I thought. His teacher didn't seem to mind that he was excluding himself.

But *this* teacher minded. Still, I wasn't sure what her point was. "Do you think it's a serious problem?" I asked. She looked at me gravely. "Oh yes," she said.

Oh yes? I wasn't prepared for that answer. As the little wooden gate of the preschool closed behind me, I started to cry. All the way home I tried to make sense of what she had said. I didn't want to believe her, but I couldn't ignore her, either. A lot of things had happened in the last few months: Evan's sister had been born, we had forced him to give up his pacifier, we had moved to a new house . . . Was his behavior caused by something other than these changes? The teacher's tone had been so somber, so ominous. She had scared me. I knew she was a good teacher, but I started thinking about how rigid and joyless she seemed. Maybe she didn't like lively, freethinking children like my difficult but delightful son.

And he was delightful. When things were going his way, Evan was wonderful company. He was cute and funny and full of imagination. He pondered big questions, like "Who made God?" and "Why do we have to have gravity?" And he was immensely loving. "I love you bigger than the whole galaxy," he would murmur as he drifted off to sleep, or, once after a difficult day, "I love you more than you are mad. I love you more than anything."

He wasn't perfect, but he wasn't a problem child, either. *Maybe it was his teacher's problem more than his*, I told myself. *Oh yes.*

Truthfully, the moment of recognition probably didn't come until a year and several parent conferences later. Evan was getting ready for bed one night after a particularly ugly battle over I-don't-remember-what. Turning off the TV or taking a bath, perhaps, or it could have been brushing his teeth or washing his hair. Our lives were full of argument and dissent about the simplest everyday things. Whenever his father or I told him to do anything, it seemed, he would ignore us. If we persisted, he would complain, whine, fall on the floor, or scream at the top of his lungs and cry.

Nothing was easy at our house. Everything was hard.

On that particular night, I was worn out. I had yelled at him. Now he was crying and insisting that I had hurt his feelings worse than anyone in the whole world. "You make me sad when you're mad at me," he sobbed.

I reached out and hugged him. He stiffened. I kissed the top of his head. "I know," I said wearily.

"I have more to say about this," he sniffed, standing in front of me looking down at the floor. My precocious, stubborn, incomprehensible boy.

"Go ahead," I sighed.

"I don't think you want to hear what I have to say."

"I do," I insisted. "Go ahead." I pulled him on to my lap.

"I wish I weren't a real boy," he said. "I wish I lived on TV." He looked up at me with tears streaming down his face. His burden was so heavy, his helplessness so complete. I could barely meet his gaze.

"Why?" I asked, a knot tightening in my stomach.

"Then no one would get angry at me," he explained. "Everyone would be happy all the time."

More than anything, I wanted to ease his sadness, relieve his frustration, and give him the key to getting along better in this world. That was my job as his mother, wasn't it? As I sat there holding him, silently rocking, I suddenly realized that Evan's wish was my wish, too. I didn't want to be a real mom if this was how it felt. I wanted to live in a family where I didn't have to repeat and argue and threaten and yell. Where my son would say, "Okay, Mom" and "No problem" and "Sure thing."

My life as a real mom was overwhelming and unmanageable. It was too much hard work. *Every mother feels this way from time to time*, I told myself. *Every parent hits bottom*. But this moment felt different from a temporary bout of exasperation. As a mother, I'd used all the tricks I knew. As a psychologist, I had no ideas left. Like Evan, I wanted out.

That might have been the moment when I knew that we were in trouble. But I can't be sure. There were so many other moments of resignation, anger, disbelief, sadness, and desperation. Toilet training was a bizarre, nightmarish experience. Giving medicine required the equivalent of a straitjacket. And every time I washed Evan's hair, he screamed so loudly that I half-expected to see a protective services worker at our front door. Even the things that most children love—riding a bike, swimming, watching TV—always ended in tears for us. We were living in a state of nearly constant frustration.

My efforts at compromise rarely worked. One morning at 3 A.M. Evan woke me up. He was coughing in that repetitive, hacking way that just borders on choking, and I knew he was going to throw up if it didn't stop. I also knew that he wouldn't take cough syrup because it was what he called "fizzy." I went to the kitchen and made him some hot water with lemon and honey. As I climbed the stairs to his bed-room, I told myself to be calm and patient, to wait out his resistance.

At first he refused to sit up or even hold the cup. "No, no, no," he yelled. Then he held it but wouldn't put it near his face. He cried, "I can't." I insisted, "You must."

"I don't know how to," he replied.

"Of course you do," I said.

He cried some more. Eventually he put his mouth on the rim of the cup and whined, "I don't like it."

"You don't know that," I retorted. He howled, "I don't know what to do!"

Finally, he swallowed the tiniest amount, then fell over backward on the bed as if he had been shot. That was it. I knew I couldn't force him to drink my homemade remedy. It was the middle of the night, and I was sleepy and grumpy, but I was also worried about him. Why wouldn't he let me help him?

I was accustomed to giving advice, not receiving it, but I started ask-ing for suggestions from anyone who would listen—a grandmother in line at the drugstore, a 12-year-old babysitter, acquaintances at cocktail parties, friends, neighbors, family members. My mother-in-law insisted that laughing is always better than crying. More often than not, though, I just couldn't find the humor in our situation. What's funny about yelling, screaming, and crying? What's funny about failure?

And she didn't find it funny when he refused to hug and kiss her. At the end of every visit when it was time to say good-bye to his grand-mother at the airport, Evan would duck away, dodge, hang his head, plainly refuse to allow her to embrace him. She would playfully threaten and plead with him. Once she even told him she was going to cry if he didn't give her a hug. I watched him struggle with the impli-cations of that one, and even though it broke my heart, I didn't know whose side to take. Her request didn't seem unreasonable, but his resis-tance was rock solid.

I worried that the world of 5-year-olds was passing him by. At the swimming pool, other children would leap into the water while Evan held firmly to the side. They would splash and squirt and dunk and dive, but Evan complained if his face got wet, and he didn't like the floaty feeling of his feet leaving the bottom of the pool. On the playground, he never joined the kids who were playing catch or kicking a ball around. He preferred to play fantasy games based on cartoons or Disney movies. Riding bikes with friends was not fun for him. He was cautious and tentative, and he had no interest in giving up his training wheels. His friends, in contrast, could pop wheelies, race each other up and down hills, and literally ride circles around him.

So, when Evan asked to join a soccer team, I was surprised. It seemed like a good idea, since a friend of ours was the coach and we knew several boys on the team. At the first practice, though, it became obvious that this, too, was going to be a struggle. He didn't follow the drills the coach set up. He kicked over the cones on the practice field. He complained about waiting his turn. He sat down and ate peanuts when it was his turn to run. And he yelled whenever another player took the ball away from him. Once he tried to get laughs by throwing the ball over the fence; then after the other kids got mad at him, he came home saying, "Everyone hates me."

As he got to know the game and the coach got to know him, he became more cooperative. Still, he couldn't sustain interest in the game for four quarters. He would whine and complain if he couldn't leave the game when he got tired. Then he would whine and complain if he couldn't go back when he was ready. From my self-conscious position among the other parents on the sidelines, I noticed that Evan was almost never where the action was. Sometimes he would lie down on the field while the rest of the players raced after the ball. If he was the goalie, he would hang by his arms and swing from the top bar of the goal cage, seemingly oblivious to his surroundings. Then he'd pout after the game, saying, "I don't ever get a goal" or "I'm not a very good kicker."

We asked ourselves whether we should let him quit. I didn't want to give in to him, yet I worried that he was turning his teammates against him. I was afraid that the other parents were getting tired of him. He was his own worst enemy on the field and his attempts to fit in with the team were backfiring.

At school the problems intensified. Every afternoon, Susan, his Montessori teacher, greeted me with a frown. She had a characteristically calm disposition, so her furrowed brow was a telltale sign that something was wrong. I always felt like ducking around the playground and racing for the parking lot when I saw her coming toward me. Instead, I forced myself to stand before her like a child waiting to be scolded.

Daily she would catalog the many ways in which Evan had refused to follow the routine, respond to directions, or make any apparent attempt to stay out of trouble. Her list was long: he was bumping into other children, stepping on their work, constantly making noise, jumping up and down, wandering aimlessly around the room, refusing to choose an activity or join a group. When she gave him options, he refused all of them. When she isolated him from the group, he exploded. When she forced him to talk about his misbehavior, he showed little remorse and avoided looking her in the eye.

All of this from a child who was bright, creative, and extremely verbal. A child who seemingly had every advantage. Most of the time Susan couldn't engage him in age-appropriate activities. He complained that the work was too hard. At other times he got so engrossed in a task that he would refuse to move on to the next activity, despite gentle reminders and predictable consequences. Instead of thriving in this rich, supposedly child-friendly school I had heard so many good things about, Evan was being sent to the office for refusing to cooperate. Why didn't he enjoy being there?

I would listen to Susan's complaints silently. I had nothing to say to her, even though I'd heard many parents describe similar behavior in my therapy office. My practice was full of parents and children burdened by a sense of failure. I'd made scores of recommendations to them about how to handle problems at home and at school, basing my efforts to help them on the unspoken belief that good parents raise good children, despite the inevitable problems that come their way. But now *my child* was failing and I was questioning whether I knew how to be a good parent.

Even worse, Evan was unhappy. He was starting to complain about going to school. He was refusing to talk about what happened there. He was shutting down. One Sunday night I reminded him that the next day was a school day. "Oh no," he moaned.

The next morning, as I was driving him to school, he said, "I wish Maria Montessori was in my class." I looked at him curiously. "Maybe then I could have a good day," he explained. As he saw it, only the founder of his preschool, the benevolent spirit who smiled kindly at him from a photograph on the wall of his classroom, could help him. The rest of us were clueless.

A week later he was sent home from school for slapping Susan in the face. He had been uncooperative in class, and she had taken him out on the porch to talk to him about his behavior. As she leaned down to look him in the eye, he slapped her hard across the cheek. According to Susan, Evan had seemed as startled and upset by his attack on her as she had been.

His father brought him home, and he began to cry as soon as he saw me. "We have to take down the school," he sobbed. "We have to, Mom. All the boards and all the nails. We have to take it down."

I held him in my lap and tried to comfort him. "Why?" I asked.

"Because I'm *always* bad there," he replied.

Although I'd never considered taking down the school, I had wondered whether a Montessori classroom was the right fit for Evan. I worried that we were taking up more than our share of Susan's time, patience, and goodwill. She was an excellent teacher, and I knew that she cared about Evan, but how could I expect her to tolerate his almost constant disruptive influence on the class?

At the beginning of the year, just after he had turned 5, Evan had made a spectacle of himself at the parents' breakfast. While his classmates stood in two straight lines singing Woody Guthrie favorites, Evan rolled around on the floor with a goofy grin on his face. Despite my dirty looks and whispered threats, he refused to stand up and join the group. The director of the school had nodded knowingly and characterized him as a "contrarian." He meant this in a vaguely complimentary way, and, at the time, I actually took some comfort in his description. I could imagine a contrarian growing up to be a political activist, an artist, or even a Pulitzer prize winner.

But over the course of the year, the director's view of Evan's future began to take a turn. He started describing him as "a student with a continuing pattern of disruptive behavior," then as "aggressive," and, after he slapped Susan, as "violent." He hinted that his school might not be the right place for us and suggested that we get a behavioral analysis at the University Psychology Clinic. I was both furious and relieved that he didn't seem to remember that I analyze behavior for a living. I had analyzed this endlessly, and it just didn't make sense.

We don't take kindly to children who refuse to do what they are told. I know this, because I work with these kids every day. Sometimes their parents bring them to me as early as age 3 or 4, asking for advice about how to stop the battles at home. Other families don't seek help until the children run into trouble at school. There, where the rules don't bend, kids who push against the system are punished for their resistance. After all, it is inconvenient, disruptive, and very challenging to accommodate an uncooperative child. In order for classrooms to run smoothly, children must conform to the system. Parents, as well as teachers, want their children to learn how to sit on a mat, stand in a line, fit into a group, and follow directions.

When they are young, we refer to these kids with euphemisms such as difficult, willful, or spirited. But if their defiance persists, we label them as problems. We send them to the principal, the school counselor, or a psychologist; sometimes we send them to a physician and a pharmacist. They might be given a psychiatric diagnosis, a behavioral program, an individualized education plan, or one of several different prescriptions. These interventions work for many children but not for all. When our efforts fail, we don't really know what to do next. We call those kids maladjusted, antisocial, or delinquent. We kick them out of the system and send them to the judge, the parole officer, and the warden.

I remember clearly the day my father asked me if Evan might need to see a psychiatrist. His well-intended suggestion landed on me like a slap in the face. From his point of view, Evan's misbehavior seemed pathological. I knew that our family was in trouble, but as I saw it the standard psychiatric tools were unlikely to be helpful. I was trained in psychiatric diagnosis and I knew that this was not depression or anxiety. It was not posttraumatic stress disorder, pervasive developmental disorder, or attention deficit hyperactivity disorder. *Maybe* it was oppositional defiant disorder, but what was a psychiatrist going to do about that?

The standard treatment for oppositional behavior is parent training: teaching parents more effective ways to reward and punish their child's behavior. I knew all about this. I could do it in my sleep. It's not as though I hadn't applied these principles to our family. We used stickers as encouragement for positive behavior. We hung a daily schedule on the refrigerator. We put pasta in a jar whenever Evan followed directions, then went to the movies when the jar was full. I created a checklist that Susan filled out each day, tracking whether he had done his work, controlled his body, used a quiet voice, and respected others. We gave short-term rewards. We gave long-term rewards. I had been well trained in these psychologically sound methods and I knew they could be very effective. Why weren't they working for my son?

Psychologists and sociologists suggest that oppositional behavior is frequently a harbinger of other problems to come. Peer difficulties. School dropout. Drug and alcohol abuse. Trouble with the law. Millions of dollars have been spent studying these problems, and many good minds have theorized about the mechanics of the downward spiral from difficult to delinquent. Still, the available explanations for why some kids won't do what they're told were not very satisfying or helpful to me as I struggled to understand Evan.

Based on the observation that troublemaking tends to run in families, some people believe that a genetic predisposition toward defiance might be the problem. Not well documented at the biochemical level, this explanation is just slightly more twenty-first century than the old notion of the "bad seed." Perhaps the long-awaited map of the human genome will clarify the connection between a troublemaker's DNA and his behavior, but for now a genetic alibi offered me no clues about how to live with my difficult-to-manage child.

Other explanations for misbehavior read like a laundry list of ways in which parents can fail their children. Maybe the child has been raised in a disadvantaged or violent home. Maybe the parents have been neglectful. Perhaps they have been too harsh or even abusive. Maybe they have been well intentioned but misinformed—that is, maybe they don't understand how to discipline effectively and have been overindulgent or inconsistent. Or maybe the child has been acting out some unresolved tension within the family—marital stress, sibling rivalry, an intergenerational family feud. There are endless parent-blaming explanations for why a child might be a behavior problem.

Mistreatment clearly damages children, and incompetent parenting and family dysfunction certainly contribute to misbehavior, but not all uncooperative children come from difficult, disadvantaged circumstances. Some kids who are well loved and well raised—like Evan—still won't go along with the most reasonable demands of daily living. They just don't do what they are told, despite their parents' best efforts to entice and/or coerce them to do so.

Parents who have lived with a difficult-to-manage child understand the chicken-and-egg conundrum. A reasonable parent can become a near lunatic if pushed hard enough for long enough. What starts out as good parenting can deteriorate into bad and quickly complicate the situation. So, who is to blame? And where does the solution lie?

On days when I was not inclined to blame myself, I found fault with my husband. Evan was a chip off the old block. He was following in the footsteps of his father, an independent sort whose insistence on ignoring other people's expectations of him was something I both admired and disliked. I had married a rabble-rouser, and now I seemed to be raising one. I began to imagine that my life would be spent clearing a path for my rebellious son in this world. A path where he wouldn't be penalized for his rebelliousness.

The problem was that I didn't feel up to the job. I was tired and discouraged. And Evan hadn't even gotten to kindergarten yet.

The possibility never occurred to me that Evan was doing the best that he could: that he was actually *trying* to do what he was told. It never occurred to me that he was not to blame for his failure to follow directions. Nor did it occur to me that my husband and I were not to blame for our inability to make him mind. My training as a psychologist had led me to believe that any behavior could be changed with the appropriate combination of rewards and punishments. It was a simple, straightforward formula that ought to work in my family. Why wasn't it working?

I never imagined that *my way of thinking* might be the problem until the school director showed up at one of our parent–teacher conferences and asked a simple question that I couldn't answer: *Why didn't Evan, with everything he had going for him, enjoy himself more? Why wasn't it fun for him to ride a bike? Why didn't he want to kick a soccer ball around the playground? Why weren't the classroom activities interesting and rewarding for him?* As the director saw it, Evan's resistance was a clue. His unhappiness was a sign.

I left that meeting with a newfound curiosity about my son. It was true: Things that were naturally pleasing to most kids were upsetting to Evan. And that didn't make sense. Things that came free and easy for most children required hard labor and determination for him. And that wasn't normal. What I knew about children couldn't explain my own son.

Still, I was slow to digest the notion that my way of thinking about Evan was flawed. I clung to the idea that I could change him by controlling him. I was determined to win this battle. His whole future seemed to be at stake.

Then, almost on a whim, I followed a colleague's suggestion and called her son, a newly licensed neuropsychologist. He had just opened a small practice and had time to talk. My understanding of the field of neuropsychology was sketchy—theorizing about brain processing seemed like highly technical guesswork to me. I came to this conversation with a very limited vocabulary and low expectations. And yet, as a mother, I was interested in any fragment—any shard of a solution—that might make our lives easier.

What I learned from him was encouraging. He told me that there were new neurological explanations for the kinds of problems Evan was having. Researchers in a number of fields were moving beyond traditional childhood diagnoses and describing these problems with new language, such as *nonverbal learning disabilities, regulatory disorders,* and *sensory integrative dysfunction.* There was a whole body of literature out there that I hadn't read.

I hung up from that conversation and called one of my former graduate professors, a well-known pediatric neuropsychologist. He was happy to share his thoughts on the current state of brain-behavior research. When I asked him specifically about the possible relationship between behavior and sensory processing, he said, "Here's my best professional opinion on that: I have no idea." He went on to say that he had read many research proposals on this topic and that the theoretical basis for them was not well developed. "However," he added, "I've read enough to know that something is going on there. I just don't know what it is."

He admitted that clinicians often catch wind of a phenomenon long before academic researchers can meaningfully describe it from a scientific perspective. He explained that occupational therapists (OTs), rather than psychologists, were the clinicians who concerned themselves with sensory processing, and he gave me the name of an OT who might be willing to talk to me. I'd heard her name before, and I knew that she was well respected. It couldn't hurt to give her a call.

This is how we came to Rebecca. Cautiously. Skeptically, even. I knew that occupational therapists sometimes worked collaboratively with psychologists, yet in five years as a staff psychologist at one of the leading pediatric hospitals in the country and eight years in private practice, I had never met an OT. I had a vague notion that they helped babies with eating problems, children with fine-motor delays, and survivors of traumatic injury. What could an OT do for Evan?

In my first conversation with her, I sensed that Rebecca knew something about children that I didn't know. She listened to my descriptions of Evan and seemed to understand him in a way that I didn't. She said that he certainly wanted to please me but possibly couldn't. She suggested that in most situations he was probably doing his best—that many things I considered simple and reasonable might, in fact, be impossible for him. She felt confident that there were reasons for everything he did and didn't do. She thought that she could help us. After several weeks of deliberation, I decided to see if she could.

That's how I found myself sitting on a metal folding chair in the corner of Rebecca's clinic watching Evan misbehave. He was being tested, but he wasn't cooperating. She asked him to imitate a simple sequence of hand movements. She tapped the child-size table where they were sitting with her right hand once, then with her left hand, then with her right hand once again. He flashed her a beautiful grin as he beat out his own rhythm on the table. I cringed. She calmly repeated the instructions and tried again with no success.

Next, she demonstrated a sequence of foot stomps. He ignored her and asked if he could play on the mats in the center of the room. I was trying not to interfere, but I wondered if he understood her directions. I suggested that I show him how to do it. Rebecca indulged me, and I carefully copied her alternating foot movements. Evan laughed at us both and ran across the room.

I rolled my eyes. These were familiar battle lines. Rebecca brought him back to the table and reminded him of the rules. He insisted that he needed a snack. She bargained with him, promising him a break after more work. He fell out of his chair onto the floor. She asked, "Does it feel good to fall?" He didn't answer, but the question intrigued me. What was she getting at?

Over the course of two days, Rebecca tested him on seventeen different tasks that measured visual skills, coordination between the right and left sides of his body, balance, sensitivity to touch, accurate positioning of his body in space, imitation of movement, and the ability to follow a sequence of instructions. Initially, the tasks were nonverbal but highly visual, like recognizing a picture embedded within another picture or copying geometric designs. Then she asked him to do things like move his finger from one spot on a map to another without looking at the map, or stand on one foot with his eyes closed. At first, he seemed to do pretty well, despite his reluctance to participate. But when he was forced to rely on touch, balance, and sensory information coming from his muscles and joints rather than his eyes and his ears, he flatly failed. For example, when Rebecca lightly touched one of his fingers without allowing him to look at his hand, then asked him to identify which finger she had touched, he couldn't do it. In most instances, he chose the wrong finger.

I didn't know how to make sense of what I was seeing. As a psychologist, I'd done a lot of testing with children, but I'd never seen tasks like these before. They weren't measuring traditional intellectual abilities like verbal expression, visual-motor coordination, or abstract reasoning. I had never thought of Evan as anything other than gifted, because he was so engaging, so analytical, so verbally talented. I didn't know what it meant when he couldn't imitate facial expressions or stand on one foot without closing his eyes. Rebecca was tapping into a mystifying weakness.

"He escapes into language," she said at the end of the testing. "He uses it as a distraction from tasks that are too difficult." Tasks too difficult? For Evan? With that comment, my understanding of him began to shift.

Several days later, my husband and I sat with Rebecca in her clinic. She reminded us that she had not evaluated Evan's intelligence, only his ability to process sensory information. She confirmed that she had, in fact, found evidence of what she called sensory processing problems. He was extremely sensitive to touch, but he often couldn't tell where he was being touched. As a result, he responded to tactile sensation defensively. His balance was shaky and his upper body was weak, so he often bent his left arm and held it close to his body to stabilize himself. Because of this, he didn't use the right and left sides of his body in a coordinated manner. He also had a great deal of difficulty with what Rebecca called motor planning—the ability to set up and carry out new or unfamiliar movements. She explained that these weaknesses interfered with his ability to pay attention, follow certain basic directions, participate in group activities, and engage in purposeful, independent activity. She thought they were also connected to his emotional reactivity, his resistance, and his sense of helplessness.

According to Rebecca, Evan was not oppositional by nature. Nor had he been poorly parented. Instead, he was at the end of his rope, trying to meet the demands of his world without the necessary neurological foundation. He was trying—but failing—to please the adults at school and at home as we dragged him through his life, oblivious to the challenges he faced each day.

Rebecca talked to us about *dysfunctional sensory integration*, which she described as a malfunction in the brain's translation of sensation into meaning and action. As an example, she explained that Evan's brain might not automatically recognize that pressure on the skin and muscles of his abdomen is coming from a too-tight waistband. It might not judge accurately whether the sensation is important or trivial, dangerous or benign. Therefore, he might not respond to it logically or efficiently. He might avoid getting dressed or refuse to put his pants on. He might be irritable and jumpy for no apparent reason. He might have a full-blown tantrum.

For most of us, the delicate interaction between the brain and body known as sensory integration is nothing short of marvelous. It allows us to move purposefully through the world without being driven to distraction by the cacophony of sensory experience that bombards us each moment that we are awake. When brain-body connections are intact, the lower brain constantly interprets input from sensory receptors all over the body and responds with motor reactions. Those actions create more sensory feedback, which provides self-correcting information to the brain in a never-ending cycle. Thankfully, this occurs outside of our awareness in most instances. We are free to focus on conscious thoughts while our subcortical brain and its agents literally keep us from bumping into walls.

According to Rebecca, children like Evan are not so fortunate. They may vacillate between states of over- and understimulation, and, as a result, act in ways that seem erratic and inconsistent. Everyday tasks—washing their hair or brushing their teeth—can quickly overwhelm them. Complex tasks—learning to ride a bike or cleaning up a messy room—may totally confound them. They may withdraw and avoid. When pushed, they are likely to resist. They may become discouraged, irritable, whiny, even explosive.

In most cases, we assume that these children are capable of doing what we ask them to do—after all, they have no obvious difficulty seeing, hearing, talking, walking, or understanding. We see no reason for their seeming misbehavior. We tell ourselves *they're just spacey, stubborn, or strong-willed*. In fact, they may be all of those things *but for a reason*. The reason—faulty sensory processing—is unseen by us and unrecognized by them.

I was flooded with sadness and relief as I listened to Rebecca's descriptions of Evan. Through her eyes, I saw a boy who couldn't—*absolutely couldn't*—stop thinking about the seam of his sock or the waistband of his underwear or the tag on the back of his shirt. A boy who couldn't button his pants, zip his jacket, or fasten his seat belt because he wasn't able to tell which of his fingers were touching the things he was handling. A boy who constantly made noise in order to screen out noise. A boy who bumped into things and moved around a lot in order to maintain his balance. A boy who felt under attack by his skin, by smells, by noises. By his friends. By his father. By me. No wonder he was pushing back. His body was in a constant state of alert, and he was putting out tremendous effort just to get through each day.

It was the first explanation of Evan's behavior that made sense.

Still, I struggled to grasp the concepts Rebecca was describing. Was this explanation legitimate? Why hadn't I learned about dysfunctional sensory integration in my clinical training? Were we just putting new labels on an old set of problems, or were we headed into new territory?

I called my best friend, Karen G., in Chicago. She, too, was a psychologist. Years ago, she had been told that her son, Ben, who was now 11, had sensory integration problems. I knew that Ben had seen an OT when he was 4 years old, but I couldn't remember the details. When I told Karen that Rebecca thought Evan had sensory processing problems, she was surprised. She was well aware of his struggles. Still, she hadn't made a connection between the problems Evan was having and the kinds of problems Ben had had as a preschooler. Neither had I. How had we missed it?

The truth was that Ben and Evan were very different kids. Ben had come screaming loudly into this world: as a baby, he cried whenever he was laid down for a diaper change, or if he was raised high into the air, or if someone put her face too close to his, or if he heard a loud noise like the coffee grinder or vacuum cleaner. As a toddler, he propelled himself along with a wiggly tummy scoot that we called an army crawl, he refused to climb stairs, and he spoke his own language—we called it *ben-ese*—that was very engaging but completely incomprehensible. In preschool, he had trouble with fine-motor tasks. He refused to wear socks, sit with the group at circle time, or take a time-out when he misbehaved. Yet he was good-hearted and completely engaging. We all knew that Ben was his own little person. He got away with things partly because he was so cute but also because Karen worked so hard to understand and accommodate him. Still, when an OT at the hospital where Karen worked said that Ben had sensory integration difficulties, she had no idea what the OT was talking about.

In contrast, Evan had been a calm, seemingly well-regulated baby. He passed all the developmental milestones at the expected times. He was a go-along toddler, always game for whatever we were doing or wherever we were going. As long as he had his pacifier, that is. Without it, he would cry, whine, and insist single-mindedly that he needed his "plug." We were as dependent on it as he was and would rush around frantically looking for it on those rare occasions when it was lost. It wasn't until we took the pacifier away from Evan at age 4 that we learned he couldn't soothe himself without it. By then we already knew that he was strong-willed, but we hadn't realized the extent to which his plug was holding him together.

Could Ben and Evan have the same problem when their behaviors appeared so different? Ben was more physiologically reactive, whereas Evan's behavior seemed to be the problem. Ben had obvious speech and fine-motor difficulties, whereas Evan's developmental weaknesses were hidden. Ben's sensitivities seemed particular and specific, whereas Evan generally had trouble moving through the day. How could poor sensory processing account for such a broad range of problems? Karen and I weren't sure what to think of this. Didn't all children have sensory processing problems at one time or another? We were unconvinced that dysfunctional sensory integration was anything more than a wastebasket category for kids who were hard to diagnose. Still, we were curious, despite our reservations. Something about this explanation of our sons struck a chord. Something about it rang true.

My husband and I began to recognize some fairly obvious examples of sensory interference in Evan's life. Perhaps his consistent, adamant refusal to hug his grandmother was not rude; instead, it might be related to his fear of losing his balance and the confusion and discomfort that light pressure on his skin created. His resistance to taking medicine might not be stubbornness; perhaps it was an almost primal defense against the taste. His extreme reaction to the least little bump, scrape, or cut no longer seemed like an act. When he shrieked and screamed, "It feels like it's bleeding on the inside," we began to realize that his body was experiencing pain more intensely than normal.

Over time, with Rebecca's guidance, we learned to anticipate Evan's reactions to the sensory experiences he found assaultive. Whenever we got stuck in a no-win battle, we looked for ways to relieve the pressure for him and for us. When he dove under the dining room table to escape the smell of fish, collard greens, or even fresh bay leaves, we didn't stubbornly insist that he sit in his chair. We tried to avoid the severe meltdowns that typically followed crowded, noisy birthday parties by taking him home before he got overwhelmed. In order to prevent bath-time screaming, we asked Rebecca how to make hair washing less threatening. So many of these everyday situations required hidden competencies—unconscious, lower-order neurological skills—that Evan just didn't seem to have.

I thought about Evan in his Montessori classroom where twenty-six children were expected to work independently on twenty-six different activities. I thought about the constant movement, the bright lights and the chatter, the squawking of the class parrot, the maze of mats spread across the floor in an ever-changing patchwork. I thought about the visual array of work lined up on the shelves in tidy order. I thought about Evan's difficulties with motor planning, spatial organization, and tactile discrimination. And I began to understand Susan's complaints. She said that Evan might try an activity once, but if he got confused or frustrated, he would put it back on the shelf. Then he would wander around the room looking for something else to do, getting into trouble along the way: bumping into other kids, stepping on their mats, acting silly. I asked him about this and he replied, "When Susan says 'Find some work,' that's hard for me, Mom." I started to believe him.

I thought about Evan on the soccer field. Everything about that game was a challenge for him: being pushed and bumped, following the ball, running and kicking simultaneously, anticipating the next move, maintaining his balance. No wonder he was never where the action was. No wonder he preferred the safety of the sidelines and the goal cage. I began thinking of him as the most valiant player, just for being willing to show up for the games.

I thought about what Rebecca called our sensory diet—that is, our family's daily sensory intake. It was sedentary, cerebral, and media dominated. Even though we lived in a small town where it was safe to roam our neighborhood, we spent most afternoons inside, reading, watching TV, and playing games. On weekends we usually wandered around the house barely dressed, like zombies. We didn't play sports; we didn't exercise regularly; we rarely went outside at all! And yet, when we did, Evan was a different child: enthusiastic, active, and adventurous rather than grumpy, lethargic, and argumentative. Some of our best times together had been spent outside—going on a flashlight walk after dark, sitting in a parking lot during a thunderstorm, playing hide-and-seek, looking for flowers, picking strawberries. According to Rebecca, Evan needed to become more active, more playful, more tuned in to his body—and we did, too.

We started taking him to Rebecca for twice-a-week occupational therapy sessions, where she worked with him on developing foundational sensory processing skills. She predicted that he would respond well to treatment but that it would take time—at least a year. This was not magic, she insisted: it was hands-on, developmentally oriented therapy based on the notion that our brains are influenced by our experiences. Through elaborate play activities, Rebecca provided Evan with sensorimotor challenges difficult enough to be appealing but easy enough to be attainable. She said that these experiences would build upon one another, gradually laying the pathways between body and brain that were necessary for more efficient sensory processing.

My husband was apprehensive. He worried that alteration of Evan's sensory processing networks might change his personality in unacceptable ways. Would he be less creative, less spontaneous, less sparkly? Frankly, I didn't worry about this. I wanted the problems to go away as quickly as possible. Looking back now, I wonder why I wasn't more dubious about Rebecca's claims.

Perhaps it was because she was so confident that she could help him and because he responded to her so enthusiastically. When they were together, it looked like they were just having fun—crawling through tunnels, spinning in tire swings, diving into bean bags, tooting on horns, jumping through hoops. But with practice I began to see that she was deliberately working on decreasing tactile sensitivity, increasing upper body strength and postural stability, encouraging bilateral coordination, and practicing motor planning. He was building self-confidence and developing a sense of mastery.

"I believe that children want to please their parents," Rebecca told me early on in our work with her. "If they're not behaving, it's because something is preventing them from doing what they're being told to do. It's our job to figure out what it is and find ways to help them be successful."

It seemed so obvious when she said it, but I realized that I hadn't been treating Evan like a child who wanted to please me. I'd been treating him like a troublemaker. I'd come to assume that he didn't care about doing the right thing—or, worse still, that he got some secret thrill from misbehaving. It was liberating to once again see him as a child who wanted to do well, as a boy who wanted to behave.

Still, life at our house continued to be difficult. Power struggles persisted and temper tantrums were a regular occurrence, usually just before dinner when the accumulation of the day's irritations crashed in on us all. Even though we couldn't always figure out what was causing him to crumble, we no longer blamed Evan for his frustration. We eased up and tried to listen.

With encouragement, he began to describe the peculiarities of how his body worked. Over a peanut butter snack one morning, he said, "Andrew is allergic to peanut butter, but I'm allergic to things on my skin." After we gave in to his request to wear the same pair of orange cotton knit shorts day after day, he practically shouted, "I love smooth! It's my favorite thing." When I asked him what happened when kids at school accidentally bumped into him, he replied, "Oh, I have to fall down to get away from them."

One of the children I wished he could get away from was a boy in his class named Mike, who was loud, disruptive, and annoying—Evan was drawn to him like a magnet. Each morning, just as Evan was settling into some methodical Montessori-style activity, Mike would cavort by, chanting some nonsensical rap, tapping him on the head, and knocking over his carefully arranged work. Evan would be off in a flash, and the two of them would bound around the classroom, working each other into a frenzy that would usually get them both sent to time-out. I knew I was being unfair, but I blamed Mike for the trouble he and Evan caused each other.

I was fighting my unfriendly feelings one afternoon as Mike stood in front of me in a new hooded sweatshirt. I dug deep to find something nice to say. "That's a great red jacket," I offered lamely. Teresa, his mom, overheard me.

"Mike has just started treatment for sensory integration problems, and we've discovered that he's very sensitive to noise," she explained. "He likes to wear jackets that he can pull up over his ears, even when he's inside."

I was stunned. I had been wrong about Mike. I had dismissed him as a troublemaker, making the same assumptions about him that I was afraid other parents were making about Evan. No wonder he and Evan couldn't resist one another—their predicaments were similar.

Teresa told me that Mike had been a difficult child from early on. As an infant, he didn't sleep, he couldn't breast-feed, and he was restless, hyperactive, and difficult to settle. From the first moment that he could crawl, he sought out small, enclosed spaces where he could hide. Even though she had raised two older children, Teresa didn't know what to make of Mike's unusual behavior. Before she knew about dysfunctional sensory integration, she had gone to see a family therapist who had recommended a behavior modification program to decrease Mike's "aggressive behavior." It hadn't worked—just like the behavior charts I'd designed for Evan hadn't worked.

"I felt desperate," she said. "I didn't know what to do. I had this underlying fear that if we didn't do something, we were headed for medication."

Mike was 5 years old when a family friend told Teresa about dysfunctional sensory integration. She had Mike evaluated and immediately started him in therapy with Rebecca. For the first time since her son was born, Teresa felt hopeful.

Fortunately for both Mike and Evan, Susan was interested in learning about sensory integration. She read everything that she and I could find about school-based interventions for kids with sensory processing problems. She created work spaces away from the noise and activity of the busy, open classroom. She allowed us to set up an old refrigerator box as a sensory shelter, which we decorated and called the chill zone. She tracked Evan and Mike closely, always mindful of the possibility of sensory challenges in problematic situations. She responded creatively and constructively to bumping, rolling, falling, touching, and noise-making. Whenever their opposition to a task puzzled her, she consulted with Rebecca. Most importantly, she maintained her composure and her compassion in the face of their sensitivities.

Within a few months, Evan stopped hating school. He started to recognize his own weaknesses, which made it easier for him to calm himself when he got upset rather than exploding or disintegrating into a crying heap. When the din of the classroom became too intense and he started to get jumpy and loud, he asked for permission to go into the refrigerator box for a break. As his sensory processing became more efficient, he was able to focus on learning and enjoy its natural rewards.

"I'm so busy doing work at school that I don't have to try to be a good boy," I heard him tell my mother one afternoon.

His body was now working for him rather than against him, and he gradually developed the ability to ignore little discomforts. Because he was less sensitive to touch, getting dressed was no longer a painful chore. One morning, with wonder in his voice, he told me, "Mom, when I put on my underpants, they were too tight. But by the time I got downstairs, they were just the right size." Habituation—the brain's automatic modulation of sensory awareness—is no small miracle, when you think about it.

A vulnerable side of Evan began to emerge. One night at dinner he was arguing and ignoring my ongoing litany of commands: "Lower your voice. . . . Don't lean back in your chair. . . . Stop teasing your sister. . . . You may not sing at the table. . . . Don't interrupt me." Suddenly, my patience ran out, and I yelled at him before I could stop myself. He immediately collapsed and began to cry inconsolably, a wellspring of discouragement and self-doubt.

"Come on, Evan," I said, trying to undo the damage I'd done. "You're just having a bad night."

"I hate it when this happens," he cried. "I haven't been having a bad night in a long time."

"That's true," I agreed. "But everyone has a bad night every now and then."

Rather than reassuring him, this comment seemed to set off a panic that he had slipped back into old ways. Frantic, he asked, "What if I start having bad days every day? What if all my nights are bad nights?"

Increasingly, I heard this subterranean insecurity in Evan's voice whenever he felt that he had failed to meet my expectations. "I don't want anyone to be mad at me," he insisted if he thought I was the least bit irritated. "I didn't mean to do it," he cried when he accidentally slammed a door. One day after refusing to take his medicine, he asked, "Are you mad at me?" This was the boy I had so recently thought of as impervious to my wishes. It was now painfully obvious that he had always wanted to please me.

In my therapy office, I began to recognize children who were similarly misunderstood. Children described as angry sounded hopeless; kids whose parents complained that they were stubborn seemed stuck. Defiance became a red flag for me, as did explosiveness and even hyperactivity. I began to wonder if being out of control might be a sign of sensory overload for some kids.

I found myself comforting, rather than correcting parents who blamed themselves for not being in charge of their children. I could relate to their rage and guilt. I understood their sadness. I told them that having a difficult child was not evidence of personal failure. I gave them permission to ease up, back off, give in. I encouraged them to accept their children as they were, rather than as they wished that they would be.

I began talking to families about sensory integration, but I didn't always know what to say. I was still learning myself, and I wasn't always certain if sensory processing was a reasonable framework for understanding behavior problems. I discussed the possible connection between disruptive behavior and dysfunctional sensory integration with physicians, teachers, and therapists, many of whom are considered authorities on the topic of difficult-to-manage behavior. Not one of them was well informed about sensory integration theory. Most of them dismissed it out of hand because it has not yet been validated empirically.

It was true: there was no scientific evidence to indicate what caused dysfunctional sensory integration, nor were there any well-designed studies to evaluate its treatment. However, there was a lot of anecdotal evidence to suggest that children with a variety of diagnoses—including specific learning disabilities, behavior disorders, pervasive developmental disorders, and attention deficit hyperactivity disorder—were benefiting from treatment based on a sensory integration framework. It also appeared to be helpful for many children without a specific diagnosis. Children like Evan, Ben, and Mike.

As a psychologist, this left me with a lot of unanswered questions. As a mother, it gave me hope.

Part

One

CHAPTER ONE

|||||||||||||||||||||||||||||||||||||||||||||||||||||||||||||||||||||||||||||||||||||||||||

Making Sense of Our Senses

We live on the leash of our senses.

— DIANE ACKERMAN
A Natural History of the Senses

Your brain is all over your body.

— EVAN,
at age 6

WE EXPERIENCE the world through our senses—sounds, sights, tastes, smells, physical sensations. A 7-year-old gets a present in the mail from her grandparents and her first comment is "It smells like Grandma's house." We, too, remember our grandmother's house—the smells of chicken soup, onion and garlic, aging plaster and musty incinerators; the caress of cool air on our skin as we entered her dark hallway from the steamy outdoors; the patterns of the wallpaper; the muted colors of the tile; the sounds of life behind the apartment doors. We cannot separate our grandmother from our sensory memories of her. All our transactions with the world are mediated through our senses.

There is even more of the world that we do not experience. It is blocked out before reaching our awareness. Everything need not be seen, heard, or smelled. When it comes to knowing our world—making sense of it, you might say—less is often more. In her beautifully written book *A Natural History of the Senses* Diane Ackerman explains,

The world is a construct the brain builds based on the sensory information it's given, and the information is only a small part of all that's available. . . . The body edits and prunes experience before sending it to the brain for contemplation or action. Not every whim of the wind triggers the hair on the wrist to quiver. Not every vagary of sunlight registers on the retina. Not everything we feel is felt powerfully enough to send a message to the brain; the rest of the sensations just wash over us, telling us nothing.

If it weren't for this pruning and editing, this process of simplification, we couldn't function. Our brains would be awash in a sea of confusion. The world would come flooding in on us, relentless and incomprehensible. We would rush to defend ourselves at the snap of a twig or the breath of a breeze. We'd be continuously distracted and disoriented, and we quite literally would not know whether to come or go. Fortunately, we only apprehend what we really need to know. The rest of it escapes our consciousness.

GETTING STARTED

Imagine a typical morning. When the alarm goes off, you get out of bed, take a shower, dress yourself, and begin breakfast. You perform this simple set of tasks without any conscious awareness of the complex interplay between brain and body that moves you along. You are on automatic pilot, already listing in your head the many things you need to accomplish that day. You don't give a thought to the abundance of sensory cues that guide you from your bed to the breakfast table. Nor do you think about the myriad distractions that you unwittingly ignore.

First, the sound of the alarm explodes into the silence of your sleep. Loud, jarring, it carries a message—it is time to start the day. As you rouse yourself, you become aware of other sensations: the sun on your face, the shadows playing on your bedroom walls in the early morning light, perhaps the muffled sounds of your children waking. Your brain tunes out the unimportant sensations: cars honking down the block, a dog barking, birds chirping. You raise your body in bed, effortlessly negotiating the downward pull of gravity as you move from a prone to an upright position and swing your feet to the floor. Again resisting the force of gravity, you stand. The bottoms of your feet touch the floor—

smooth, cool wood, then scratchy, warm carpet, and, in the bathroom, cold, slick tile.

There, your brain is assaulted by different sensations. The glare of the lights, the chill of a morning draft, the sound, pressure, and temperature of the water—you tune in to these while balancing on one foot to step into the shower. All the while your brain is aware, somewhere, that it must be on the alert for the ring of the telephone or the cry of a child. You feel the soap gliding along your body and the water beating down on your head, helping to waken you. You again balance as you step out of the shower. You dry off and feel the terry rub of your towel on your skin. You grimace at the too-cold water as you brush your teeth and at the tug of knots in your hair as you comb it. There is the sensation of light on the walls and on your skin, the smell of coffee and toast from the kitchen, and the sound of the radio playing in your bedroom.

Outside, morning noises are increasing: buses rumbling, leaf blowers whining, more dogs barking. As you move to get dressed, you scan your closet and drawers and run your fingers through clothes that are soft or stiff, smooth or rough, light or heavy. You make your choices and pull on soft cotton underwear, wool pants, a knit sweater, and your favorite pair of warm socks. You fasten hooks, slip buttons through buttonholes, and lace your shoes, all the while instructing your 5-year-old to start his own morning routine. You notice, in passing, that your pants feel a bit snug. Your sweater smells a bit musty. But your focus stays sharp as your sense of purpose moves you through your morning.

You glance at the digital clock beside your bed and move down the stairs toward the smell of that coffee. Within ten minutes, you have made two lunches, signed a permission slip for your teenager's field trip, and eaten a bowl of crunchy granola laced with sweet strawberries. As you glance at the headlines of the newspaper, your brain automatically filters out the grinding of the garbage truck beyond your kitchen window but instantly tunes in to the whimpers of your baby. Walking into her room, you are greeted by the aromatic cocktail that is uniquely her: the sweet and sour of talcum powder and wet diapers, the sudsy smell of soap, and the tangy perfume of baby wipes mingling in the humid warmth of her room. You lean over and lift her from her crib. There is nothing on earth that feels quite so luscious as a baby. You brush your cheek against hers. So soft. You look into her eyes and smile.

Suddenly, you hear the front door opening. You hurry into the hall to say good-bye to your older children. They look good: shoes tied, faces clean, coats on, lunchboxes in hand. You will be out the door behind them in five minutes.

In the hour since waking, you have taken in a vast array of information through your senses. Your brain has filtered, organized, and translated it into an ongoing series of messages to your body that has gotten you through your morning routine without a hitch. You are ready to face the day.

LOOKING BACK

Our senses not only give meaning to the immediate present but also color how we remember the past. Think about a childhood memory, such as coming inside from playing on a chilly autumn afternoon. The memory is encoded through your senses: The hint of burning leaves and the crispness in the frosty air gave way to the aroma of a roast cooking in your mother's oven. The animated voices of your friends playing in the street yielded to the drone of the evening news on the television. Your stiff, cold fingers tingled as they slowly warmed over the stove. Your father was in the shadows, smoking a cigarette behind the newspaper at the kitchen table. Your mother handed you a fresh-baked sugar cookie while talking on the phone. Your brother's saxophone was squawking in the basement and your sister was laughing down the hall. You eased your body, tired from running and jumping rope, into the cushioned chair in the living room. Aaaah. You were home.

Collections of these memories, made vivid by the sensations that accompanied the events, comprise our sense of who we are and where we belong in the world. Because they are experienced on a level that does not involve language, very few people are talented enough to describe them with words. That is the gift of great writers. However, the powerful connection between sensation, memory, and identity can be experienced when you walk into your mother's house twenty years later on a chilly autumn afternoon and smell a roast cooking in the oven.

The sights and smells of her kitchen can instantly evoke deeply held, perhaps temporarily forgotten, emotions from your childhood: feelings about your mother and father, regrets about a long-lost friend, confusion or resentment about your place in your family. Your most fundamental beliefs about yourself may be encompassed in a single sensation-packed memory.

Our senses can evoke negative as well as positive emotions. Karen G. recalls her stepdaughter Sarah's first trip to the Field Museum in Chicago. A special exhibit about the Maori included a native hut, songs, dances, and ceremonies that Karen and her husband were sure 5-year-old Sarah would enjoy. Inside the hut, the air was damp and smelled strongly of the earth. It was dark, and an unfamiliar instrument played a strange, shrill melody that echoed throughout the chamber. Sarah was told to take off her shoes. As soon as she did, she began screaming hysterically. Ordinarily a calm child, she shrieked as though her life depended on it. Baffled, her parents grabbed her and took her outside. When they asked Sarah what had scared her, all she could say was, "It smelled bad." Once outside the museum, she stopped crying as quickly as she had begun, and the three of them spent a lovely day playing along the Chicago lakefront.

Years later, while talking to Karen about the Field Museum, Sarah, who was 18 at the time, said, "I hate that place! Remember that exhibit you guys took me to? It was horrible in there." She remembered little about the native hut or her reactions to it, but her feelings about the museum were indelibly colored by the threatening sensations she experienced there.

In more extreme situations, sensations and the memories associated with them bring considerable pain, discomfort, and anxiety. A hallmark of human response to trauma is that the memories of a horrifying experience can be triggered by sensory cues reminiscent of the traumatic event. The backfiring of a truck can send a war veteran diving for cover on a city street; the acrid smell of smoke in the air can transport a Holocaust survivor back to Auschwitz; the sensations associated with sexual intercourse can retraumatize a rape victim. In these cases, the sensations set into motion a series of physiological responses that leave the victim feeling as though she is actually reliving the traumatic experience.

FROM SENSATION TO ACTION

Understanding how the human sensory system influences our ability to perform daily tasks smoothly and competently was the life work of Jean Ayres, an occupational therapist who developed the theory of sensory integration. Through her work at UCLA's Brain Research Institute in the 1960s and 1970s, she became convinced that the efficient organization, interpretation, and use of sensory information underlies all other aspects of human behavior. In *Sensory Integration and the Child*, Ayres wrote about the role the senses play in normal development. She described the first seven years of life as a critical period for "a child to learn to sense his body and the world around him and to rise up and move effectively in that world." As the child's brain develops, it becomes more efficient at using sensory information to generate motor output. This process of sensory integration facilitates effective interaction between the child and his world.

Ayres's ideas were purely theoretical in the 1970s. At that time, there was little research to support her observations and clinical impressions about the connections between sensory processing and brain functioning, although other developmental theorists such as Jean Piaget had also maintained that early sensorimotor experiences laid the foundation for later learning. A quarter century after Ayres first developed her theory, we continue to amass evidence that the brain is shaped by experience. Connections between the cells of the brain are formed in response to the sights, smells, sounds, tastes, and physical sensations that a child experiences. His brain learns to receive these sensory messages, then to pass them from one area of the nervous system to another. These relay systems, known as neural pathways, support the development of many skills, including perception, attention, speech, memory, and abstract reasoning. Every response to sensation initiates or strengthens connections in the brain. In effect, then, the child's sensorimotor experiences actually help to build his brain. As author Jane Healy says in *Your Child's Growing Mind*, "Every child weaves his own intellectual tapestry, the quality of which depends on active interest and involvement in a wide variety of stimuli."

Ayres intuitively understood that some children's tapestries are less efficiently woven than others. She coined the term *sensory integrative dysfunction* to describe a sensory processing breakdown, or in her words "a traffic jam in the brain." It was her observation that irregularities in the brain's responses to sensory information can contribute to an array of problems that are rarely recognized as sensory based. These problems can include difficulties with attention, emotion regulation, motor coordination, activity level, perceptual abilities, peer relationships, and, not surprisingly, academic achievement. We are not generally aware of the sensory underpinnings of normal behavior, and sensory processing problems often go unrecognized. An exact understanding of the brain, how it sorts and integrates sensory information, regulates attention and arousal, and moderates our emotional responses, remains elusive. We do know, however, that the point of entry to the brain is through the seven senses.

THE SEVEN SENSES

Sensations are disparate pieces of information that must be organized and interpreted by the nervous system so that our body and mind can adapt to the world around us on a moment-to-moment basis. We experience the world through the conscious awareness of sight, hearing, smell, taste, and touch and the unconscious monitoring of balance/ movement, and body position.

Walking down an unfamiliar city street on a hot summer day, we are acutely aware of the bright colors of people's clothing, the shapes of their bodies, the height of the buildings, the color of the sky, the density of the crowd. We hear music playing in a store, people talking at a sidewalk café, sirens blaring. We may be assaulted by the stench of garbage coming from an alley, intrigued by the smell of incense and spices, or attracted by the aroma of baking bread wafting out of a bakery. Lunch might be a slice of hot garlic-scented pizza washed down with icy cold lemonade, or a pastrami sandwich and a too-sweet cream soda, or wasabi- and ginger-loaded sushi with green tea. These sensations are the building blocks from which we construct our experience of the day. Was it pleasant or unpleasant, relaxing or stressful, fun or frustrating? Our sense of well-being, our mood, and even our interactions with others are strongly affected by these sensory experiences.

We have long recognized the critical contribution of the senses to mental health. For centuries, sensory deprivation has been used as a means of torture. Psychological experiments have shown that individuals exposed to sensory deprivation for prolonged periods of time experience disorientation followed by mild hallucinations. Studies of institutionalized children from the 1940s and more recent studies of children adopted from Eastern European orphanages document the debilitating effects of sensory deprivation. Infants who are left in their cribs for days with minimal human stimulation develop a range of emotional and behavioral difficulties, including disturbed social relationships, difficulty regulating emotions, disturbances in attention, and oppositional behavior. Researchers have documented that these children not only have aberrant developmental patterns but that their brain chemistry has actually been altered so that they produce higher levels of cortisol (a stress-regulating hormone) than noninstitutionalized children.

Other studies have shown that certain sensory experiences have positive effects. The knowledge that blues and greens are calming while reds are arousing has influenced the interior decoration of hospitals and other institutions for decades. Researchers at Yale have discovered that the smell of spiced apples can reduce blood pressure, while the scent of lavender can stimulate metabolism and increase alertness. And it doesn't take a scientist to demonstrate the connections between music and our emotions. The therapeutic use of music is gaining acceptance in many settings, including classrooms, intensive care units, and infant nurseries. A simple melodic line can send our spirits soaring, touch deeply concealed wells of sadness, or make us get up and dance. Some music just cannot be resisted: it has been shown that joggers will stay on a treadmill longer when they are listening to invigorating music. The American advertising industry has exploited these connections between sounds, images, and our sense of well-being. Advertisements for cars are routinely paired with popular songs that make us feel young, daring, or light of heart. Vacation ads are shot against soft sunset skies and backed by romantic tunes.

Surprisingly, perhaps, the three sensory systems most essential to our daily functioning are the ones we take the most for granted: the tactile (touch), vestibular (balance and movement), and proprioceptive (body position) systems. You may not have heard of the vestibular and proprioceptive systems. When we think of our senses, we typically only consider the five that we are consciously aware of: touch, sight, sound, taste, and smell. Actually, though, there are seven senses, and without the continuous integration of information from the other two—the vestibular and proprioceptive systems—along with one of the five—touch—we would be completely unable to function. The simplest activity, like sitting in a chair, would require constant concentration. We would not understand how far we could lean back in that chair without falling over or how hard we could hug our baby without hurting her.

TOUCH: IT'S A MATTER OF LIFE AND DEATH

The tactile system is the sentinel between our bodies and the world. It governs our reactions to whatever touches our skin. According to Ayres, it is one of the most important of the seven sensory systems. After all, it covers our entire body. Seventy percent of our sensory receptors are located in our skin.

We all crave touch. As adults, we walk arm-in-arm, pay for massages, nuzzle our babies, and indulge in sexual pleasure. Children snuggle with stuffed animals, rub their fingers over their "blankies" for comfort, and rarely tire of tickling games. In fact, without tactile stimulation, babies are less likely to develop normally. In a famous set of experiments in the 1950s, Harry Harlow demonstrated that infant monkeys raised in cages with surrogate mothers made of terry cloth developed more normally than infant monkeys raised with wire surrogates. The infant monkeys with the terry cloth "mothers" hugged and clung to their cloth surrogates, receiving tactile stimulation and comfort; the infant monkeys raised with wire "mothers" received no tactile comfort. These tactilely deprived monkeys grew up to be aggressive, highly abnormal in their peer play, and maladaptive sexually. These experiments have been cited repeatedly as evidence of the importance of human touch in the development of healthy infant–mother attachment.

Many researchers have documented the benefits of infant massage and shown that touch facilitates healthy development. Premature babies who are regularly massaged gain weight as much as 50 percent faster than babies who are not massaged. They are also more active, alert, responsive, better able to tolerate noise, and emotionally more in control. You could say that their neurological systems are better integrated, and, as a result, the babies are better able to calm and console themselves. Tactile input is helping them learn an essential survival skill: regulating their responses to the world.

Tactile receptors are exquisitely tuned to warn us when we are at risk for being harmed. Consequently, it is very difficult to ignore unusual, aggravating, or startling sensations on our skin. We all have been annoyed by the tickle of a cobweb, threatened by a bump in a crowd, or bothered by a particularly scratchy label or fabric. These sensations demand that we pay attention and take action to protect ourselves from whatever has gotten "under our skin." If a child is bumped from behind but cannot tell exactly where or how hard she has been touched, she may feel a gentle touch as a rough one and misinterpret the action as hostile. Developmental researchers have noted that aggressive children are more likely than others to miss social cues that might help them interpret intent. They also attribute hostile intent to ambiguous cues. One hypothesis about the source of these differences is that aggressive children think differently about their peers' actions as a function of past experience. An alternative hypothesis, however, is that something about the way they physically experience bodily contact causes them to respond aggressively. What they sense colors what they think as well as what they do.

THE HIDDEN SENSES

The vestibular and proprioceptive senses are the least present in our conscious awareness. Ayres referred to them as the "hidden senses" because, for the most part, they operate at an unconscious level. We tend to become aware of them only when they go awry.

The Vestibular System (Balance and Movement)

The vestibular system is located in the inner ear and is stimulated by head, neck, eye, and body movements. It responds to the pull of gravity and registers where our bodies are in relationship to the earth—information that Ayres considered the bedrock of physical and emotional security. Vestibular input helps us maintain our balance by telling us whether we are at rest or in motion, how fast and in what direction we are moving, and also by registering the movement of objects around us. Healthy vestibular functioning allows a child to know how high he can swing without going over the bar or how fast he can spin without falling over.

Life can become very difficult if your nervous system doesn't integrate vestibular sensations efficiently. Have you ever had a middle ear infection? If so, you have some appreciation for how much you depend on normal vestibular functioning. Actions you take for granted—getting up and sitting down, walking in a straight line, moving your head from side to side—may have become so compromised that you were unable to accomplish basic daily tasks such as cooking, reading, driving, even getting dressed. Perhaps you became uncharacteristically irritable, and as time wore on, increasingly depressed. After having such an infection, one father whose 13-year-old son had vestibular processing difficulties told Karen G. that he was overwhelmed by a newfound awareness of the magnitude of his son's daily struggles.

The Proprioceptive System (Positioning of the Body)

The term *proprioceptive* comes from the Latin stem *proprius,* which means "one's own," and it is through proprioceptive input that we know our own body, where it is, and how it is moving. Proprioceptors send information to our brain from our muscles, joints, and bones. Because there are so many joints, muscles, and bones in our body, this system is almost as large as the tactile system. It sends continuous information to the brain, but even when we try to pay attention to what our muscles and joints are telling us about our body position, we can only feel a fraction of the sensation that is generated by the proprioceptive system.

Have you ever walked down the aisle of an airplane with a carry-on bag slung over your shoulder? As you made your way to your seat, you undoubtedly found yourself apologizing repeatedly to other passengers for bumping into them with your bag. If you're like most of us, you experienced a "body map" problem. You bumped into people because a lifetime of knowledge about how much space you occupy, where your body ends and the rest of the world begins, was challenged. If you had kept that bag on your shoulder for several hours, you would have bumped into people less and less as the day wore on. With repeated feedback, your brain would have begun sending more accurate messages to your body about how to move through space. Operating outside your conscious control, your vestibular and proprioceptive systems would have enabled you to adjust to the experience of increased weight and bulk. This new body map would allow you once more to move through space safely and efficiently.

Karen S. was reminded of the importance of the hidden senses when she observed Evan in his preschool Montessori classroom. Children were working on projects on mats that were spread across the classroom floor, creating a mosaic of bodies and materials in irregular patterns. Karen watched as Evan tried to thread his way through this maze, looking out for little fingers and carefully constructed projects, while still maintaining his balance. As he stepped on mats, bumped into bodies, and knocked over projects that he just didn't seem able to avoid, Karen realized how difficult it was for him to walk from one side of the room to the other—a task that most children accomplish effortlessly.

Together the vestibular and proprioceptive systems quite literally keep us grounded. They regulate our posture and muscle tone. They tell us whether we are standing or sitting, slouching or squatting, bending, straightening, or stretching. They help us negotiate our distance from other people and things. As a result, we are able to move through space without falling or bumping into things. We can right ourselves against gravity, move through a doorway, sit on a chair without falling off the edge, and balance ourselves as we ride a bicycle or walk along a narrow curb. We can stand in a crowded, moving subway without tumbling into the people around us.

Watching young children at play, you see them pushing the limits of these two systems, experimenting with how far they can go and enjoying the thrill of the challenge. A preschooler spins around and around until she falls to the floor. Instead of crying, she picks herself up, dizzy and laughing, and begins to spin again. She craves this activity! By engaging in it repeatedly, she learns the limits of her body's ability to resist gravity. Almost all playground activities—running, jumping, climbing, spinning, and swinging—excite the vestibular and proprioceptive systems. As children slip and slide, twist and twirl, jump and bump, they come to understand where their bodies start and stop and how to move through physical space without crashing into other people or things.

SENSORY INTEGRATION:
HOW IT ALL COMES TOGETHER

Like the cacophony of notes coming out of the orchestra pit before a concert, sensory information has little meaning in its raw form. A flash of light. Colors. Patterns of movement. A vibration. Deep pressure on skin. The brain analyzes, organizes, and interprets these bits of information: *My teacher just touched me.* Where? *On the back.* How hard? *Medium hard. Not a tickle. Not a punch. Like a pat.* Further analysis is required: What was the meaning of her touch? *Congratulations? Punishment? Reminder? Accident?* The brain will use its interpretation of that sensory input to plan and carry out a response. *Should I defend myself? Run away? Ignore it? Smile? Tune in to what she is saying? Shift the focus of my attention? Do something else?* And on an unconscious level, the brain has already responded by sending messages to muscles and joints that keep the child from flopping over in response to her teacher's touch. This complex interaction between brain and body is what Ayres referred to as sensory integration. For purposes of explanation, sensory integration can be broken down into three complementary processes: *sensory modulation, sensory discrimination,* and *motor planning.*

Sensory modulation is the brain's automatic adjustment to the intensity with which sensory stimuli are experienced. When sensory modulation is efficient, the nervous system responds to some input while disregarding other sensations. We are able to tune out or tone down annoying or distracting stimuli. This process, explained further in Chapter Five where we elaborate on brain functioning, accounts for differences in the intensity of stimulation that we can tolerate. In any family, there are differences in people's tolerance levels. Mom can work at the computer while the TV is on, but Dad needs complete quiet to concentrate. One sister sleeps easily under a heavy down comforter, whereas the other cannot adjust to the weight of the covers and throws them off. These differences are often thought of as preferences or characteristics of personality. It becomes family lore that Dad has a short fuse or that Jane is a restless sleeper. Actually, these outward signs reflect internal physiological differences in how each person's brain responds to sensory input.

Our ability to modulate sensory stimulation may vary over time, with the circumstances, and depending on how we feel. Loud music may be intolerable to Dad when he is trying to read the newspaper after a difficult day at work, but it might be welcome, even energizing, when he is working in the garage on a Saturday morning. Most of us know our limits, and we choose levels of stimulation that feel comfortable to us.

As adults, we have considerable autonomy in managing the sensory characteristics of our surroundings. We intuitively know how well we modulate sensory input, and we choose environments that are a good match for us. We can work alone or with others, live in the city or the country, play classical music or rock, turn the volume up or down. Children do not have this freedom. For the most part, adults impose their preferences on children, whether they "like" it or not.

The child with sensory modulation problems who does not easily adjust to different levels of sensory input may spend much of his day in a state of discomfort. His classroom may appear too busy or too bright, too crowded or too colorful. His teacher's voice may sound too loud or too shrill. The other children might feel too boisterous or too close. Before he has even been given an assignment, he may be overwhelmed by his inability to adjust to the intensity of sensation he experiences in the classroom.

Sensory discrimination is the ability to distinguish one sensory experience from another. It is how we know that an itch on our arm is not an itch on our lower back, that a siren is coming toward us rather than moving away from us. It is the ability to distinguish sweet from sour and cold from hot. It makes it possible for us to tie our shoes in the dark and button a shirt without looking at our fingers because we can tell where we are touching things even when we can't see them. Sensory discrimination allows us to judge whether sensations are threatening or benign, important or insignificant. By providing information about the intensity and tonal quality of a baby's cry, sensory discrimination allows us to make the judgment that our infant is in pain. It also allows us to distinguish the sounds of a garbage truck outside (which clearly does not need our attention) from the sound of a bookshelf crashing inside (which certainly might). It is an essential component of our ability to organize our daily lives.

The third component of sensory integration, **motor planning or praxis, is the ability to translate sensory input into organized, purposeful motor output.** The process of motor planning includes (1) coming up with an idea about the action, (2) having an accurate sense of where the body is, (3) starting the action, (4) executing the steps in the appropriate sequence, (5) making adjustments as needed, and (6) knowing when to stop the action.

When motor planning is efficient, sequenced movements are executed smoothly; over time, we no longer have to think about how to do them. The 2-year-old who is just learning to talk concentrates hard on the movement and positioning of his tongue and lips in order to make sounds that will be understood. With practice, he will speak effortlessly without contemplating how to form the words. Motor planning makes it possible for a school-age child to respond to a series of directions from his teacher. *Take your spelling book out of your desk, get a clean sheet of paper, put your name in the upper right hand corner, and number down on the left side from 1 to 10, leaving a line between each number.* His brain and body work together in a coordinated manner to move him through that sequence of tasks. Motor planning is the process whereby a child is able to write legibly, hit a baseball, and walk down a flight of stairs. Motor memory allows him to ride a bicycle successfully even if he hasn't been on one since last summer.

Young children spend a great deal of their time mastering motor planning activities through repetition. A child who is learning to pull herself up in her crib will be delighted to discover that she can stand holding on to the rails. Once she has had this experience, she will raise herself over and over until it is no longer challenging, until it becomes "mindless." Then she will move on to master another feat.

Motor planning also underlies the combination of several familiar, well-rehearsed steps into a more elaborate movement, like an aerobics routine or a line dance. Remember learning how to swim? First, you learned to kick while holding solidly to the tiled edge of the pool. You let your feet rise up behind you, but only briefly, as you first felt the weightlessness of floating. With practice, you learned to kick so hard that you splashed water out of the pool. Then, using a kickboard, you began to propel yourself from one end of the pool to the other, using the flutter kick to move you along. Next, you stood still and practiced breathing in the water by blowing bubbles and moving your head from side to side. You made a few mistakes, swallowed a bit of water, gagged, coughed it up, and tried again. You played around with putting your face in the water, dunking your head all the way under, holding your breath, and opening your eyes. You might not have liked the feeling of water in your nose, and it probably took you a while to learn how to breathe out through your nose to prevent water from coming in. Later, you combined breathing with arm movements while standing still. Ultimately, the challenge was to combine this seemingly bewildering variety of individual motor skills into a sequenced and purposeful set of movements that efficiently moved you down the swimming lane. Miraculously, once you mastered it, your motor memory never let you forget it.

During the early school grades, sensorimotor activities are the primary vehicle for learning. Being able to write, color in the lines, cut and paste, construct three-dimensional objects, and put together puzzles all require motor planning. Developmental specialists argue that these early forms of motor learning establish the foundation upon which higher-order thinking is built.

Together, the processes of modulation, discrimination, and motor planning make sensory integration possible. It is this silent interaction between our brains and bodies that enables us to move through the day in a purposeful manner. We do not think about the sounds we are not consciously noticing, the mechanics of sitting in a chair, or the location of the third finger on our right hand as we slide a button into a buttonhole. Instead, our brain does this work for us outside the realm of consciousness. It receives and sorts countless tidbits of sensory information, then allows only an essential fraction of it to pass to the thinking parts of our brain.

Because of this well-choreographed dance between brain and body, between sensory receptors and motor effectors, between gray matter and muscles, joints, skin, and bones, we glide through our day consumed by our thoughts and mostly lost to our senses. Unbeknownst to us, the processes of sensory integration are keeping us alert, out of harm's way, and literally moving in the right direction.

Some children, however, are not so fortunate. For reasons not clearly understood, they do not process sensory information efficiently. They are painfully aware of sensations that other children do not seem to notice. Or they have difficulty discriminating and integrating sensory input in a manner that leads to smooth and efficient motor output. These kids may look clumsy and disorganized. They may be silly and excitable. They might crash into things despite their protests that others are crashing into them. They may complain about noise but make lots of it. They can be controlling, irritable, anxious, or difficult to manage.

Conversations with our own children and experiences with our clients have convinced us that the child with poor sensory integration often feels assaulted by his environment, betrayed by his body, and misunderstood by everyone. He might not automatically recognize that a classmate's touch on the shoulder is benign rather than threatening. He probably can't explain that the seams of his socks paralyze him or that the bristles of the hairbrush feel like fire on his scalp. His parents, exhausted and exasperated, do not understand why the simplest everyday task is a challenge in their home. For this child, and many like him, life is a constant struggle.

|||||||||||||||||||||||||||||||||||||||||||||||||||||||||||||||||||||||||||||||||||

CHAPTER TWO

Betrayed by Their Senses:
Dysfunctional Sensory Integration

*Whenever I try to ride my bike, I see a black wall coming up
in front of my face and I'm afraid I'm going to run into it.*

— BEN,
at age 8

I don't like that shirt. It's too spicy on the inside.

— SALLY,
at age 4

GETTING STARTED

Imagine a typical morning for the child with dysfunctional sensory integration. The morning routine we described in the last chapter becomes an obstacle course replete with challenges if his brain is unable to modulate and discriminate sensory input and translate it into organized, meaningful movement.

First the alarm goes off. An assaultive sound for all of us, it is louder, more irritating, and perhaps even frightening for the child with auditory sensitivities. It may also be disorienting, especially when combined with the dissonant sounds coming from outside his open window. You tune these out—the sounds of cars honking, garbage trucks grinding, and neighbors talking—but the child with auditory modulation or discrimination difficulties cannot ignore them so easily. For this child, the morning routine requires greater effort and concentration. His thoughts do not translate automatically into action even though he has completed these tasks hundreds of times. Rather than getting up, he lies in bed staring into space, playing with the shadows on the wall, literally lost in his own thoughts.

You get out of bed and walk to the bathroom without a thought, but the child with sensory integration difficulties may be more cautious about moving from a prone to an upright position. As Evan's occupational therapist once said, "Evan has to think about gravity all the time." For a child with sensory modulation problems that affect movement and balance (the vestibular sense), the challenge of sitting up, swinging his feet to the floor, and walking down the hall in a straight line may be the equivalent of a high-wire circus act. It takes tremendous concentration.

Once this child makes it to the bathroom, he may feel assaulted by many of the sensations he experiences there. He turns on the shower. If he is temperature sensitive, the water may feel too hot or too cold. If he is tactilely defensive, the pressure of the water cascading over his head may feel like needles pricking his scalp. He may hate the feeling of soap on his body or the rough texture of the towel against his skin. Leaning over to dry off his legs might make him dizzy and he may lose his balance, crashing to the floor. Brushing his teeth may be painful. The bristles of the toothbrush feel sharp on his gums, and the balancing act of keeping his head stable while moving the toothbrush up, down, and around may literally make him feel sick. He has not even gotten to the point of getting dressed and already he feels irritable, frustrated, and put upon. More likely, he has resisted doing these things. His mother has checked on him two or three times and found him back in his room, sitting on the bed, looking at his clothes. Irritation has crept into her voice. He has started to whine and complain. It has been only fifteen minutes since the alarm went off, and both of them already feel the day's goodwill slipping away.

Their battle is likely to continue as the child reluctantly gets dressed. His jeans feel too stiff and his socks are uncomfortable. He cannot button, snap, or zip his pants or tie his shoes. This annoys his mother because she knows that other children his age can easily do these things. She wonders: *When is he going to grow up? Should I refuse to do these things for him? Why doesn't he want to be more independent?* Meanwhile, the cries of his baby sister in the next room distract him from the unpleasant task at hand. He puts his hands over his ears, loses his focus, and forgets what he is supposed to be doing. When his mother returns to check on him, he is still only partially dressed. He has not eaten breakfast or packed his backpack and they have to be out the door in five minutes. She explodes, and her son, hurt and confused, bursts into tears.

To an observer, there might be several possible explanations for this boy's failure to get ready for school. The most common psychological theory is that his parents may have been inconsistent in their discipline or unclear in their demands and that they have rewarded his negative, uncooperative behavior. Inadvertently, the theory goes, his parents are paying more attention to negative behavior than to positive behavior. Their ineffective discipline methods have increased rather than decreased the likelihood that the undesirable behavior will recur.

This explanation assumes that the child is capable of performing the necessary task but has experienced a history of negative interactions that interfere with the likelihood that he will. However, the child with sensory integration difficulties is *unable* to meet his mother's demands because he is having difficulty translating sensory information into an efficient, organized, and adaptive morning routine. He is not manipulating his mother, and he is not seeking negative attention. He wants to please her, but he literally cannot get it together. Unfortunately, neither he nor his mother knows why he is having so much trouble getting started. A greater understanding might allow them to move toward a more productive resolution of their conflict.

Difficulties with sensory integration are not the same for all children. The behavioral manifestations of these difficulties differ depending on (1) which sense is involved and (2) whether they are related to inefficient modulation, discrimination, or planning. Most children with sensory dysregulation have difficulties in more than one of these areas. However, rarely do children have difficulties in all areas of sensory functioning unless they are otherwise significantly impaired. The following lists are based on the work of Lucy Miller and her colleagues, a group of occupational therapy researchers who are attempting to more clearly define what is meant by the term *dysfunctional sensory integration*.

SENSORY MODULATION DIFFICULTIES

As we stated in Chapter One, sensory modulation is the ability to turn the volume up or down on our experience of the world. Depending on the ever-changing demands of the moment, we adjust our awareness of louder or softer noises, gentler or rougher touches, more or less pleasing odors. Difficulties can result from over- or undersensitivity to input from one or more of the seven sensory realms. One child might experience problems with auditory stimuli, whereas another might only experience difficulties with vestibular modulation. Furthermore, their behavior may appear erratic if they are oversensitive to some stimuli and undersensitive to others. Or their sensitivities might vary depending on other factors such as sleep deprivation or illness. The problem is one of dysregulation—that is, the child's inability to *adjust to* the input and moderate her response.

Imagine a radio with poor reception. At times the signal comes in too loudly, whereas at other times it comes in too softly. Sometimes it is clear; other times it is full of static. If you turn the volume down while it is too loud, you won't be able to hear a thing when the reception shifts unpredictably. Because it shifts in and out, it is impossible to find a volume level that will allow you to listen comfortably. In this way, the erratic input affects your ability to respond in a meaningful way. Similarly, the child with sensory modulation difficulties experiences the world as an uncomfortable, out-of-control place in which it is hard to figure out how to respond.

Have you been to a movie theater recently? If so, you have undoubtedly had the experience of settling into your chair as the lights go down only to be blasted by the unpleasantly high volume of the movie previews. You wince, you wiggle in your seat, and you frown at your companion. Perhaps you even consider getting up and complaining to the manager of the theater, but after a few minutes you are able to focus on the substance of the plot and follow the action without being disturbed by the intensity of the sound. Your brain has habituated to the noise. With no conscious effort on your part, your sensory feedback system has adjusted. You are no longer annoyed.

For the child with auditory modulation difficulties, this habituation may not take place. The noise may continue to irritate him, even though he may not be aware of the source of his irritation. If he remains uncomfortable throughout the movie, he may squirm in his seat and talk over the noise, annoying people seated around him and embarrassing his parents. Karen G. recalls taking Ben to the IMAX when he was 4 years old. As soon as the image was projected onto the screen and the musical accompaniment began, Ben's body became rigid and he started shrieking. The abruptness and intensity of his reaction was frightening to Karen and her husband, who had long ago become accustomed to his crying when they were grinding coffee or vacuuming. The auditory and visual intensity of the IMAX was not only irritating but also deeply threatening to Ben. As soon as his family left the theater, he calmed quickly, but it was years before he would consider a return trip.

Tactile Modulation Difficulties

Many young children are sensitive to the labels on their clothing or the seams of their socks. The child who has tactile modulation difficulties finds a much wider array of textures distressing. One mother described an exhaustive and expensive search for sheets comfortable enough for her son to settle in for a night's sleep. Another mother purchased multitudes of socks in a futile effort to find a brand her toddler could tolerate. Finally, giving up, she allowed her son to wear water shoes everywhere until the discomfort of the snowy Chicago winter made sockless feet more uncomfortable than the texture of the socks themselves. Forced to choose between ice-encrusted toes and scratchy socks, he overcame his resistance to the socks.

In our offices, we have come to recognize these children from the stories their parents offhandedly tell about them. They refuse to wear jeans. They wear their T-shirts inside out. They will only wear pants with elastic waists. They wear the same pair of knit shorts every day whether dirty or clean. They will not put on a coat. One mother reported that whenever she found a comfortable pair of pants or shoes for her child, she bought them in enough colors and sizes to last for the next several years. Other parents report that as soon as they get into the house their children kick off their shoes or strip off most of their clothes. Some prefer to run around the house naked. Although this might be acceptable to parents when their children are young, it becomes awkward when they get older. It can also lead to complaints from older siblings who are embarrassed by this behavior, especially when their friends are visiting. Insisting that these children wear clothes can lead to irritability, power struggles, and tension for the entire family.

Parents recognize tactile hypersensitivity because children's over-reactions to certain materials or experiences are directly observable; however, they are less likely to understand behaviors related to hypo-sensitivity. Children who are hyposensitive or undersensitive to touch frequently miss tactile cues that should alert them that their clothes are askew or that they have food on their faces. These kids often crave tactile input and plunge into messy materials such as finger paints, sand, or clay with such abandon that parents may forbid these activities because the child does not use the materials properly. This is unfortunate because these children may need this stimulation. They crave these activities because, unlike good sensory processors, they do not get enough tactile input in the natural course of their daily activities.

Tactile modulation difficulties can cause eating problems. Parents who know that their child is a picky eater may not have made the connection between food preferences and food texture. A child may eat very soft foods such as pasta, bread, or mashed potatoes but refuse anything with a more substantial textural feel. In the most extreme cases, only liquid diets are acceptable to the child. In contrast, a child who is undersensitive to touch might crave crunchy or hard foods that give her deep tactile feedback. A child with sensory modulation difficulties in the tactile realm may behave in one or more of the following ways:

- Aggressively responds to touch or imagined touch
- Has difficulty with dressing, bathing, hair brushing, nail cutting, or tooth brushing
- Shows peculiar and particular responses to food textures
- Constantly touches or pokes others
- Gives high fives too hard; hugs too tightly
- Craves cuddling (hyporesponsive) or arches away from cuddling (hyperresponsive)

- Crashes into people or walls
- Is excessively ticklish
- Overreacts to ordinary childhood bruises or underreacts to pain
- Craves messy activities or refuses to play with messy items such as finger paint and clay
- Constantly "fingers" or "mouths" things such as food, hair, clothing, and objects
- Has trouble with group situations such as circle time
- Resists wearing certain materials, long sleeves, or pants
- Strips clothes and/or shoes off whenever possible
- Is sensitive to waistbands, belts, collars, sleeves
- Becomes controlling with others in an attempt to decrease overwhelming input

Auditory Modulation Difficulties

Parents easily recognize auditory modulation difficulties when a child reacts strongly to sounds. An infant may scream or cry at the sound of the garbage disposal or a hair dryer. A preschooler may place his hands over his ears in a loud restaurant or at a fireworks display. Other situations that might be stressful for the child sensitive to noise are less easily identified by parents. A child may react negatively because the voice his mother is using sounds like a "yelling voice" even though she is actually not yelling. Or a child may become irritable if the noise level in a room is high enough to grate on her but not so loud that she complains or covers her ears. Think of a really noisy place (a preschool birthday party, a crowded bar, a rock concert). If you were trying to concentrate on reading a book or mastering a new skill in that place, you might feel grumpy and irritable after a while. You would be likely to overreact to little things that usually wouldn't bother you. Children with auditory modulation difficulties feel and act like this when they are overloaded.

Ironically, these children are often loud themselves. Parents wonder why a child who is sensitive to sound would be so loud herself. When you are in a really noisy place or you are talking to someone with a loud voice, don't you generally talk louder? Many of these children feel that others are always shouting at them, so they shout back. They also make their own noise to block out noises around them. They bang on things, hum, sing, or make sound effects—driving everyone around them to distraction—so that they can concentrate. One third-grader who hums constantly while he works complained that he was having a "personal problem" with the boy seated at the desk next to him. When his teacher asked what the problem was, he replied, "He's always telling me to be quiet." Needless to say, noise-making in the classroom is considered disruptive, and if it continues after several requests that it stop, it is seen as oppositional. A child with sensory modulation difficulties in the auditory realm may behave in one or more of the following ways:

- Has difficulty filtering noise in a classroom and elsewhere
- Overreacts to loud sounds, frequently covering her ears with her hands—for example, when she hears sirens
- Constantly complains that others are screaming at him
- Produces excessive amounts of repetitive noise with hands or mouth
- Hears noises that others do not hear—startles in response to sounds that may not even be heard by others.

Olfactory and Gustatory Modulation Difficulties

Modulation difficulties in the realms of taste and smell often result in difficult or unusual responses to foods. Children who are hypersensitive to taste are very picky eaters. They only eat very bland foods and are unwilling to try new foods because they have learned that this is frequently an unpleasant experience. In contrast, children who are undersensitive to taste and smell prefer spicy, pungent, or stronger-tasting foods. One mother reported that her son insists on loading every bite of food with several shakes of salt and pepper. Another mother described jalapeño peppers as her son's favorite snack.

Preschoolers are known for their difficult and picky eating habits; however, for children with inefficient sensory modulation, these sensitivities go beyond preference. No matter where they are or how hungry they feel, no matter what threat or reward they have been offered, they will refuse to eat the foods whose smells or flavors they find overwhelming. One mother reported that even though her son loved eating dinner with his family, he always took his plate into another room and ate by himself when his parents ate shrimp because he could not tolerate the smell. Another mother described an unexpected tantrum at the door of a restaurant the family wanted to try. When she asked her daughter what the problem was, she screamed, "It smells yucky!"

Children's comments about smell are easily misinterpreted by adults as impolite or disrespectful. In a consultation with Karen S., one teacher described a kindergartener as rude because he always held his nose in the school cafeteria. A father reported being taken aback when his son matter-of-factly said to him, "Something stinks, Dad. I think it's you." The following behaviors suggest modulation difficulties with taste or smell:

- Reports that all food tastes the same
- Craves unusual tastes—for example, very spicy or very salty
- Will only eat bland foods
- Sniffs people or objects
- Does not notice offensive smells (hyposensitive) or reacts violently and inappropriately to offensive smells (hypersensitive)
- Refuses to go near strong-smelling foods
- Dislikes certain people or pets because of their smell

Visual Modulation Difficulties

Children with visual modulation difficulties may react strongly to light, color, or complex images. They may avoid bright sunlight, as in the case of one boy who told his mother that his favorite weather was "gray and cloudy." Another boy complained that "the grass is too green." A typical elementary classroom, with its fluorescent lighting and visual clutter, is a stressful environment for some children. Before the teacher has given the first direction, these children are often jittery and out of sorts.

Other children may be sensitive to direct eye contact. They become overstimulated when someone holds their gaze for too long, or when a person puts her face too close to them. One mother recalled leaving her 2-month-old infant with a good friend for an afternoon. Upon her return, she learned that every time her friend had caught her baby's eye he had cried inconsolably. By trial and error, her friend had discovered that he calmed only when she turned his body away from her. The two women concluded that he had been disturbed by the emotional and visual intensity of this direct gaze. Seeking visual stimulation on his own terms allowed him to modulate this intensity. A child with visual modulation difficulties may show the following behaviors:

- Difficulty shifting gaze from one object to another
- Difficulty copying from the blackboard or books
- Avoidance of visually stimulating environments
- Avoidance of eye contact
- Preference for dim lighting
- Preference for sunglasses
- Tiring easily or irritability when attending to visually complex tasks
- Squinting, rubbing eyes, or getting headaches after reading but not requiring glasses

Vestibular-Proprioceptive Modulation Difficulties (Problems with Balance, Movement, and Body Position)

Modulation difficulties in the vestibular and proprioceptive realms are the least obvious to parents but the most likely to have a negative effect on a child's ability to move productively through the day. Children with these sorts of modulation difficulties frequently misperceive where their bodies are in space. As a result, they appear clumsy. They tumble along, bumping into people, crashing into walls, flopping out of their seats. They have difficulty standing in line without touching others. They knock over their drinks. "Can't you see where you're going?" and "Watch what you're doing!" are constant refrains from those around them. They are generally unaware of how much force they use when touching other people or handling everyday objects. They hold hands too tightly. Their hugs are painful. They break toys inadvertently, poke holes in their paper while writing or erasing, and put down things they are carrying with a crash.

These children avoid some playground activities but crave others.

Movement of certain types—swinging or hanging from a bar—may nauseate them, while an activity that makes other kids sick—such as spinning—may be soothing. One mother of a 3-year-old said that her child loved to be spun around in circles on the tire swing at the playground. She described him as so mellow after fifteen minutes of spinning that he "looked like the patron of an opium den." Other children are reluctant to join in playground activities for fear of being bumped or jostled. They do not want to be forced to go on slides or swings that make them feel ill. One father reported that his son literally vomited the first time he walked on a beach. The vestibular disequilibrium caused by the shifting sand under his feet was too much for his extremely sensitive system to handle.

In contrast, children who are understimulated in the vestibular-proprioceptive realms crave feedback to their muscles, joints, and inner ear. They deliberately crash into people and things. Whenever possible, they run, climb, bounce, lean back, tilt, spin, and hang upside down. They love rough-and-tumble play, and they usually play too rough. They jump on the furniture regardless of their parents' exasperated warnings. They are easily misjudged as being aggressive and oppositional because they "do not learn from their mistakes." Identifying behaviors for a child with modulation difficulties in the vestibular-proprioceptive senses include:

- Poor balance
- Difficulty going up and down stairs at an age-appropriate level
- Frequently rocking or hanging upside down
- Slouching off to one side; trouble maintaining a seated position with good posture
- Afraid of heights and/or vigorous, fast-moving activities
- Preference for spinning activities
- Fear of escalators, open staircases
- Avoidance of sports or difficulty learning them
- Bumping into things a lot

SENSORY DISCRIMINATION DIFFICULTIES

Sensory discrimination is the ability to recognize differences in sensory information. Is a thing close by or far away? Dangerous or benign? Relevant or irrelevant? Sensory discrimination difficulties can create a great deal of confusion in a child's day-to-day life. He may have difficulty determining the meaning of a sensation, and he may need sensory input from more than one source to interpret the information accurately. Is that sound coming from behind or in front of him? He may need to look around to locate it. Did someone just touch him on the shoulder or the back? He may startle if he didn't see that person approaching. Was her touch friendly or hostile? He may need to look at her face or listen to her voice to judge whether to respond defensively.

Children with sensory discrimination difficulties often have problems with fine-motor tasks. One mother reported that her son's teacher reprimanded him for his refusal to join the class in table projects. For this child, the demands of those activities—manipulating scissors, coloring inside the lines, assembling tiny pieces of paper into a whole— were overwhelming, so he retreated into fantasy play rather than face tasks he was sure to fail. Another teacher complained about a kindergartener who "won't do anything I tell him to do." When his classmates were busily working at table projects, he usually hid under the coat rack. Karen S. inquired about whether he might be avoiding tasks that were too difficult. "No way!" the teacher insisted. "He can do this work. It's just cutting and coloring."

Tactile Discrimination Difficulties

Children with tactile discrimination difficulties have trouble making sense of their own touch and the touch of others. They cannot tell exactly where they are being touched, which makes it difficult for them to determine whether the touch is friendly or frightening. Mothers of these children frequently describe them as aggressive, and teachers report that they strike out at other children without provocation. Indeed, their lashing out often appears unprovoked. For example, if a child with discrimination and modulation difficulties is accidentally bumped by a classmate, he cannot tell where the physical sensation is coming from. He also may experience the bump more as a blow, which will alert his brain stem, the most primitive, defensive part of his brain. Bypassing reason, he attacks because he believes that he has been attacked. However, the objective onlooker sees the accidental bump and the overreaction to it and considers the child's response to be an act of aggression.

These children frequently have difficulty with fine-motor tasks because they cannot always feel which finger is which or where each one is located. This makes it hard for them to use their hands in a well-coordinated way. As a result, they have trouble learning to button, zip, and buckle clothing and to tie their shoes. One mother reported her relief and excitement when a shoe company extended the manufacture of Velcro shoes to larger sizes. Her third-grade son would be able to put on his own shoes!

Many self-care tasks are extremely difficult for these kids. Take tooth brushing, for example. In addition to setting off sensory modulation alarms, this task requires accurate tactile discrimination. You cannot guide the toothbrush with your eyes when it is in the back of your mouth; instead, you have to feel where it should go. But if a child says, "I can't," when he is told to brush his teeth, most parents hear that as "I won't." "Don't be ridiculous," a mother might reply. *"Of course you can!"* Thus begins a daily conflict between a misunderstood child and a frustrated parent.

One mother reported that getting her son into the car each morning was an ongoing battle. While all the other children in the carpool easily settled into their places, her son would delay the trip to school by refusing to wear his seat belt. She didn't realize that he was refusing for a reason. He couldn't see the buckle under the bulk of his coat, and he couldn't feel it either—he literally couldn't buckle his seat belt. To make matters worse, the tactile sensation of the seat belt tightening around his abdomen caused profound discomfort for him. No wonder he wasn't jumping happily into his seat! Behaviors indicative of tactile discrimination difficulties may include

- Consistent avoidance of or difficulty with fine-motor tasks such as writing or cutting, buttoning, zipping, tying shoes

- Aggressive or startle responses to being touched from behind
- Need to look at objects in order to correctly identify or manipulate them

Auditory Discrimination Difficulties

Auditory discrimination difficulties interfere with a child's ability to make sense of what she hears. She may not be able to tell where a sound is coming from or how far away it is. Adults may find themselves repeating requests several times before she responds. She may not pick up subtle sound cues that are necessary to distinguish between words with similar sounds, so she may hear things incorrectly. In circumstances where there is a lot of background noise, such as a classroom or a crowded kitchen or anyplace where a TV is playing, she may not be able to pick out the important sounds and ignore the rest. She may be accused of not listening, not paying attention, or not following directions. At school, she may be criticized for being off task or for looking at other students' papers to see what she is supposed to be doing. Teachers may describe her as being in a fog or having her head in the clouds.

Many times these children are diagnosed with attention deficit hyperactivity disorder (ADHD) because their auditory discrimination problems are identified as auditory inattention. This is a tricky distinction and there are no clear guidelines yet to help us understand the overlap between sensory processing problems and some of the symptoms of ADHD. In trying to sort out the difference, one father of a child with auditory modulation and discrimination difficulties explained, "It seems to me that children with ADHD are like Odysseus trying to resist the Sirens: they are drawn to the things that distract them. But my son is infuriated by distracting noises. He is overwhelmed by them and he becomes irritable and angry because they are interfering with his ability to concentrate on the task at hand." A child with inefficient auditory discrimination may display difficulties in the following areas:

- Understanding or attending to what is said
- Differentiating and remembering certain sounds or words
- Judging the source of sounds

- Judging location and distance by sound
- Focusing on or recognizing particular sounds in the context of background noise
- Responding consistently to verbal requests or commands
- Following age-appropriate commands with multiple steps

Olfactory and Gustatory Discrimination Difficulties

Taste and smell are closely related, and together they determine what we describe as the taste of our food. Children with discrimination difficulties in these senses have trouble identifying foods unless they can see what they are eating. They may also have difficulty distinguishing particular tastes or smells. One mother described a science experiment in which her second-grader had to chew crackers for varying lengths of time, then report on the shifts in sweetness as a function of the time chewed. Although this task was easy and enjoyable for most of the children in the class, her child could not do it. He detected no differences in the taste of the cracker no matter how long he chewed it. A child with discrimination difficulties in the areas of taste and smell may show the following behaviors:

- Difficulty differentiating smells and tastes without visual cues
- Seems oblivious to the relevance of certain smells (e.g., burning toast)

Visual Discrimination Difficulties

Of all the senses, sight is probably the most precious because we rely on it to navigate, to feel safe, to relate to others, and to understand the world. We say, "Oh, I *see* what you mean," when we comprehend what someone is saying. Unlike other primates who rely primarily on smell or hearing to gather information about their environment, we depend most heavily on our vision to negotiate our world. Children have long flirted with the scary feelings related to loss of vision by inventing games such as "Blind Man's Bluff" and "Pin the Tail on the Donkey" in which one blindfolded player has to perform a task. Games of "Peeka-Boo" and "Hide-and-Seek" similarly delight children because they allow them to ponder the mysteries of life without vision.

Life can be very confusing for children with visual discrimination difficulties. Their behavior can also be confusing to others. Although their eyesight may be perfect, they act as if they cannot see clearly. They may have trouble identifying numbers and letters, perceiving forms, or understanding how individual forms relate to each other. For example, learning the difference between the letter E and the letter F, figuring out how to space words in a sentence, or constructing a poster for school with neatly spaced pictures poses a significant challenge for these children. Learning to read can be difficult. Adding a tactile component to letter discrimination tasks provides information from more than one sensory channel and often makes it easier for them to distinguish the letters. Occupational therapists sometimes recommend letting them "write" in sand or shaving cream or rice.

Picking something out of an array of objects may also be challenging for these children because they have difficulty discriminating among visual choices. It may take them longer to accomplish simple tasks that require them to find things (e.g., finding a pair of shoes on a messy bedroom floor, finding a homework paper in a backpack, finding the butter in the refrigerator). "It's not here!" they holler, as they seem to look right past it.

Karen S. recalls that Evan used to wander aimlessly around his Montessori classroom each morning, getting into trouble rather than starting an activity. One day he complained, "When Susan says 'Choose some work,' that's hard for me, Mom." At the time, she didn't know what he meant. After all, there were many enticing possibilities displayed on shelves all around the room. Later she realized that he was describing a visual discrimination problem. There were so many choices that he literally could not see what his options were.

Translating pictures into three-dimensional objects and seeing relationships between parts and a whole (e.g., building a toy from a set of instructions or putting a puzzle together) may cause these children great frustration. One mother described watching her 14-year-old son try to use a manual can opener. Despite repeated instruction, each time he tried to open a can he acted as if he had never seen the can opener before. She watched him struggle to make sense of the different parts of the opener and to properly align it against the edge of the can. He stuck with it, because he knew this was a task most 14-year-olds could easily accomplish, and he eventually succeeded. His mother, however, was struck by the difficulty he experienced. It transported her back in memory to the times when as a preschooler he struggled unsuccessfully to place various shaped blocks through their corresponding holes in a child's toy. A child with sensory discrimination difficulties in the visual realm may have difficulty with the following tasks:

- Perceiving forms, shapes, and the relationships between objects
- Recognizing, matching, and categorizing color, shape, texture, and size
- Scanning visual sequences and following rapid movement with their eyes
- Using vision to guide gross and fine-motor movements (it might be very hard for this child to learn a line dance)
- Recognizing symbols and gestures; he might misinterpret nonverbal interpersonal cues such as facial expressions
- Perceiving depth, distance, location of boundaries, and space between objects; much of her experience may seem like optical illusions
- Differentiating foreground from background images

Vestibular-Proprioceptive Discrimination Difficulties (Difficulties of Balance, Movement, and Body Position)

We are least aware of the vestibular and proprioceptive senses, even though they allow us to move efficiently through space. Children who have discrimination difficulties in this realm trip, fall, and bump their way through each day. They slip off their chairs for no apparent reason. They lose their balance standing on firm ground. They do not seem to be able to judge where their body stops and the rest of the world begins. Childhood games that require balance, such as walking along beams, avoiding cracks in the sidewalk, and hopping on one foot, elude them. This gravitational insecurity causes them to rely heavily on vision and touch to determine where they are in space. Therefore, they are extremely "touchy" and may seem to ignore the unspoken rules of personal space.

One mother told the story of being called into school to deal with her 8-year-old daughter's disruptive behavior in the halls. Despite repeated admonitions from her teacher, Jenny was bumping into trash cans and knocking things off the wall as her class traveled in a line down the hall to the cafeteria each day. The students were told to keep their hands to themselves, but Jenny was always touching something or someone. Children complained that she would bump into them or hit them when she was behind them in line. Her teacher had tried rewarding and punishing her, but she continued to cause problems in the hallway. Fortunately for Jenny, her mother knew why she was doing what she was doing. She realized that Jenny was touching the wall (and the garbage cans and her classmates) to determine her position in space, using the tactile feedback to keep herself on track. Without it, she would have literally been lost in space. Jenny's mother suggested that her teacher assign her a line partner: someone whose hand she could hold as they walked down the hall. This simple solution kept her on track and out of trouble. A child with vestibular-proprioceptive discrimination difficulties may have problems in the following areas:

- Maintaining balance, particularly when he is moving
- Knowing the position of her body in space and its relationship to her surroundings
- Maintaining an upright posture or sitting in a chair for a long period of time
- Differentiating right from left after age 7
- Enjoying playground equipment or amusement park rides—these kids prefer to have their feet firmly planted on the ground at all times

MOTOR PLANNING DIFFICULTIES (DYSPRAXIA)

Motor planning is involved in all aspects of "doing." When we tell a child to find something to do, that requires praxis—the process of planning, sequencing, carrying out, and ultimately remembering motor movements. It is the adaptive response, the motor output, which results from efficient sensory processing. Difficulties with motor planning, generally referred to as *dyspraxia* (from the Greek root *dys*, meaning "bad," and *praxis*, meaning "to do"), can affect a child's ability to engage in a wide range of motor activities. He cannot easily join other children in the world of physical play. He may not feel comfortable on the playground and he may not enjoy sports. He may look and feel awkward. He may have trouble in the world of work—keeping up with the classroom routine, finding his way around the school, and following a complicated series of directions.

These difficulties can begin early. Some children never crawl properly, or they may learn to walk late. Speech development can be delayed due to the difficulty they have moving their tongues and lips in the proper sequence to form words. As preschoolers, they may have difficulty learning to ride tricycles, string beads, or assemble crafts. As they get older, operating the combination lock on their school locker, filling in the bubbles on standardized test forms, and playing team sports pose significant challenges.

One mother of a 12-year-old dyspraxic boy really had to fight with his physical education teacher for the accommodations her son needed in gym class. Not only were the physical activities themselves difficult for him but he also needed more time than other kids in his class to get dressed and undressed. To make matters worse, he usually arrived in the dressing room late, because walking up and down the stairs to the gym was difficult for him. Despite this mother's efforts to explain her son's hidden disability to his gym teacher, the teacher insisted that he try everything at least once. Sometimes pushing a child to persevere at difficult tasks makes sense; however, in this case, the effort it took for this boy to attempt the task and the embarrassment he experienced at his failure caused him to shut down for the rest of the school day.

Karen G.'s husband, Norm, vividly remembers teaching Ben to ride a bicycle. Ben was much older than most kids are when they first learn, and still it was a considerable challenge for him. "It was like teaching him to ride in a box in which the sides were too close, even though we were in the middle of the street," said Norm. "It was as if he had to fight off visual obstacles, things we don't even notice when we're in the street, like a tree on the parkway or the front stairs of each house. To make it worse, he acted as though the sidewalk was coming up at him." He added, "I finally suggested that we move to a large field, thinking that might help."

Ben concurred, "Until we moved to that big field, everything was way too small, way too skinny. I kept thinking I was going to crack my head open."

"Even after we moved to the field," Norm continued, "it was hard for Ben to do any three things at once. Braking, steering, and pedaling together presented a real challenge. He also had to stay in his seat and maintain his balance—and I realized that he was trying to make himself as small as possible on the seat. Any time he had to make an adjustment, like if he had to go around something, he panicked. He would stop suddenly or fall off his bike. I finally realized that the only way we were going to be successful was for me to let Ben teach me how to teach him."

Ben agreed. "Parents should listen to their kids," he said. "Their kids can guide them."

Dyspraxia also has an ideational or conceptual component that involves the ability to mentally plan a series of activities or organize materials to create a product. The child with ideational dyspraxia is not very good at planning out her activities for the day or getting started on a project requiring the use of many materials and the assembly of multiple parts. At the most complex level, neuropsychologists refer to this as executive functioning: the ability to organize, plan, and execute a program of action in accordance with an idea. A child with dyspraxia may have difficulty in both the ideational and motor realms when it comes to

- Deciding what to do and how to do it
- Getting started on projects
- Translating ideas and images into action
- Organizing a series of actions to produce an intentional movement
- Figuring out how to play a new game or incorporate new actions or movements into an old pattern of activity

- Combining several steps of an activity even though he can complete each individual step successfully
- Learning and executing novel motor activities such as riding a bicycle, swimming, or playing tennis
- Transitioning from one body position to another with appropriate sequencing and timing
- Smoothly executing fine-motor movements required to complete activities such as tying shoes, fastening clothes, writing, and cutting
- Coordinating tongue and mouth movements, resulting in problems chewing and swallowing, sucking, and blowing
- Using appropriate facial movements to convey feeling and meaning
- Coordinating eye-hand movements
- Recognizing the movement of his own body in relation to the movement of others—he may think someone else bumped him when, in fact, he bumped into the other person

IS THIS MY CHILD?

The list of behaviors that can be related to inefficient sensory integration is lengthy, seemingly contradictory, and at times confusing. It is difficult to know when a behavior problem is sensory based and when it isn't. Parents may ask: *Isn't everyone sensitive to noise and crowds some of the time? How do I know if my child has a motor planning problem or is just stubborn? What about learning disabilities and attention deficit hyperactivity disorder? Are they the same as sensory integration problems?* Their fervent hope, of course, is that a correct label will bring with it a prescribed, well-established, and effective treatment. But correctly identifying sensory processing problems is a challenge. Many professionals bypass this potential explanation, focusing instead on more traditional ways of thinking about children who are out-of-sorts or difficult to manage. As a result, many children are misunderstood and their problems remain unresolved. In Chapter Three, we will describe the diagnostic process and propose a way of thinking about these children that leads directly to a comprehensive treatment plan.

||||||||||||||||||||||||||||||||||||||||||||||||||||||||||||||||||||||||||||||||||||||

The Prevailing Sensibility: Sensory Processing Problems and Psychiatric Diagnosis

Expertise, I was reminded, isn't seeing all there is.
Expertise is knowing what you're looking for.

— ADAM GOPNIK,
New Yorker

I'm hoping you'll tell me I'm not
the worst mother in the world.

— JESSICA,
mother of Tony

T HE YOUNG mother of an unmanageable 4-year-old boy rattled off a list of situations in which her son was likely to throw a temper tantrum: getting dressed, brushing his teeth, washing his hair, eating a meal, moving through the day, preparing for bed. "We have to negotiate everything with Tony," she said. "That's all we do."

Her training as a teacher led her to believe that her son was bright. She called him a "computer wiz," and he was already reading. She was impressed by his quick sense of humor, cracker-jack memory, and exceptional attention span. She felt certain that he understood what he should be doing; nevertheless, he never seemed to be doing what he should.

She and her mother, an elementary school principal, had no idea what to make of Tony's constant commotion. "He's always angry," she marveled. "He never stops whining and crying." Her husband was puzzled, as well. Was Tony jealous of his 10-month-old brother? Was he unhappy with his babysitter? Was he just a difficult child?

Tony himself was full of good intentions and promises that he couldn't keep. No sooner would he sincerely proclaim "I want to be good," than he would suddenly throw a tantrum about something. Seemingly unprovoked, he would refuse to sit at the dinner table, put on his shirt, or let his mother clip his fingernails or blow-dry his hair. How could he behave when so many things upset him? The sun was too bright. His shoes were too tight. Even ice cream was too cold.

Now he found himself wedged between his parents on a therapist's couch, listening to their descriptions of his uncooperative, out-of-bounds behavior. Hearing his mother ask this stranger if she is a bad mother. Watching his father shrug his shoulders. Feeling the helplessness in the air and wondering why, once again, he was in trouble. There sat Tony, like so many other children who have been in the same position.

ANALYZE THIS

Disruptive, uncooperative behavior is the most common reason why young children are referred to mental health clinics. Typically, these children and their families arrive at a therapist's office in a cloud of frustration. One or both parents describe the many situations in which the child has misbehaved—at home, at school, at the grocery store, in church or synagogue. The therapist asks in detail about the parents' failed attempts to manage their child's difficult behavior. Throughout this conversation, the child may busy himself with a shelf of toys, wander distractedly around the office, or sit glumly in a chair trying to tune out his parents' complaints: "He doesn't listen." "He always has to have things his way." "Nothing I do makes any difference to him." It is the therapist's job to make sense of this litany of failure and confusion.

Parents of a child who is not following directions can reel off a dizzying array of suggestions they have received from people they have turned to for help. Family members may have advised them to surrender to the cosmic justice of getting the same sort of grief they gave their own parents a generation ago. In an attempt to reassure, friends may have offered annoying aphorisms, like *Boys will be boys* or *Spare the rod, spoil the child.*

Parents who have gone to the bookstore for help have stepped into an ongoing debate among the experts. Authors of popular parenting books contradict each other: *Take charge of your family,* insists one; *Celebrate your child's inner spirit,* asserts another; *Turn off the TV!* shouts a third. Which one to listen to? A parent has to wonder.

If they have spoken to their pediatrician about the problem, chances are good that they've been told *Don't worry. He'll grow out of it.* Many pediatricians haven't been trained to recognize emotional and behavioral difficulties in children. Research studies indicate that pediatricians rarely refer children to mental health specialists. It is not until they are face-to-face with an out-of-control child and a parent who doesn't know what to do that pediatricians pass the problem to a child development expert, a psychologist, or a family therapist.

The problem for Tony, the chronically upset 4-year-old with the too-tight shoes, and his parents is that a therapist could join the long line of people who do not entirely understand him. Why? Because she will attempt to answer the question, *What's wrong with Tony?* by viewing him through the diagnostic lens she has acquired from years of training—a lens that focuses on the *Diagnostic and Statistical Manual of Mental Disorders* (fourth edition), or DSM-IV.

DIAGNOSE THIS

The DSM-IV is the latest version of a classification system developed to describe an assortment of problems that have come to be recognized as psychological in nature. It is a listing of symptoms that have been shown through careful research to cluster together in groups. These groupings of symptoms, labeled as disorders, can be consistently distinguished from other disorders and reliably identified in a small subset of the population. Researchers have investigated the relative effectiveness of particular kinds of psychotherapy and various medications with groups who have been diagnosed with these disorders. Therapists are guided by these results when they recommend treatment to their patients; however, the relationship between diagnosis and treatment is not always straightforward. Children's emotional and behavioral difficulties are rarely simple.

The use of the word *diagnosis* is somewhat misleading. Most of the disorders listed in the DSM-IV cannot be explained *medically*. DSM-IV diagnoses are not generally based on physiological findings or on theories of mental illness. Rather, they are based primarily on carefully researched clusters of observed behaviors. There are no tests that can determine conclusively if your child has a particular diagnosis (as there are for medical illnesses such as strep throat or mononucleosis). Rather, the diagnosing clinician gathers information from several different sources, including yourself, your child, and your child's teacher. She then draws on her training, her understanding of your child, and her knowledge of the DSM-IV to determine whether your child should be given a specific psychiatric diagnosis.

In attempting to understand your child, the clinician using the DSM-IV runs into a few difficulties. DSM-IV categories are not sensitive to developmental changes in behavior. A 4-year-old with attention deficit hyperactivity disorder (ADHD), for example, is unlikely to act, think, or feel the same as an 8-year-old with ADHD. A symptom such as hyperactivity may be more acceptable in the younger child than in the older one. The parents of the 4-year-old might be hopeful that their child will outgrow the problem and choose brief parent–child therapy as a treatment. However, because the potential educational and behavioral consequences of hyperactivity are more damaging for a third-grader, the parents of the 8-year-old might opt for medication. In either case, the diagnosis of ADHD does not explain the *source* of the problem. It simply labels it.

The therapist attempting to understand Tony must consider which DSM-IV diagnoses are potentially relevant to a bright, funny 4-year-old boy who rarely does what he is told. She will ask herself: *What sort of problem is this? Is his intellectual, language, or social functioning significantly impaired? Does he appear particularly anxious or fearful? Is there evidence of depression or other forms of emotional disturbance? Are his thoughts bizarre or his behavior aggressive?*

By gathering information from Tony's parents, spending time with him in her office, and observing him in his preschool class, she will discover that this particular boy is not intellectually or socially impaired. He is not anxious or depressed. And he does not think in a bizarre way or behave aggressively. Rather, his behavior is best described in DSM-IV terms as *oppositional*. She will develop an impression of when and where he refuses to cooperate, what his lack of cooperation looks like, how frequently it occurs, and what happens as a result of it. Guided by that impression, she will look through her diagnostic lens and attempt to answer some specific questions outlined in the DSM-IV:

A. *Has Tony exhibited a pattern of negativistic, hostile, and defiant behavior lasting at least six months and including at least four of the following:*
— *often loses his temper?*
— *often argues with adults?*
— *often actively defies or refuses to comply with adults' requests or rules?*
— *often deliberately annoys people?*
— *often blames others for his or her mistakes or misbehavior?*
— *is often touchy or easily annoyed by others?*
— *is often angry and resentful?*
— *is often spiteful or vindictive?*
B. *Does this behavior occur more frequently than is typically observed in other 4-year-old boys?*
C. *Is this disturbance of behavior causing clinically significant impairment in his social, academic, or occupational functioning?*
D. *Is he psychotic or depressed?*

The answer to A will be yes; B, yes; C, yes; and D, no. Therefore, Tony is likely to be given the diagnosis of *oppositional defiant disorder (ODD)*. This diagnosis applies to children whose noncompliance and negativity exceed the bounds of what is generally considered normal at a given age. Once the therapist arrives at this diagnosis, she will look through her broader psychological lens to determine the cause of his behavior and what to do about it. Applying what she knows from a large body of theoretical and research literature, she will look for patterns that are common in children with this diagnosis. She will also look for patterns that characterize the families of these children. Is Tony temperamentally difficult, or does he have a learning disability that makes it hard for him to understand what they are asking him to do? Are Tony's parents inconsistent in disciplining him, or do they give him attention for negative behavior and ignore his positive actions? Do they get caught up in power struggles and escalating cycles of coercive discipline? It is often impossible to determine the sequence of events in the development of a problem. Poor parenting can lead to unruly child behavior, but it's also true that an unruly child is hard to parent.

In this case, Tony's parents have good parenting skills. The psychologist finds no evidence that they are inadvertently reinforcing negative behavior. They are not locked in a pathological power struggle with their preschooler, but they are at their wits' end. He does seem temperamentally more difficult than other children, but he appears bright, and they believe that he understands everything they ask him to do. How should she advise them? The diagnosis of ODD, though accurate, does not tell these parents anything new about their son's behavior, nor does it help them understand why he is so difficult to manage. Even more discouraging, it offers this family no helpful suggestions. Why? Because the theoretical explanations that appear through a psychological lens do not adequately describe their situation.

WHAT IF . . .

Let's assume for just one moment that this boy with caring, competent parents has a good reason to be angry and resentful. Let's then ask ourselves what that reason might be. Why does he lose his temper so often? Why does he argue so much? What causes him to routinely defy the requests of the adults he so desperately wants to please? And what about his touchiness—why is he like that?

If we look through a sensory lens, we might pick up a number of clues: his sensitivity to hair washing, tooth brushing, and cold foods. More information about Tony's sensory processing capabilities might illuminate his (admittedly) oppositional, defiant behavior. We might ask: *Are there common sensory characteristics in the situations in which he becomes agitated? Might his anger and resentment, his argumenta-*

tiveness and defiance, or his "touchiness" be related to sensory modula-
tion or discrimination problems? Is it possible that he becomes uncoop-
erative when he is feeling threatened by his senses, that his behavior is
defensive rather than defiant, that he is pushing the outer limits of his
processing capabilities rather than challenging his parents' authority?

Investigating these questions would lead the therapist to recognize
that Tony's story is more complicated than the categories of the DSM-
IV would suggest. As is often the case for children who end up in a
therapist's office, a single diagnosis doesn't tell the whole story. A more
comprehensive explanation of Tony's situation would include information about him that is not captured by a diagnosis (or even by multiple
diagnoses) but that offers insight into his inability to function in everyday life. Careful listening led Tony's psychologist to view his behavior
through several lenses: diagnostic, psychological, *and* sensory. She
asked herself: *What if inefficient sensory processing is interfering with*
his ability to behave appropriately? What if he is saying no for a reason?

Viewing Tony's oppositional behavior through a sensory lens helped
his parents change their thinking about their son. Surrendering their
belief that he was willfully disobeying them opened up a whole new
range of possibilities for this family. For the first time in their struggle,
rather than believing that Tony was deliberately oppositional and defiant, Tony's parents recognized that he was doing the best he could!

THE CHICKEN AND THE EGG

Another boy found himself sitting with his parents in a therapist's office
listening to a similar but different set of complaints. Jorge was older—a
first-grader—and he had been in this position before. "He has ADHD,"
his kindergarten teacher had told his mother. At her insistence, his parents had taken him to see a psychiatrist who had quickly agreed with
the teacher's categorization of the problem. After a brief conversation
with Jorge's mother, the doctor wrote out a prescription for Ritalin,
which his parents reluctantly filled. They gave Jorge the medication for
the last several weeks of kindergarten, but they were uneasy about the
drug and uncertain about the diagnosis he had been given so hastily.

When problems surfaced again the next fall, Jorge's parents decided to get a second opinion from a psychologist. "It takes him twice as long to do everything as any other kid," they told her. "Getting dressed in the morning, doing homework, whatever. We have to stay on him constantly. At school, he never does what he's supposed to do. He doesn't finish his work and he doesn't stay in his seat. He daydreams constantly." Yet they also described him as sweet tempered, smart, and very lovable. They were convinced that he wanted to do the right thing, so they were baffled by the way in which he turned molehills into mountains.

"It just doesn't make sense," they said to the therapist. "We *know* he can do these things, so why is he constantly dragging his feet?"

The psychologist shared their curiosity about this unfocused boy who seemed to march to a different drummer. She decided to observe Jorge in his classroom to get a look at how he operated in his world. What she saw there shed additional light on the problem.

WHAT DID YOU LEARN IN SCHOOL TODAY?

Jorge attended an inner city public school where forty children, two teachers, and an aide were assigned to his first-grade class. The room was cramped, crowded, and cluttered with the personal belongings of forty-three individuals on a winter day in Chicago. Forty desks were arranged in tightly packed rows, so moving from one place to another required children to move sideways, shuffling between desks and stepping over each other's book bags, which were slung over the backs of their chairs or spread out on the floor. Many children stood beside their desks rather than sitting in their chairs so that they could look back and forth between the two teachers' desks and the blackboards to the side and behind them. The nearly constant chatter of the children and the buzz of the fluorescent lights were frequently punctuated by abrupt announcements on the PA system. It was warm and stuffy. The overhead lights flickered and glowed.

In the midst of the hubbub, there sat Jorge working on a holiday art project. For a full hour, the curious psychologist watched him try to cut, glue, and piece together a holiday character with movable arms and legs from a predrawn pattern mounted on one of the blackboards. He couldn't use the scissors efficiently, so his efforts to cut out each body part were laborious. He couldn't figure out how the parts fit together, so he carried each part to the board, where he would match each arm and leg to the example hanging on the wall. Then he wound his way back to his desk through the maze of children, tripping on backpacks, bumping into people, and knocking things off of their desks.

He couldn't open his glue bottle, so he asked another boy for help. His friend opened it, then started using it and forgot to give it back. Meanwhile, Jorge lost track of who had taken it, so he went wandering from desk to desk looking for it. Back at his place, as he was concentrating on his project, he gradually slipped to one side of his chair, then crashed to the floor. He constantly knocked his supplies off of his desk. His pencil box, scissors, or the parts of his project periodically fell to the floor, and as he bent over to pick up one thing, something else slid off in another direction. It was as though he were trying to steer a rudderless boat on stormy seas.

Not surprisingly, perhaps, Jorge was the last child in the class to finish. A project designed for fun by the teacher had posed tremendous challenges to this smart, capable boy. He had worked steadily and his attention had not wavered, yet what he had to show at the end of the hour wasn't pretty. A busy, well-intentioned teacher could easily misunderstand and misjudge his efforts. She would remember seeing him out of his seat, talking to other students, wandering from place to place, bumping into people and things, and creating a disturbance. She might look at his poorly constructed project and conclude that he hadn't tried very hard.

IF THE SHOE FITS . . .

A parent or psychiatrist or therapist relying on information from that teacher would be well on the way to assigning Jorge the diagnosis of ADHD. After all, her descriptions of his behavior match the symptoms of inattention listed in the DSM-IV:

— *often fails to give close attention to details or makes careless mistakes in schoolwork*
— *often has difficulty sustaining attention in tasks or play activities*
— *often does not seem to listen when spoken to directly*
— *often does not follow through on instructions and fails to finish schoolwork*
— *often has difficulty organizing tasks and activities*
— *often avoids, dislikes, or is reluctant to engage in tasks that require sustained mental effort*
— *often loses things necessary for tasks or activities*
— *is often easily distracted by extraneous stimuli*
— *is often forgetful in daily activities*

Her descriptions also match some of the symptoms of hyperactivity-impulsivity:

— *often fidgets with hands or feet or squirms in seat*
— *often leaves seat in classroom or in other situations in which remaining seated is expected*
— *often runs about or climbs excessively in situations in which it is inappropriate*
— *often has difficulty playing or engaging in leisure activities quietly*
— *is often "on the go" or often acts as if "driven by a motor"*
— *often talks excessively*
— *often blurts out answers before questions have been completed*
— *often has difficulty awaiting his turn*
— *often interrupts or intrudes on others*

Also in keeping with the DSM-IV description, the symptoms were present before age 7; impairment is present in two or more settings; there is clear evidence of clinically significant impairment in social and academic functioning; and he is not psychotic or autistic. It is understandable that both the kindergarten teacher and the psychiatrist labeled Jorge as ADHD. He fits the description!

However, after observing him in his classroom, the psychologist was struck by a number of things not immediately evident in his teacher's descriptions of Jorge's behavior. Although he had been the last to finish his project and he had created a disturbance by knocking things off his desk and moving around the classroom, Jorge had never once wavered in his single-minded attention to the task at hand. He had put forth a great deal of effort, even though his final product was relatively poor compared to those made by his classmates. He had clearly tried his hardest. The problem, it seemed, was not just distractibility and inattentiveness but that he could not do the job any better *under the sensory circumstances.*

Based on his parents' responses to a sensory checklist and her observations, the psychologist was able to construct a more comprehensive explanation for the behaviors that others had labeled solely as ADHD. She could offer Jorge's parents some sensory-based answers to the questions they had been asking themselves. Much of Jorge's off-task behavior was a function of motor planning difficulties. Simply making his way through the maze of desks and objects on the floor around the classroom slowed him down considerably. His seeming distraction resulted from his need to continuously check himself physically as he attempted to follow a sequence of directions. Furthermore, his vestibular and proprioceptive difficulties made it hard for him to stay in his seat.

Research suggests that approximately 30 percent of children with ADHD may also have sensory integration difficulties, so it is not surprising that Jorge was given a diagnosis of ADHD. It is possible that a medication such as Ritalin would help him focus his attention and organize his work; however, it is unlikely that medication would improve his difficulties judging where he is in space, bumping into other kids, assembling objects, or knocking things off his desk. To address these problems, the psychologist, his parents, and his teacher would need to view his behavior through a sensory lens.

A NECESSARY BUT INSUFFICIENT EXPLANATION

A third child found himself in a psychologist's office at age 9. Unlike the two children described earlier, David arrived with a mother who knew a great deal about sensory integration difficulties. Early on, David had been an unusual, difficult-to-manage child. He was clumsy and uncoordinated, had difficulty learning to write, frequently overreacted to loud noises, resisted transitions, and had a hard time letting go of a series of obsessional interests. After an exhaustive search for answers, his mother had taken him to a neurologist. This doctor identified several motor difficulties, including clumsiness, difficulty with handwriting, motor sequencing problems, and motor memory deficits. He diagnosed David with dyspraxia (motor planning problems).

Through her own reading on dyspraxia, his mother learned about other difficulties associated with dysfunctional sensory integration. In David's case, these difficulties included hypersensitivity to noise, touch, taste, and smell. For the next several years, he worked with a speech therapist, an occupational therapist, a social worker, and several special education teachers. His mother arranged for appropriate accommodations in the school setting and tried hard to create a home environment in which David would feel comfortable. Despite this intensive intervention and energetic advocacy on his behalf, he continued to have problems.

"I have anger all the time," he announced to the psychologist after listing the many ways in which he felt assaulted at school. The lights hurt his eyes, the chatter irritated him, writing was hard, and organizing his work was impossible. His desk was difficult to slide into and he had trouble sitting appropriately (back straight, feet on the floor) in his chair. Moving from classroom to classroom also presented a challenge, as the crowds in the hallway were disorienting to him. Finding a seat in the crowded chaotic lunchroom left him feeling overwhelmed.

David's teacher complained that he repeatedly and somewhat obsessively engaged in inappropriate sex talk with other students and told sexual jokes to teachers. He interacted with his peers in a one-sided, stereotyped manner rather than using more reciprocal two-way communication, and he had considerable difficulty working productively with others on group projects. He seemed disorganized, was frequently missing homework assignments, and sometimes refused to do his assignments in class, especially if they involved writing. Long-term projects, such as book reports, were especially difficult for him. Although he was bright and very sociable, David was experiencing little success in school or with his peers.

This raised several questions in the psychologist's mind: *Was the diagnosis of dyspraxia incorrect? Was it correct but incomplete? Was something else going on? Were there other things that could be done for David?*

NOTHING IS SIMPLE

Specialists are experts about the subject in which they specialize. About other subjects, they typically know less. Therefore, a great deal of expertise remains compartmentalized by discipline. We look through the lens with which we are most familiar. A neurologist looks for neurological dysfunction. Since David's motor deficits were the most "neurological" of his symptoms, the neurologist selected a diagnosis that described his observable difficulties with motor planning. This diagnosis led his mother to the writings of occupational therapists who described dysfunctional sensory integration and suggested occupational therapy as a treatment.

The psychologist knew that sensory processing problems can affect a child's emotions, academic achievement, and social relationships; however, she wondered if David's social and learning difficulties might be problems in and of themselves. She wondered if he might have *Asperger's syndrome,* so she took out DSM-IV and looked through her diagnostic lens. Matching David's observable characteristics with the behavioral descriptions in DSM-IV, she considered the diagnosis of Asperger's syndrome. Did he demonstrate the following:

    A. *Qualitative impairment in social interaction, as manifested by at least two of the following:*
- *marked impairment in the use of multiple nonverbal behaviors such as eye-to-eye gaze, facial expression, body postures, and gestures to regulate social interaction*
- *failure to develop peer relationships appropriate to developmental level*

— *a lack of spontaneous seeking to share enjoyment, interests, or achievements with other people (e.g., by a lack of showing, bringing, or pointing out objects of interest to other people)*
— *lack of social or emotional reciprocity*

B. *Restricted, repetitive, and stereotyped patterns of behavior, interests, and activities, as manifested by at least one of the following:*

— *encompassing preoccupation with one or more stereotyped and restricted patterns of interest that is abnormal either in intensity or focus*
— *apparently inflexible adherence to specific, nonfunctional routines or rituals*
— *stereotyped repetitive motor mannerisms (e.g., hand or finger flapping or twisting, or complex whole-body movements)*
— *persistent preoccupation with parts of objects*

C. *The disturbance causes clinically significant impairment in social, occupational, or other important areas of functioning.*

The psychologist's answers to A, B, and C were yes. The diagnosis of Asperger's syndrome took into account David's ongoing social awkwardness, his perseverative behavior, his difficulty with transitions, and his somewhat idiosyncratic use of language. And despite the fact that they are not included in the DSM-IV description of Asperger's, sensory processing problems are common in children with autistic spectrum disorders such as Asperger's. Still, this diagnosis did not tell the entire story.

Results of testing revealed a significant discrepancy between David's language abilities and his nonverbal reasoning skills. For example, he was much better able to define vocabulary words and recite factual information than he was able to put puzzle pieces together. This type of test profile is consistent with a particular type of learning disability called a *nonverbal learning disability*. Children with nonverbal learning disabilities frequently have difficulty interpreting social cues such as facial expressions, organizing themselves, completing long-term school assignments, and writing in a sequentially logical and coherent fashion. All of these difficulties were a part of David's story.

The psychologist realized that David, like many of the children she sees in her office, did not fit neatly into a single diagnostic category.

Experts from different professional backgrounds had focused on different aspects of his problems. Was he dyspraxic? Did he have Asperger's syndrome? Was he struggling with a nonverbal learning disability? Were all three diagnoses appropriate? Although the symptoms of these disorders overlap, the experts who had been working with David had not taken a holistic, multidisciplinary approach to his treatment. Instead, each professional had viewed David through a single lens.

WHICH WAY TO GO?

When experts disagree, it is very difficult to make choices about whose advice to follow. We are bombarded by facts and figures daily, many of which appear contradictory and a great deal of which seem meaningless. We look to the experts to interpret that information for us. When we have a problem that needs a solution—which car to buy, which stock to dump, which pill to take—we want an authoritative voice to tell us what we should do.

Parents come to psychologists looking for answers. Their children are in trouble, and they do not want equivocation. They want the problem fixed. After all, scientists can map the human genome, clone sheep, split the atom—surely there is a solution for a child who won't follow directions! However, in psychology—the science of behavior—there are very few clear answers.

Most of the time when parents ask why their children aren't doing what they should, there are many possible answers. Depending on which experts they ask, they may hear about brain structure and chemistry, rewards and punishments, negative thought patterns, learning styles, skill deficits, processing channels, intergenerational patterns within the family, power dynamics, or sociocultural influences. They may receive one diagnosis here, another diagnosis there. None may answer their most basic questions: *What should we do about our uncooperative child? Should we try medication? Should we bribe him to be good? Run his life like a boot camp? Does he need a tutor? Is he bored? Should we take him to therapy? Tae kwon do? Yoga? Would it help to change his diet? Take away sugar, preservatives, wheat? Will any of this make a difference in the quality of our daily lives?*

As psychologists, what we have to say is not always satisfying. Some children respond in a dramatically positive way to medication. Others do not. Sometimes a strict behavioral approach to a problem helps tremendously. Other times it seems to backfire. Occasionally there are family dynamics—tension in a marriage, favoritism between siblings, depression of a parent—that contribute to a child's behavior problems. But it's often hard to tell which came first: the behavior problem or the family dysfunction. After all, living with a difficult-to-manage child is stressful for everyone in the family.

WILL THE REAL DIAGNOSIS PLEASE STAND UP?

Tony, Jorge, and David are confusing to their parents and to the professionals trying to help them because they do not fit neatly into a clearly definable box. Although their behaviors objectively meet DSM-IV criteria for oppositional defiant disorder, attention deficit hyperactivity disorder, and Asperger's syndrome, these diagnoses alone do not adequately describe their difficulties. All three boys also have sensory processing difficulties that significantly affect their ability to function well at home and at school. Dysfunctional sensory integration is not a psychiatric diagnosis. Rather, it is an explanatory concept that helps us understand a whole range of problematic behaviors. Sometimes sensory processing problems occur simultaneously with psychiatric disorders; other times, they occur alone. When they go unrecognized, misunderstandings abound.

In order to help a child with dysfunctional sensory integration, we have to look beyond the DSM-IV, beyond narrow fields of expertise, and beyond the limitations of our current body of knowledge. We have to think beyond categories. We have to operate from a multidisciplinary perspective, assembling a team of professionals who together understand the child's difficulties. In Chapter Four we will lay out a framework that will place sensory processing difficulties in the context of a child's everyday life. It will provide a starting point for you to think about where, when, and how you can take action to make your child a happier, more successful person.

||||||||||||||||||||||||||||||||||||||||||||||||||||||||||||||||||||||||||||||

A Sense of Hope:
How Change Happens

*I don't know what to do anymore. I don't want to be angry at
my daughter all the time. She's not a bad kid, but she acts like
one — and it breaks my heart to see the way she turns people
against her.*

— DENISE,
mother of an 8-year-old girl

WHEN WE ask parents about their hopes for their children, we hear the same phrases over and over: *I want
him to be happy. I want her to be successful. I want her
to be able to fulfill her dreams. I want her to feel good about herself. I
want him to have friends. I just don't want life to be so hard for him.*

In response, we tell them that a child's sense of happiness and self-
worth is the natural developmental outcome of good relationships with
others and success in the areas of work (school) and play. Whether this
is achieved depends largely on the match between a child and her
environment. As adults, we select partners, friends, work, and home
environments that contribute to our feelings of comfort and success.
Childhood, in contrast, is a time of imposition. Children have little
control over the circumstances in which they find themselves. When a
child's circumstances are a bad match for her particular sensitivities,
abilities, or passions, her struggles affect the course of her development.
For example, a child with a learning disability might suffer immeasur-
ably in a classroom in which there is no recognition of her particular
needs. She would likely feel stupid and worthless, and eventually she
might become disorderly or depressed. In a school with a well-developed

learning disabilities program, the same child might thrive, gaining strength and a sense of her own competence by conquering difficult subject matter.

Mental health has been described as the ability to love well, work well, and play well. It is also the ability to anticipate well, to expect that good things will come your way. These achievements can be compromised for children with sensory processing problems when they struggle with the simplest everyday tasks and the most basic aspects of their social lives. Facilitating healthy growth in these children is not just a matter of arriving at the right diagnosis. Rather, it requires a comprehensive look at their specific struggles. Saying that a child has dysfunctional sensory integration is just a start. The term itself is much too broad and encompasses too many subcategories to be helpful to parents looking for specific advice on how to help their particular child. After all, think about the many differences between Evan, Ben, and the other children you have already met in this book. Understanding your child's particular sensory processing problems will help you understand the challenges she faces in interacting with her world.

In this chapter, we describe the dynamic interaction between what the child brings to her world and the environment in which she finds herself. Specifically, we examine the impact of sensory processing problems on four critical components of healthy development: intimacy, peer relationships, academic mastery, and cultural rituals. These examples illustrate the extent to which sensory difficulties can complicate your child's life. We offer a sensory lens through which you can view your child's individual strengths and weaknesses and the sensory characteristics of the environment in which she lives.

This method offers you a portable set of tools for identifying your child's sensory vulnerabilities and managing her out-of-bounds behavior in various situations. By learning to ask questions about your child's sensory sensitivities and the sensory components of her life, you will discover new solutions to an old set of problems.

HUGS AND KISSES: THE WORLD OF INTIMACY

Touch is a critical component of human existence. It is through hugs and kisses and other forms of intimate touch—tickling, wrestling, snuggling—that parents and children express their love for one another. A parent's hand on a child's shoulder telegraphs comfort and security, and the whole world can be set right again by the achingly deep reassurance a child receives from that simple physical contact.

From the first moments of a baby's life, physical contact with her caregiver begins to shape her understanding of the world and her place in it. Is the world friendly or hostile, predictable or unreliable, benign or dangerous? Is she important, lovable, secure? The attachment that forms between the infant and her primary caregiver becomes an unconscious blueprint for how this child will relate to other people. Although attachment is based on many more responses than physical comfort, hugs are one element of this interplay.

In studies that measure the quality of parent–child attachment, the most important indicator of attachment is the child's response to the mother after a period of stressful separation. The child who raises his arms to his mother and responds to her embrace by literally molding his body into hers is considered to be securely attached. An insecurely attached child either does not approach his mother at all or allows himself to be lifted up but receives no comfort from her touch, arching his back and pulling away from her embrace. Many studies indicate that securely attached infants are much more likely than their insecurely attached counterparts to develop into children who can tolerate frustration, delay gratification, solve problems, soothe themselves, and relate well to peers.

Tactile modulation difficulties complicate the attachment dance. Children who are tactilely defensive may dislike cuddling and may not be soothed by hugs. Conversely, children who are hyposensitive to touch may cling in a quest for tactile input and cry when they are put down. It takes parents longer to learn how to touch these easily irritated babies—with what level of pressure and in what spots—in order to comfort them. Because they are difficult to soothe, they leave their caretakers feeling less effective as parents. Parents of children with tactile modulation difficulties often report that their children were difficult babies whose irritability created stress for everyone in the family. Whether or how this affects the quality of the attachment relationship is an open question.

A child's discomfort with hugs and kisses creates ripples beyond the parent–child bond. Grandmothers and grandfathers, aunts and uncles, cousins, brothers, and sisters expect hugs. Family gatherings frequently begin and end with a round of physical affection. If Josh is uncomfortable with touch, he may find these exchanges extremely difficult. Insistence that he "give Aunt Velma a hug" can lead to outright refusal. This puts his parents in a tight spot. They want to please their family and they want Josh to be loved and indulged by them. If only he would give in, but he won't! Not only are these parents stressed by their own relationship with their stubborn, hands-off son but they also have to listen to the comments of their extended family about how difficult he is.

Family labels get assigned early, and they stick. Josh becomes the "difficult child" or the "unaffectionate one." He is a "mama's boy" because he will only let his mother hold him. His grandparents may hesitate to care for him, even though they readily take care of his cousins. Other relatives may pull back, extending less and less effort to develop a bond with Josh because they feel rebuffed by him. If this pattern persists, he may internalize a sense of himself as less worthy, less attractive, and less lovable than other children in his family.

ON THE PLAYGROUND: THE WORLD OF PEERS

Our well-being is deeply affected by our interactions with others. Availability of social support has been identified as a primary buffer against depression as well as a significant factor in recovery from physical illness. Given the importance of social relations, it is no surprise that positive peer relations have been shown to be one of the most significant predictors of adjustment in children. Those with poor peer relations are at greater risk for aggression, academic failure, and drug and alcohol abuse. Social interaction even affects our biology. In a now famous set of experiments, Martha McClintock demonstrated that close female friends who live together eventually begin to have synchronous menstrual periods.

Children begin to be sociable at a very early age. The social smile—a smile in response to the pleasure of interacting with others—is present within the first few months of life. As children grow older, they become increasingly interested in others, and by the preschool years, peer interaction is very important to them. Much of the play between young children is sensorimotor in nature. Although children younger than age 4 do not engage in very much cooperative play, they love to run, chase, tumble, and climb together. It is often on the playground that children first approach same-age peers, ask their names, and begin to learn the rudimentary process of making friends.

For the child with sensory integration difficulties, these early interactions are often problematic. Playground activities can be daunting for the child with vestibular and proprioceptive difficulties. He may be afraid of swings, or, conversely, he may like to swing so much that he has a hard time giving others a turn. He may have trouble with noise and disorganization, both marked aspects of playground play. If he cannot accurately judge his distance from others, he might get too close or touch others too frequently or too hard in group games or during one-on-one interactions.

Parents of these children frequently voice strong concerns about their child's peer relations. They are aware that he is socially out of step and seems to miss the nuances of social interaction. Or they complain that his behavior careens out of control when he is overstimulated and that he doesn't know when to stop. Or they notice that he hangs back, afraid to join the whirlwind of activity.

As these children get older, their social difficulties increase. They lag further and further behind other children who are becoming more socially adept, better able to regulate themselves emotionally, and better at responding to subtle social cues. However, their difficulties are hidden, not readily apparent to others, so their peers are less forgiving of their social gaffes. They have difficulty themselves understanding why they have so much trouble making and keeping friends.

The implications of these social difficulties are far-reaching. As he moves into middle childhood, a child's self-esteem is strongly tied to social and academic mastery. Since a child with sensory integration difficulties often looks awkward playing sports, may misinterpret nonverbal social cues, or may have difficulty participating in group activities, he will stand out among his peers. In middle school, where social comparison is rife and conformity is a must, teasing or rejection by peers is often the fate of a child who appears different.

SCHOOL: EARLY MASTERY EXPERIENCES

When children enter school, they move from the safety and security of the family environment and the freedom of preschool play to the highly structured world of the classroom. There, the child who marches to a different drummer confronts a set of universal norms that she is likely to find particularly challenging. In our offices, we have listened to many parents as they have agonized over the choice of a kindergarten setting for their child because of fears that she will not fit in and that her first school experience will batter her self-esteem.

Over the past half century, formal schooling has begun earlier and earlier for American children, and the demands for early academic achievement have increased. The movement of women into the workforce and the increasing number of families with two wage earners has led to a dramatic growth in the number of children in day care settings. Kindergarten now runs full days rather than half days in many communities, and junior or prekindergarten has supplanted nursery school. The emphasis is on earlier and earlier development of school readiness skills such as cutting, identifying and reproducing letters and numbers, and understanding simple arithmetic concepts. Children are also expected to be behaviorally ready for school at earlier ages. They are expected to be able to sit and cooperate with group activities, manage their frustrations, and regulate their emotions.

School, with its demands for focused attention, multiple transitions, fine- and gross-motor agility, and peer interaction, is stressful for all young children. However, the school environment presents many hidden challenges for children with sensory integration difficulties. The gap between their strengths and weaknesses is often more pronounced, and many of them may also have learning disabilities. The typical elementary classroom is a beehive of activity: loud, bright, cluttered—a constant sensory assault for the child with poor sensory modulation. Furthermore, the expectations that she sit for long periods of time, organize her work, and carry out complex sequences of fine-motor tasks (required for the production of written work) are particularly challenging for her. If she needs sensory stimulation or movement to organize her thinking, if she cannot sit on a certain type of chair, or if she has difficulty organizing her belongings, she might be seen as disruptive, lazy, or uncooperative. As this child experiences repeated academic failures, daily behavioral challenges, and negative comparisons between herself and her classmates, school is likely to become a setting for disappointment.

Achieving success is essential for the development of an integrated sense of identity, healthy self-esteem, and a willingness to persevere in the face of future challenges. It is fundamental to learning to anticipate well. Children whose sensory processing problems interfere with school mastery are likely to be at risk for escalating emotional and behavioral problems and early school dropout.

CULTURAL RITUALS

All families have rituals. These patterned behaviors emanate from each parent's family of origin, but they are also shaped by cultural norms and religious practices. Some of these rituals, like your child's bedtime routine, are performed daily. Others occur at holidays or mark the achievement of particular developmental milestones. These celebrations—holiday dinners, marriages, baptisms, bar mitzvahs—generally include members of the extended family and close friends, and the traditions accompanying them acquire a sacred aura. These rituals, documented by photographs and videos, become defining moments in the life of a family and in the memory of children. They are the stuff of which family myths are made, and, as such, they help define who we are and where we fit in the world around us.

Whereas the structure and predictability of daily rituals are often helpful for children with sensory processing problems, these larger events can be disastrous. They occur infrequently, generally involve a large number of people and specific expectations for behavior, and are emotionally intense for all involved. Parents of children with sensory problems come to dread them! In our offices, we hear many complaints and concerns about the ways that these children stand out at parties and family gatherings. They may withdraw from the special activities, refuse to talk to unfamiliar relatives, complain about the food, play too rough with the other children, or run uncontrollably around the house.

Let's imagine Thanksgiving dinner for the child with sensory integration difficulties. Mom wakes up early to start cooking. As Patty wakens, she is greeted by the smells of her mother's cooking—perhaps pleasing, or, more likely, offensive to her sensitive nose. In the absence of the usual morning routine, she is left to her own devices while other family members dress, clean the house, or otherwise get ready for the company, so she wanders aimlessly in her pajamas or turns on the TV. Although she is pleased not to have to put on clothes, the sedentary activity of sitting in front of the television deprives her of the sensory input she needs to get herself organized for the day. As the morning progresses, she remains inactive, lounging around while her parents prepare dinner. Sometime in the early afternoon, she is told to get dressed—not in her everyday sweats but in stiffer, less comfortable clothes. This may take several reminders and stern persuasion.

Soon the guests begin to arrive. Grown-ups—bigger than she is, smelly with perfume and aftershave—crowd the front hallway. They exclaim loudly and demand hugs and kisses. Or they ruffle her hair, pat her on the back, or jostle her playfully. She is beginning to feel overwhelmed just as her cousins arrive. They race into her bedroom and begin to go through her toys. Excited themselves, they are loud and unpredictable. They start pulling her things out of cubbyholes and drawers. They pretend to shoot guns or imitate ambulances coming to the rescue of imaginary patients. Feeling assaulted by the noise, the smells, the bodies, and the invasion of her things, Patty strikes out. She hits her cousin, who begins to cry.

When her parents come in to see what is happening, they yell at her for being a poor hostess. Feeling betrayed by the people she hopes will understand her plight, she yells back defensively. Hearing the ruckus, her grandmother walks in and chastises her loudly for talking to her parents in that tone of voice. Feeling utterly attacked, Patty disintegrates into tears. Her grandmother turns to her daughter, Patty's mother, and says, "What is wrong with that child?" When the adults leave the room, Patty begins to jump on the bed. (On some level, probably unconscious, she has learned that jumping calms her.) Immediately, her cousins crowd onto the bed to join her not because they *need* to jump as she does but because it looks like fun. It is only minutes before the adults return to the room and she is in trouble again.

Over the course of the evening, Patty must manage the noise, tolerate the smells and tastes of the food that is placed in front of her, and ignore her cousins' jostling. By evening's end, she is running around wildly, impervious to adult demands that she calm down. She is irritable and uncooperative.

Her parents go to bed exhausted and frustrated, wondering why Patty can't behave like her cousins. Her mother knows that her sister and parents talk about Patty when she is not around and that they consider her to be a difficult child. She also knows that Patty is aware of their disapproval. More and more, Patty has begun to ask her parents if she is a bad girl and why nobody likes her. They are worried about her, but they are also angry and confused, wondering why she always has to be so difficult. They want to be able to answer her grandmother's question: "What is wrong with that child?" More importantly, they want to know what to do to stop the downward spiral that seems to engulf the entire family.

USING THE SENSORY LENS: WHO? WHERE? WHAT?

In order to know what to do, Patty's parents need to look through a sensory lens. This will help them organize their thoughts about the problem. This lens takes into account Patty's individual sensory characteristics *(who she is)*, the sensory characteristics of the environment in which she finds herself *(where she is)*, and the sensory demands being placed upon her *(what is expected)*. This lens will help her parents identify the changes that need to take place for Patty to be more successful in any given situation.

Patty's parents can visualize this framework as follows:

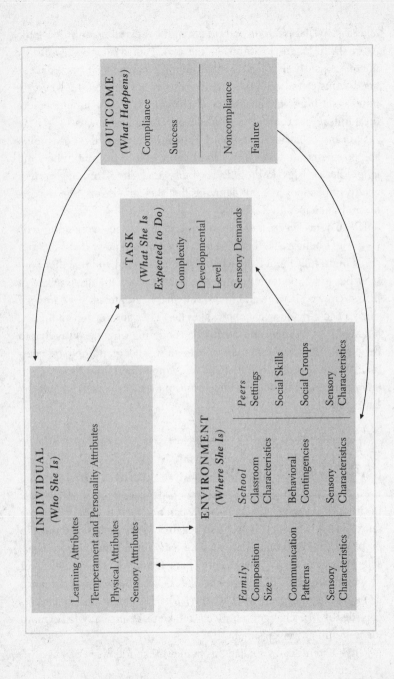

Note that sensory issues are important at all three levels. At the individual level, Patty's parents must think about her particular difficulties with sensory processing. *Does she have problems with balance and movement modulation, tactile discrimination, auditory modulation, or motor planning? Does she have a learning disability, attention deficit hyperactivity disorder, or a physical difficulty such as low muscle tone? How do her particular individual characteristics make Thanksgiving dinner difficult for her?*

Next, what are the environmental constraints within which Patty is operating? Is Patty's household always noisy and chaotic, or just when the extended family is coming over for holiday dinners? Is she accustomed to dressing herself, or do her parents usually give her extra help buttoning and zipping her clothes? Do Patty's parents usually agree on how she should behave on special occasions? Are they likely to make similar decisions about how to manage Patty's behavior when she gets disruptive? Are they consistent?

Finally, Patty's parents must think about the specific characteristics of the particular tasks that she is faced with on this Thanksgiving day. *Are the tasks too difficult for her developmental level? What are the sensory characteristics of the tasks? Given Patty's sensory processing weaknesses, is the task reasonable? Or is it so challenging that she is unlikely to be successful?*

PATTY'S THANKSGIVING REVISITED

Let's reexamine Patty's Thanksgiving in the context of this sensory framework. First, Patty's parents must ask themselves which of Patty's individual characteristics are likely to have an impact on her ability to manage this event. They note that Patty has a motor planning problem that makes it hard for her to organize herself without a lot of structure and specific step-by-step instructions. She has an expressive language problem that makes it hard for her to speak when other people are talking quickly. Her fine-motor skills are also delayed and she has difficulty with tactile discrimination; therefore, she can't independently button her blouse or zip her skirt. Patty has sensory modulation difficulties in the auditory, olfactory, and tactile areas, so her parents know before the day even begins that it will be hard for her to tolerate noise, smells, and the feel of her dress clothes on her skin.

Having identified their daughter's individual vulnerabilities, Patty's parents must now think about the challenges of Thanksgiving dinner in the context of these individual characteristics. Given her particular needs, what can they do to make the day easier for her? Can they plan ahead so that one of them will have time to help her get dressed? Can they forego the dress clothes and let her come to dinner in her favorite sweatpants? To help provide some structure to her day, Patty's mother can take a moment to involve her in something fun while she prepares dinner. Later, her father can structure some activity when her cousins arrive so that she will not have to assert herself verbally in a large group. They can plan some quiet activities so that she will not be over-whelmed by noise and chaos. They can explain to their relatives that Patty doesn't like hugs and give her permission to say hello to Grandma in a way that feels comfortable to her. By planning ahead in this way, Patty's parents will make the day easier for Patty and themselves so that they are all in a better state of mind when their guests arrive.

Next, Patty's parents must analyze the environment. They have wisely decided to have Thanksgiving dinner in their home, where Patty feels most comfortable and where they have greater control over the environment. So, whom have they invited to dinner? They know that Patty's loud and rambunctious cousin is particularly problematic for her; however, they also know that Aunt Ruth will be insulted if she isn't invited to dinner. Patty's mother is mindful of Patty's difficulties coping with this particular cousin, and she anticipates her sensitivity to the noisiness of Aunt Ruth's loud, boisterous family. She provides Patty with a Walkman so that she can control her adjustment to the auditory input coming at her. She also recognizes that Patty needs a place to retreat when the swirl of activity becomes overwhelming. She sets up a safety zone for Patty that is off-limits to others. Before the guests arrive, Patty's mother tells her that she can go into her bedroom and shut the door if she needs some space and quiet. Her father makes a point of taking the children outside for a while so that Patty and her cousins can run and jump around without getting in trouble. Her parents recognize that playing outside gives Patty the opportunity to experience sensory stimulation that helps organize and calm her.

When everyone sits down to dinner, Patty's parents think about where to seat her. She will probably do better at the end of the table rather than in the middle, where she would be surrounded by the touch, smell, and noise of other people. Her parents also recognize that if they give her a job, such as carrying things to and from the table, she will have a legitimate reason to get up and move during dinner. This movement may eliminate her need to bounce up and down in her seat and will allow her to make a positive contribution to the dinner. Rather than getting negative comments from her annoyed relatives, she is likely to be praised for being a good helper.

Finally, Patty's parents think about the tasks they are asking Patty to complete that day. Can they really expect her to dress herself? Is it fair to ask her to wear dress clothes? Is it reasonable to expect her to organize her cousins to play a game quietly? Are there toys that she should not be asked to share? Does she have to taste the unfamiliar food on her plate? Must she sit at the table with the grown-ups for the entire meal? Will turning on the TV make things better or worse? Should she be restricted from computer games or other assaultive video experiences for the day?

Patty's parents realize that the success or failure of Patty's participation in the Thanksgiving gathering will depend, at least partially, on their ability to accommodate her sensory needs. They must analyze all aspects of the situation using their sensory lens to understand Patty and the demands being placed on her. Then, if they plan ahead and make modifications where they can, they greatly increase the likelihood that Patty and the members of her family will enjoy their holiday together.

A NEW WAY OF THINKING

We hope that Part One of this book has given you a more thorough understanding of your child's sensory processing difficulties and the broad impact they can have on his—and your—everyday life. In Part Two, we will explore ways of managing the individual, environmental, and task-related demands that make life for you and your child such a struggle. Chapter Five will teach you more about the neurobiological underpinnings of sensory processing, with a basic introduction to the relationship between your child's nervous system and his sensory integration capabilities. In Chapter Six we will discuss how to decide whether you should seek professional help and where you can find it. Chapter Seven will cover sense-able parenting strategies and other ways of modifying family life that will lead to a happier, less tension-filled home environment. In Chapter Eight we will describe modifications that can be made at school to increase the likelihood that your child will experience greater academic success. In Chapter Nine we will look at your child's social world through the sensory lens. Finally, in Chapter Ten we will examine some unanswered questions about the relationship between dysfunctional sensory integration and children's emotional and behavior problems.

Recognizing the contribution of sensory processing to your child's behavior is the first, most important step toward creating new possibilities for him. When you stop blaming him for his troubles, your relationship with him transforms from one of coercion to one of cooperation. Looking through a sensory lens, you can begin to apply your newfound knowledge about your child and his needs to the many settings in which he must operate. Learning when to accommodate his differences and how to help him succeed is what the rest of this book is about.

Part

Two

||||||||||||||||||||||||||||||||||||||||||||||||||||||||||||||||||||||||||||||||

CHAPTER FIVE

Thinking Sensibly: No Two Brains Are the Same

There is so much physical variation among people—some have strong hearts, some have weak bladders, some have steadier hands than others, some have bad eyesight—it's only logical that senses should vary, too.

—DIANE ACKERMAN,
A *Natural History of the Senses*

The sound of the waves is making me crazy in my head.

—BRITANNY,
at age 4

PERHAPS THE biggest hurdle that you face as a parent of a child with sensory processing problems is accepting the idea that his experience of daily life is fundamentally different from yours. He does not hear, smell, taste, or feel the world in the same way that you do. His relationship with gravity is not the same. He cannot move his body with the same confidence and security that you can. For him, everyday situations are full of obstacles, challenging and surprising.

Equally difficult, perhaps, is the need to respect those differences. Too often, we try to talk children out of their experience: *I'm freezing, so you must be cold.* Or we criticize it: *Stop being such a baby. It's just a scrape.* Or punish it: *If you don't settle down, you're going to lose your TV privileges.* Or just disregard it: *You cannot wear sweatpants to church. Now, stop whining and put on your dress clothes.*

In each of these instances, the unspoken message to your child is one of disrespect. The person closest to him seems to be saying that his subjective experience, his very sense of himself, is somehow wrong. In order to please *you*, he must deny, or somehow learn to ignore, his most basic instincts, his natural intuition. Almost moment by moment, he must question and resist what his own body is telling him! Suppressing his gut reactions to his different experience of the world is a constant challenge. Sometimes he can do it, but many times he can't. Those are the times when he finds himself in trouble.

Your child needs you to recognize that his body works differently from yours. He needs you to be curious about how his brain processes sensory information, how it shapes his subjective experience of the world. The development of his mind is, in fact, intricately related to his daily experiences—and this continuous, dynamic interaction between his body, brain, and world is laying the foundation for who he will become. You can help him build a solid foundation by accepting and respecting him *as he is*, a child with a unique nervous system, different from everyone else.

A PERFECT MARRIAGE: BRAIN AND BODY

There are many metaphors for the brain, most of them cold and remote. We liken our brains to storage bins, filing cabinets, or computers and we talk about information being filed, stored, and retrieved there. But when we can't remember a phone number, an appointment time, or the name of our cousin's third husband, we don't know how to find it, since we're not aware of the actual filing process. It's as if the inner workings of our mind were housed in a large restricted zone, like the reference section of a library or the back room of a dry cleaner. We trust that we'll be able to get what we need when we want it, but when something is misfiled or seems to be lost altogether, we don't have a clue how to go looking for it. For most of us, the brain remains a mystery, a vast unknown.

It has been contrasted to the body, which is frequently described in the language of the senses. We can see, smell, scratch, rub, taste, and even hear the various parts of our body. We can order them around.

Legs: run! Fingers: type! Muscles: contract! We're familiar with the ins and outs of our bodies. We feel at home there. Unless we are injured or sick, we know how to use our bodies to get what we want. Pleasure. Warmth. Rest. Exhilaration. Comfort. For the most part, our bodies do not mystify us in the same way that our brains do.

This perceived opposition between the brain and the body is false, of course. In reality, they are very happily married and perfectly matched. Our skin is the brain's outer boundary. Things we think of as bodily activities are also happening in the brain. For example, Michael Jordan's hands and feet got all the credit, but his brain made him the unsurpassable athlete that he was. Likewise, the flights of thought that we consider "brainy" would be impossible without the body. We need both, and there is nothing to be gained by our attempts to disentangle them. They are as closely entwined as lovers. Sensory integration is the meeting ground where the brain and body connect.

To better understand the processes of sensory integration and how they relate to the workings of the mind and the behavior of the body, we need to look more closely at what we know about the brain.

THE BODY ELECTRIC

The human brain is a highly organized system of communication circuits linking over 100 billion nerve cells. These cells, called neurons, are connected to one another by spider-like pathways that pass energy and information back and forth in split-second synchrony. All of human experience, both conscious and unconscious, is derived from the electrical and chemical activity that occurs between these cells. Every passing sensation, every movement of our bodies, every social encounter causes millions of neurons to fire together, forming physical interconnections between them. By way of these neural pathways, information enters the brain from sensory receptors, is channeled to various parts of the brain, then is translated into messages that are sent out to the muscles and glands. These body–brain–body connections control our daily functioning, from the basic maintenance of our bodies (i.e., heart rate, body temperature, digestion) to the sophisticated workings of our minds (i.e., speech, abstract reasoning, social interaction). The work of the brain is this relaying process—gathering, evaluating, and acting on information about our internal organs and the external world.

Beyond our ability to imagine it, the brain is an immense network of tangled intercellular connections. Information passes along these pathways in the following manner: Each neuron has thousands of branch-like receiving lines, called dendrites, which feed into a long wire-like conduit called the axon. Electrical messages travel from the dendrite down the axon to one of thousands of branch-like terminal lines. There, the electrical impulse activates the release of a chemical called a neurotransmitter that floats across the gap between this neuron and its neighbor. These junctures between neurons are called synapses, and the space from cell to cell is so small that it takes only a fraction of a millisecond for the chemical transmitter released from the sending neuron to be detected by the receiving neuron. The absorption of the neurotransmitter by a dendrite of the neighboring neuron causes an electrical impulse to fire along that axon to the nerve terminal, where a chemical signal is sent to the next neuron. And so forth. It has been estimated that each neuron is linked to an average of ten thousand other neurons. Theoretically, then, electrical activation of one neuron could set off chemical reactions in as many as one quadrillion (10^{15}) synapses throughout the brain.

The number of neurotransmitters that operate at the synaptic level is unknown, but more than a hundred have been identified. The effects of these chemicals can't be isolated because they work in combination, creating an ever-changing potion that regulates the activation and deactivation of the brain's electrical activity. Unbelievably, despite the potential for chaos, the operation of all this neural circuitry is very efficient—except when it goes awry. Sensory integrative dysfunction can be thought of as a glitch in the electrical circuitry of the brain, and the effects of this malfunction can be far-reaching.

INSIDE THE BLACK BOX: A SIMPLE MAP

Most attempts to map the mind have been controversial and less than successful, in part because brain development is variable from person to person. People differ in temperament, personality, and mental ability due to a vast array of factors that influence how our brains grow. Therefore, any anatomical map of the brain is a crude approximation of the working interconnections that may exist in a particular person's brain. Still, it is useful to have some landmarks to refer to when grappling with the brain's complexity; therefore, we suggest a simple map of the dense and ever-changing territory of the human mind.

Information about the outside world and the internal world of the body enters the central nervous system through sensory receptors. These receptors, located throughout the body, send electrical messages to the spinal cord via peripheral nerves. The information is then relayed to the brain via nerve tracts (some of which travel up the spinal cord from the body to the brain; others of which travel down the spinal cord from the brain to the muscles).

For the purposes of this chapter, we're going to discuss three basic regions of the brain. There is a great degree of oversimplification in this approach. It is much the same as dividing the United States into the North, the South, the West, and the East. Map makers, sociologists, and politicians would be unable to draw clear lines between such broadly defined categories—nevertheless, we can make some reasonable generalizations about our country on the basis of those regional categories. The same applies to our overly simplified map of the brain.

At the top of the spinal cord, the **lower brain,** sometimes referred to as the reptilian brain, receives sensory information from all over the body. Because this is the oldest, most primitive part of the brain, it is keenly attuned to matters of survival and bodily maintenance. It activates the neurons that regulate arousal, and it responds to the basic physiological needs of the body. It organizes breathing, controls the continuous activity of the heart, and regulates blood pressure. It is also concerned with sleeping and waking, relaxation and alertness. It keeps us from being disturbed by the benign drone of an air conditioner when we are asleep, but it wakes us at the sound of a footstep on the threshold of our bedroom. Its main business is to keep us alive.

As such, this region of the brain serves a gate-keeping function, determining which sensory stimuli will be allowed to enter the higher levels of the brain where it will be consciously perceived. A great deal of the work of sensory integration is done at this lower, unconscious level. When sensory integration is not efficient, superfluous sensory information may pass through the gate, creating unnecessary alarm and confusion in other regions of the brain.

If threatened, the lower brain can shut down access to higher-level thinking parts of the brain and direct behavior from a protective fight-or-flight stance. For example, a child with vestibular modulation problems and tactile defensiveness may strongly resist washing his hair. For him, the sensations associated with leaning his head backward in the bathtub are disorienting and disturbing: he feels as if he is falling. At the same time, the light sensation of water running over his face and neck is extremely threatening. He may fight and scream as if his life were in danger—and, in fact, that is the message his lower brain is sending out. There is no reasoning with this child when he feels assaulted. His lower brain is in charge, and his body is readying itself for an attack.

The **limbic system,** or emotional brain, is centrally located, where it receives input from both the lower brain and the thinking brain, or cerebral cortex, and coordinates communication between these two regions. It mediates emotion, motivation, and the individual's drive toward goal-directed behavior. It also regulates the release of hormones and some aspects of memory and attention. It integrates a range of mental processes such as appraisal of meaning, processing of social experience, and regulation of emotion.

For the tactilely defensive child who can't tolerate wet, tickly light pressure on his skin, a kiss from his grandmother is not going to elicit the same emotions as it will for his happy-go-lucky sister. She experiences the kiss as an expression of affection. She smiles and draws closer to her grandmother. He experiences the kiss as a disgusting intrusion. He grimaces and turns away, wiping his cheek. The same set of sensations, processed differently, leads to different experiences with different social consequences.

For the limbic system to operate effectively, it must receive meaningful information from the lower brain. Ayres made this point in 1979: "Few people think of emotions as functions of the nervous system. However, there is a neurological basis for every feeling of fear, anger, sadness, joy, and even love. . . . For emotions to be 'balanced,' the limbic system must receive well-modulated input from the senses." Today, brain scientists increasingly recognize the integral nature of emotions and their sensory foundations to higher mental processes.

The **cerebral cortex** mediates the more complex information processing functions of the brain such as perception, thinking, and reasoning. It consists of many overlapping layers of gray matter that have been likened to a scrunched-up wad of paper stuffed inside your skull. If it were unfolded, it would be large enough to cover a desktop! In a mature brain, about half the cortex is devoted to seeing and much of the rest is devoted to the other senses and the body's motor system. Less than 20 percent of the fully developed cortex is devoted to the mechanics of rational thought.

At birth, an infant's brain is like an open frontier awaiting settlement. As he gets to know his parents, explores his world, and becomes familiar with how his body works, groups of neurons develop interconnections based on his experiences. These networks create functional pathways that actually grow his brain. Beginning in the midbrain and expanding to the cortex, stimulation from the environment (experienced through the senses) creates more synapses and grows more dendrites, axons, and terminals. As neurons respond to what the child sees, hears, feels, and tastes, they build relay systems with neighboring neurons. Repetition of these experiences increases the strength and efficiency of these connections.

As the child gets older and experiences more and more of his world, these expanding neural connections form the specialized regions of the cortex. The occipital lobes, the regions primarily devoted to visual perception, form first. Then come the parietal lobes, which are important in interpreting touch and spatial relationships. Next, the sites that coordinate hearing and language, the temporal lobes, are formed. And finally, the frontal lobes develop. This part of the cortex is where the movement of every part of the body is planned, coordinated, and regulated.

By the time the child is 5 years old, his brain will have reached almost 90 percent of its final size, but it will keep developing well into his adolescence. During childhood and adolescence, the brain is further refined by a process of *pruning*, which eliminates excess synaptic connections. This results in a less dense but more critical network of neural connections that facilitate more efficient information processing.

This period of brain growth is also marked by continuing myelination. Myelin is a fatty sheath that acts like insulation for the nerve axon. Myelination contributes to more efficient conduction of nerve impulses. It is believed that disruptions in myelination may manifest in behavioral disruptions, but the precise nature of this relationship is unknown.

The prefrontal cortex, which doesn't reach full functional maturity until sometime after puberty, is the center of abstract reasoning, planning, judgment, social skills, and self-awareness. It has been likened to an executive system that guides, coordinates, and updates behavior in a flexible fashion, particularly in novel or complex tasks. It is also intimately connected to our emotional life. It receives direct input from the limbic system, but it is interwoven with the lower brain as well. It is a highly complex structure built on the solid neural foundation of countless dynamic transactions between the individual and her physical and social world.

ANOTHER WAY TO LOOK AT IT: INFORMATION PROCESSING

Ayres described sensory integration as "the neurological process that organizes sensations from one's own body and from the environment and makes it possible to use the body effectively within the environment. The spatial and temporal aspects of inputs from different sensory modalities are interpreted, associated and unified. Sensory integration is information processing."

Consider this example: Something moves on the skin of your forearm. An electrical signal representing this information is screened for input at the brain stem level—*more information is needed for interpretation.* Your eyes are asked to check it out. Visual input comes back—*shapes, colors, light, and shadow.* It needs further interpretation. The associational areas of the visual cortex create a perceptual representation of the critter—*looks like an insect.* You look more closely. A linguistic symbol is assigned to what you see—*mosquito.* A conceptual association is made, and you remember the last time you encountered a mosquito—*got bitten, didn't feel good.* Limbic structures send a message of alarm to the frontal cortex—*danger!* These different messages are coordinated and organized into a plan, which is translated into an output message that is sent to your hand—*swat that thing quick before it bites!*

If you had been talking to a friend or taking a math test or listening to a piano concerto when you noticed the mosquito on your arm, your attention to those tasks would have been interrupted, or suspended, while your brain alerted you to the danger of being bitten. This automatic switch in the focus of your attention is an example of *modulation*. Turning neural switches on and off to control input is one of the ways that your brain organizes its approach to information processing. So much sensory information, so little time! A brain has to set some priorities.

Modulation is accomplished through the mechanisms of inhibition, habituation, and facilitation. *Inhibition* is a reduction in sensory intake when certain kinds of information are not needed to perform a particular task. For example, ballet dancers learn to inhibit vestibular input so that they can perform pirouettes without becoming dizzy. *Habituation* is the automatic tuning out of input when it becomes familiar. After a time, people who live near railroad tracks grow accustomed to the sounds of passing trains and seem not to hear them anymore. *Facilitation* is the enhancement of or sensitization to particular sensory input. We might close our eyes (inhibiting visual input) if we want to listen closely to a piece of music, thereby facilitating our auditory processing. Inhibition, habituation, and facilitation are organizational tools that the brain uses in the ongoing work of sensory integration.

Sensory breakdown can occur at any point in the information processing sequence that we have described. At the input stage, a child may be hypo- or hypersensitive to what he sees, hears, touches, tastes, smells, or how he experiences movement and gravity. If he is hyporeactive, he will appear slow or spacey. He will need a large amount of stimulation for arousal or he may miss nonverbal cues and be slow with affective responses. He may not look, listen, process, or remember information accurately. If he is hyperreactive, he may pay too.much attention to certain kinds of stimuli, perceiving benign signals as dangerous. This hypervigilance can lead to distractibility, overreaction to nonverbal cues, or anxiety. Both hypo- and hyperreactivity can interfere with emotion regulation, social interaction, and learning.

Difficulties can also occur at the stages of analysis, organization, and storage of sensory information. Perhaps the brain doesn't receive messages from the receptors, or the messages are received inconsistently. Another possibility is that messages are received but not connected properly with messages from other parts of the brain. These missed connections can lead to misperceptions, misunderstandings, and mistaken ideas about what is happening at any given moment. A girl with an auditory discrimination problem hears her father calling her, but she cannot locate the direction of his voice. She runs off in the opposite direction, to his annoyance.

It's impossible for a child to behave normally if his body and brain are exchanging misinformation. A boy roughly pushes the child standing behind him in line. He doesn't know why he behaved so unreasonably, but when he is asked, he starts to cry and says, "She pushed me first." In fact, she did lightly brush against him, but it was an accident. His teacher insists that he is not telling the truth (the girl did not push him), and she wonders why he seems so unconcerned about his own behavior and so emotional about the girl's. What she doesn't see is *how his senses failed him.*

Impaired processing produces impaired output. Ayres predicted, "When there is an underlying deficit in the capacity to synthesize the range of sensory experiences, the child may be unable to organize purposeful actions in areas including communication, movement and play. Often perceptual thinking and the regulation of affects are impaired as well." Difficulties with emotion regulation and self-calming only exacerbate the dysfunctional patterns of information processing, making it less and less likely that the child will be able to correct the problem himself.

Modulation and discrimination problems caused the boy standing in line to misinterpret the meaning and significance of an accidental bump from the girl behind him. His response to the sensations associated with that bump was poorly modulated. It was not well planned or organized. It was defensive, but it was not malicious; nevertheless, he will be punished for it. Feeling misunderstood and mistreated, he will learn little from the experience about how to regulate himself. He may be a bright child who understands that it is wrong to push his classmate, but he is likely to repeat the same mistake.

When sensory integration breaks down, the cortex is unable to perceive, analyze, and solve problems effectively. The child is unable to organize a well-planned, meaningful response to the requirements of the moment. Limbic and lower brain processing take over, which can result in overly emotional, inappropriate behavior that the child himself cannot explain or defend. Over time, this sort of brain misorganization can interfere with normal development. Inattention, hyperactivity, irritability, explosiveness, social withdrawal, learning problems, and poor self-control can all be downstream effects of poorly regulated sensory processing. Most professionals focus on the social, academic, and family problems that emerge as if they were primary. But these efforts will not succeed if they do not take into account the piece of the problem that is specific to the child: poorly regulated sensory processing.

BORN TO BE WILD?

Traditionally, inborn differences in a child's reaction to normal, everyday events have been studied under the rubric of *infant temperament*. At the same time that Ayres began theorizing about sensory integration in the 1960s, Stella Chess and Alexander Thomas began studying the effects of temperament on how a child develops. Their research attempted to determine whether behavioral styles identified early in life, such as the difficult or slow-to-warm-up temperament, might predict later problems, like disruptive behavior or anxiety.

Over the years, temperament has been defined in a variety of ways, but it has always been assumed to be a reflection of a child's biological makeup. Researchers have related these early emotional and behavioral tendencies to some relatively stable personality characteristics. In particular, Harvard psychologist Jerome Kagan has demonstrated the enduring influence of temperament in his studies of shy, inhibited children who show persistent patterns of withdrawal in new and unfamiliar settings, shyness and anxiety in new social situations, and a preference for solitary activity and smaller friendship groups.

More recent work on temperament emphasizes variations both in the reactivity of a child's central nervous system (CNS) and her capacity to regulate those emotional reactions. This is sometimes referred to as *emotion regulation*, and it is assumed to evolve from the combined influences of heredity, maturation, and experience.

A child's level of *emotional reactivity* is both biological and social in nature. Her nervous system responds in a characteristic fashion (high reactivity versus low) to external and internal sensory stimuli such as touch, light, noises, smells, hunger, and pain. It reacts to social demands in a similar style. For example, a preschooler may react violently to the tactile discomfort of being strapped into a car seat, screaming, crying, thrashing around, and dropping to the floor. She may display the same emotional reactivity when told that she can't watch her favorite TV show. In contrast, a less reactive child might respond to both of these events in a more mellow manner. Perhaps CNS reactivity is just one aspect of temperamental differences between individuals.

Self-regulation refers to the child's ability to modulate, or balance, her responses to arousing or upsetting events. She does this by paying more or less attention to the event (approaching or avoiding it) and by finding ways to soothe herself. The infant, startled by a sudden sound, might cry and look to her mother for comfort or suck furiously on her fist and turn her head away from the sound. These are responses designed to regulate her distress. The more immature the child's neurological system, the more likely she is to need external support for emotion regulation; hence, the reliance of a baby on an adult for comfort. The adult holds and rocks her, sings and talks to her, and tries to engage her attention with a toy, a rattle, or some other distraction in order to stop her crying. As the child's brain develops, she becomes increasingly skilled at soothing herself, initially through calming activities such as thumb sucking or hair twirling, and later through distracting herself or talking about what is bothering her.

A child's emotion regulation skills develop as an outgrowth of the interplay between her biological capacities and the environment in which she is raised. Researchers have indicated clearly that patterns of reactivity can be modified by experience. In particular, parents can have tremendous impact on a child's developing abilities to modulate sensory input, soothe herself, and regulate her emotions and behavior. Kagan found that shy children become less fearful if their parents continuously expose them to unfamiliar situations. However, if parents shield their timid toddlers from novelty, the predisposition to shyness is reinforced. In this way, a child's neurobiology is actually changed by the experiences her parents provide.

Karen G. was immediately struck by Ben's hypersensitivity as an infant. Whenever she laid him down on his back from an upright position to dress or change him, he screamed and tensed up, arching backward and throwing out his arms as though he were falling out of the sky. He cried inconsolably at the sound of the coffee grinder in the morning and his clothes were a constant annoyance. This emotional reactivity, which Karen only later understood to be related to sensory modulation difficulties, affected her feelings of competence as a parent. She had no idea why he was so easily disturbed, and she and her husband struggled to find ways to teach him to soothe himself. His inborn biologically based reactions to the world created unique challenges for him and for them—and they realized early on that teaching him self-regulation skills would be their most challenging task as his parents.

Although it is unclear how sensory integration difficulties relate to what we know about temperament and emotion regulation, researchers are finding brain connections to temperamental characteristics like excitability, motor activity, and distress to unfamiliar stimuli. It is unlikely that temperament and sensory processing are one and the same. Nevertheless, it is clear that a child's ability to regulate his attention, emotions, and behavior develops in response to many influences, one of which is likely to be the efficiency with which his brain processes sensory information.

WE ARE THE WORLD

Since the early 1990s, neuroscientists have learned more about the brain than in all previous history. In the not-so-distant past, the brain was viewed as a bundle of instincts dictated by our genes, and it was assumed that genetic influences were mechanistic and inflexible. However, we now know that the mind does not mature according to a precisely programmed, predetermined genetic plan. The more than thirty thousand genes that make up our DNA are turned on and off by stimuli that come and go in our environment. In this way, our genes become the tools that experience uses to sculpt our brain as it responds to changing environmental demands and challenges. We become who we are as our brain adapts to the world around us.

This idea—that the world we live in literally helps to shape our brain—represents a relatively new way of thinking about human development. It is based on an understanding of the brain as a dynamic, complex system of neuronal interactions with tremendous potential for self-organization and change. We are coming to view the brain precisely as Ayres imagined it—as a network of neural circuits that are constructed and continually reshaped by our experiences.

Of course, we all recognize that how we feel and what we think changes in response to the events in our lives. For example, a teenager's mood can shift dramatically following an argument with a friend. A woman's sense of identity is forever altered by the experience of childbirth. A person who has been mugged sees the world differently than he did before. But now neuroscientists are discovering that our experiences change us on a biochemical level. It is a miraculously complex collaboration between our internal makeup and the external world that makes us who we are! And this process of brain building, once thought to be complete by the time a child entered school, continues throughout our lifetime.

The metaphor of the brain as a machine no longer applies. It is not a hardwired, precisely programmed instrument. Rather, it is flexible and adaptive: new neural connections are continuously being formed in response to brain–world interactions. It is opportunistic: neglected neural patterns fade away and unused neurons die. It is chaotic, like a very complicated game of Twister: neural pathways are constantly being forged in unpredictable patterns. This ongoing reorganization of the brain's microstructure, biochemistry, and function is called *neural plasticity*, and it is this capacity that allows experience to shape our brain.

In a sense, then, each of us has a uniquely formed brain, the product of our particular history. Genetic influences, biological strengths and weaknesses, and positive and negative life experiences combine in a back-and-forth exchange that makes us who we are. This is why two seemingly similar children will not necessarily develop in the same fashion. Development is too fluid and too complex to be neatly categorized or precisely predicted.

This is good news for children with sensory processing problems and their parents. A child's nervous system is malleable and open to change—and so are the brains of his parents! (Although, admittedly, neural plasticity decreases with age.) The undeniable contribution of experience to brain development is the basis of what developmental psychologist Dante Cicchetti calls "a psychobiology and neuropsychology of hope and optimism." Parents can make a difference in a child's future by observing him closely, finding out how he perceives the world, and accommodating his particular needs. Those accommodations have the potential not only to modify his behavior but also to change the neural pathways that maintain his behavior. Changes in brain functioning can affect his ability to manage tasks of daily living, regulate his emotions, and engage in reciprocal social interaction.

This is why occupational therapists and other helping professionals like to work with children and their families before negative patterns are set. Dysfunctional behavior and its underlying ineffective neural networks are both changed by positive therapeutic experiences. To be most effective, those interventions must address the child's body and brain as well as the social, behavioral, and emotional problems that emerge as she encounters the world.

||||||||||||||||||||||||||||||||||||||||||||||||||||||||||||||||||||||||||||||||

CHAPTER SIX

Helping Your Child to Help Himself

*Once the OT and I started talking, I realized that some of
Mike's behavior that I had considered odd was just his way of
staying safe and comfortable.*

— TERESA,
mother of Mike

*People say, "You have two older children. How could you not
notice?" But he tricked me for a while.*

— LISA,
mother of Stephen

OUR SON has always been extremely sensitive to loud
noises and the smell of things," a mother said of her
now 8-year-old son. "We've always avoided parties,
which seem to send him into overload." Her husband nodded. "On a
trip one time," she went on, "he went into a smelly bathroom and
immediately vomited from the smell. Certain foods he just vomits
straight back—it's instantaneous."

"He's very agitated if someone bumps into him," her husband added.
"Sometimes at the movies, he just sits there with his hands over his
ears."

They both looked at Karen S. expectantly. "How do we figure out if
he has dysfunctional sensory integration?"

There is a simple answer and a not-so-simple answer to this question.
The simple answer is this: You can fill out a screening questionnaire
(e.g., look at the "How Do I Know" questionnaires on the Web site
www.otawatertown.com) and see how well the items describe your

child. Or you can take your child to an occupational therapist (OT) and ask her to evaluate him. In order to determine whether your child has sensory processing problems, the OT will interview you. She will probably ask you to fill out a checklist and she may want to interview your child's teacher. She will also observe your child at school or in a structured clinical situation. In some cases, she may formally evaluate your child using a battery of tests developed by Ayres called the Sensory Integration and Praxis Tests (SIPT), or other tests such as the Bruininks Oseretsky Test of Motor Proficiency or the Beery-Buktenica Test of Visual-Motor Integration. Then she will give you her professional opinion about his sensory processing capabilities.

The not-so-simple answer to the question is this: it depends. The questions that you ask determine the answers that you are given. If you ask an occupational therapist whether your child has dysfunctional sensory integration, you will be given information about his sensory processing capabilities. You will also be told about the ways in which sensory processing problems might be affecting his behavior. You will not receive information about other problems or conditions that may be relevant, nor will you be told about any treatment options other than occupational therapy. In contrast, if you ask a pediatrician about sensory integration, you will probably receive a blank stare. Then you will be told whether your child is healthy and seems to be on track developmentally. You may be referred to a psychologist, who may or may not know about sensory processing problems but who can give you other information about your child's psychological adjustment.

Therefore, as a parent you must choose carefully whom you consult about your child's difficulties. By the time Karen S. knew that Evan needed help, she was almost in a panic, wanting to make up for lost time and repair the damage that had been done to his fragile self-concept. She faced the same question that all parents of a child with special needs face: Who can help him? Karen relied on her own judgment as a psychologist and bypassed some possible helpers because she felt certain that Evan's problems were not medical, psychological, or academic in nature. She knew that occupational therapists are the experts on sensory integration, so she took Evan to the best OT she could find. And she asked a lot of questions.

Looking for clues

We recommend that you do a bit of detective work before you decide whether to take your child to an OT. Your child's problem behaviors—the ones that are creating so much difficulty in her life and yours—are clues.

- Under which sensory circumstances are those behaviors likely to occur?
- What do they suggest about how she is experiencing the world?
- What kinds of sensory and motor tasks are difficult for her?
- Is there a possible mismatch between your child and her world that could be explained from a sensory framework?

Based on her developmental level and the kinds of demands that are being placed on her, different clues will appear at different ages. *Your job is to analyze the clues.* Look for signs of over- or undersensitivity to sensory input. As she gets older, the external, observable signals of dysfunctional sensory processing are likely to become increasingly complicated and problematic. She may also begin to show evidence of coexisting emotional, behavioral, or learning problems.

RED FLAGS FOR INFANTS AND TODDLERS
Sensitivity to touch: negative response to being held or cuddled; resists car seat, face washing, particular clothing; sensitive to water temperature; rejects certain foods; doesn't like cuddly toys
Response to visual stimulation: sensitivity to lights, faces, objects placed in his field of vision; distressed by busy environments
Response to movement: sensitivity to sudden, unexpected movement or postural changes (prefers upright position to prone or vice versa); fears or craves movement; uninterested in exploring or highly distressed when prevented from exploring; motor delays

Response to sounds: upset by noise (doorbell, sirens, vacuum cleaner); sensitive to voice modulation; speech delays
Ability to self-regulate: difficult response to transitions or changes in routine; fussiness, irritability; poor self-calming; unable to establish eating, sleeping schedules
Emotional attachments: resists behavioral limits; fearful of unfamiliar people; clingy

Most children seek out the kinds of sensory input and motor experiences that encourage normal brain development. Through play, they give themselves the sensory nutrition that they need. However, a child with dysfunctional sensory processing is not always able to play in such a constructive way. Her brain doesn't process the sensory input from play efficiently, and, in many instances, the sensations that other children enjoy are not pleasant for her. Swinging or climbing might be scary. Being in the midst of a swirl of noisy, running kids might be disorienting. As a result, she may avoid these activities, depriving her brain and body of the kinds of sensation and movement that, over time, might facilitate more efficient organization and better sensory processing. When this pattern continues, she may become extremely resistant to experiences that elicit uncomfortable sensations.

Evan's preschool friend, Mike, was sensitive to noise. Before his mother, Teresa, knew about his auditory defensiveness, she took him to Disney World for a family vacation. "It was terrifying for him," she said later. "He wouldn't go on any rides that were loud or dark." There they were, in every American child's dreamland, and Mike was inconsolable. Fortunately, he enjoyed swimming in the hotel pool, so the trip wasn't a total disaster. As he got older, Teresa recognized other clues. He was traumatized by the sound and feel of the electric clippers during a haircut. "After that," she said, "he wouldn't go into a bathroom if the fan was running. The sound made him totally hysterical." These clues, in combination with other signs of sensory defensiveness, raised questions in Teresa's mind.

RED FLAGS FOR PRESCHOOLERS

Sensitivity to touch: refuses to wear certain clothing; hates brushing teeth, washing hair, trimming fingernails; craves deep pressure; touches others constantly; dislikes messy feeling on hands; strong preference for certain food textures

Response to visual stimulation: avoids eye contact, especially when in trouble

Response to movement: awkward, clumsy; low muscle tone; bumps, falls, frequently breaks things; poor motor skills; fears particular kinds of play equipment; does not like feet off the ground; always on the go; fearless

Response to sounds: sensitivity to noises; excessively loud himself; speech delays

Ability to self-regulate: delayed bladder or bowel control; low tolerance for frustration; frequent tantrums; difficulty in group situations; need for sameness in routine

Emotional attachments: tests behavioral limits; less independent than peers; aggressive; resists separation from primary caregiver

Raising a child with sensory processing problems is confusing. When do you give in to him and when do you insist that he tough it out? How important is a clean room, a haircut, a winter jacket? Can you—should you—ignore his noisemaking? His surliness? His tantrums? Is he testing the limits or honestly struggling to cope?

Teresa describes Mike's first experience in a day care program when he was 2½. He was very bright and could already put together puzzles and read simple words, but almost from the first day, Mike was in trouble for pushing children away from him at the water fountain, on the playground, wherever they got too close and he couldn't escape. One day the teacher got too close to his face. "He told her to 'back off,'" Teresa recalls. "She told me that she'd never had a child speak to her like that before."

"I knew that things weren't right," she says. "But I didn't know why."

The child whose brain processes sensory information inefficiently is experiencing the world differently from other children. His misperceptions affect everything—how he thinks, what he feels, how he reacts to other people. There is an incoherence to his daily experience that is self-perpetuating—that is, he responds to the world, but his response is inappropriate (too loud, clumsy, or overly defensive) because it is based on sensory misinformation. Others react in a way that he does not expect—with complaints, criticism, or anger. His response to them is just a bit off, and, again, their reaction is not what he wants or expects. His emotions and behavior become increasingly disorganized. His interactions grow more turbulent. The world just doesn't make sense.

Very few, if any, adults are likely to recognize that he is putting forth great effort to accomplish what comes naturally to other kids. As Ayres wrote, "Working hard may help, but it is not the way to overcome the problem, and brightness is also not enough. A child may work very hard and with a lot of intelligence, but because he is working and thinking with a poorly organized nervous system, he will still have troubles." By the time he reaches school age, he has probably learned to compensate for some of his weaknesses in ways that cover up the dysfunctional sensory processing; however, these coping strategies can be misinterpreted as behavior problems. For example, a child who makes noise to screen out noise is viewed as annoying and disruptive in the classroom. The physical education teacher considers another child uncooperative because he refuses to join the hustle-bustle of a game of tag. Until the underlying sensory processing problems are addressed, these kids are likely to face significant difficulties at home, at school, and in the world at large.

RED FLAGS FOR SCHOOL-AGE CHILDREN

Sensitivity to touch: resistance to hygiene practices; difficulty with fine-motor skills such as tying shoes, buttoning, zipping, drawing; poor handwriting; unintentionally breaks things

Response to visual stimulation: difficulty with letter and number discrimination; inability to coordinate visual-motor activi-

ties (i.e., copying from blackboard to paper, organizing written work on a sheet of paper); difficulty finding things

Response to movement: poor balance and coordination; motion sickness; fidgety; seeks out spinning, twirling, swinging activities or fearful and tentative on playground

Response to sounds: easily distracted by unimportant noises; difficulty with speech articulation

Ability to self-regulate: difficulty with transitions, changes in routine, or unstructured activities; attention and concentration problems; unable to delay gratification; difficulty following school rules and rules of games, sports

Emotional attachments: difficulties with peers; low self-esteem

A whole new set of challenges arrives with the dawn of adolescence. As peers pressure him to conform to teenage codes of behavior and adults demand increased independence, the child who is different feels out of step. If he is already off-course socially and has been struggling to be successful academically, he may not feel secure enough to face the challenges of adolescence. Emotional distress, heightened by hormonal surges and physical changes in the shape and size of his body, can lead to erratic, explosive behavior. The social and academic demands of middle and high school present a unique set of dilemmas for the child who is dealing with sensory processing difficulties.

RED FLAGS FOR TEENAGERS

Sensitivity to touch: dislikes being touched; continuing avoidance of particular kinds of clothing; sensitivity to deodorant; resistance to personal hygiene routines

Response to visual stimulation: simultaneous fascination with and overstimulation by video games, television, computer graphics

Response to movement: poor posture; avoidance of sports

Response to sounds: hates the noise of others but gravitates to loud music of her own choosing; complains about noise at parties, school events

Ability to self-regulate: easily disorganized; inefficient work habits; disruptive behavior; poor problem-solving skills; explosive; concentration difficulties

Emotional attachments: difficulties in sexual relationships; may prefer safe family environment to peer activities; dislikes school trips, sleep-overs

Since any of us can become overloaded and experience a sensory breakdown given the right set of circumstances, a careful assessment of your child's sensory strengths and weaknesses will consider his capabilities across a variety of settings, in response to various task demands, at differing times of the day, and with an assortment of people. Although some kids cannot describe their sensory sensitivities, others are quite articulate, especially by the time they reach middle school, so asking your child for help in your investigation can be quite useful. Do not wait until he feels like a failure before you seek help for him. By then, he will be paying the emotional price of having an invisible, unidentified disability.

Once you have analyzed the clues his problems provide, decide what kind of help you think he needs. If you have medical questions, see your pediatrician. If you are wondering whether medication would be helpful, see a psychiatrist. If you want a developmental evaluation or behavioral consultation, see a psychologist. If you have educational questions, see a learning specialist or a neuropsychologist. However, if your question is whether your child has a sensory processing problem, you should ask an occupational therapist (OT).

In reality, the best help will probably come from a coordinated team of professionals. Although the standard treatment for dysfunctional sensory integration is occupational therapy, a more holistic approach may be necessary to address all of your child's needs. If he is having behavioral or emotional difficulties in addition to sensory processing problems, we recommend that you work simultaneously with a psychologist and an occupational therapist. A psychiatrist may also be part of that team. If learning difficulties accompany his sensory processing problems, you will want to work with a learning disabilities specialist and an OT. In any case, choose professionals who are willing to collaborate with your OT and who are familiar with sensory integration theory.

INCREASING YOUR CHILD'S JOB SATISFACTION

Occupational therapists help people develop the skills that they need for the job of living. A child's job is growing up, so to be successful she needs many different kinds of skills on the playground, in the classroom, and with her peers. You could say that OTs work toward improving a child's job performance by making her a more successful family member, student, and friend. When a child can learn, play, get along with others, and take care of her own body, she develops a sense of mastery that leads to a strong, positive self-concept.

An OT pays attention to the foundational physical skills that support the more obvious behavioral and emotional milestones of child development. For example, when an OT sees a child bumping into other children in the lunch line or flopping over classmates during circle time, she investigates the physical rather than the emotional underpinnings of the behavior: postural control, bilateral body coordination, motor planning ability. She analyzes the relationship between sensory regulation and behavior regulation, between body awareness and social awareness, between gravitational security and emotional security.

An OT analyzes all behavior from a neurobiological perspective. She asks herself: *Does this child have the physiological foundation necessary to meet the demands of his environment?* An OT trained in sensory integration theory will take it a step further and ask how the observable behavior relates to the processes of sensory integration. *Are there problems with balance or movement in a child who cannot sit up straight? Is there tactile defensiveness in a child who appears aggressive? Is a stubborn, oppositional child in fact having trouble with motor planning?*

This line of thinking will only be pursued by a therapist trained in sensory integration theory; therefore, you will want to be sure you have chosen an OT who approaches her work from this perspective. Simply call around to hospitals, early intervention centers (diagnostic programs for children ages 0–3), rehabilitation clinics, and private practitioners until you find an OT who works from a sensory integration framework. Or you can contact the American Occupational Therapy Association or Sensory Integration International (see resources in Appendix B) for a listing of sensory integration therapists in your geographical area.

Your child's OT will probably ask you to fill out a sensory checklist. Some of these checklists are standardized, with scoring guidelines based on a normative population sample — that is, ratings on these questionnaires yield scores that indicate whether the child's behaviors and sensory reactions are significantly different than those of his age-mates.

Other checklists are informal measures that provide a quick, impressionistic look at some behaviors associated with sensory processing problems. Many occupational therapists use these informal checklists as a preliminary check for sensory processing problems. By looking over the parent's responses to the checklist, the OT decides whether more formal testing would be appropriate.

The Sensory Integration and Praxis Test (SIPT) is the only standardized battery of tests available to identify specific types of sensory integrative dysfunction. This collection of seventeen subtests can be administered to children between the ages of 4 and 8. Computer scoring of the test profile yields a description of a child's strengths and weaknesses in different sensory modalities, which can be used to set treatment goals for the occupational therapist. An OT must be trained and certified to administer this particular battery of tests. A listing of SIPT-certified OTs can be obtained from Sensory Integration International or Western Psychological Services (see resources in Appendix B). In addition, the OT may use other standardized tests like the Miller Assessment of Preschoolers, the DeGangi–Burke Test of Sensory Integration, the Bruininks Oseretsky Test of Motor Proficiency, or other developmental measures.

With all of this information at hand, your child's OT will try to identify which sensory systems are underreacting and which are overreacting. She will also look for signs of specific problems in the processes of modulation, discrimination, and motor planning. For example, an OT might conclude that a child's avoidance of written schoolwork is related to fine-motor delays stemming from tactile discrimination problems. She may see evidence of this same processing deficiency in dressing difficulties and in sensitivity to unexpected touch. On the basis of her analysis, she would plan therapeutic activities geared toward improving the child's ability to tolerate tactile stimulation, such as drawing with a vibrating pen or searching for treasure in a box filled with dried beans.

REBUILDING YOUR CHILD'S BRAIN

The goal of sensory integration treatment is to improve a child's sensory processing capabilities by normalizing his responses to sensory input during play and everyday activities. Based on the notion of neural plasticity, treatment activities are designed to improve the way the child's brain works. Ayres described it in this way:

> In sensory integration therapy we want the child to use as many synapses as he can comfortably. We especially want him to use the synapses in his brain stem in which many types of sensations come together. The child may look as though he is merely playing, but the work goes on within. It may not seem that he is improving in the area of his problem, but he is learning how to use his brain more effectively and easily. Growing new interconnections. Facilitating certain messages and inhibiting others. Learning to direct information to the proper places in his brain and body. Putting all messages together into useful perceptions and behavior. Learning to organize his brain so that it will work better.

Of course, there is no way to test whether occupational therapy actually reorganizes a child's brain. We cannot see neuronal pathways. We cannot locate specific connections. Therefore, it is very difficult to evaluate the claim that sensory integration treatment works at a neurobiological level. However, we know that the brain continues to grow and change throughout our life span, and we know that experience plays a powerful role in directing that growth. It is not a big leap to suggest that sensory integration treatment has the potential to change the way a child's brain functions.

Here is how it works: The therapist presents the child with an active physical challenge that requires a response just a little more difficult or neurologically mature than what the child is normally able to do. Because the task appears simple and fun, the child is willing to give it a try. If it is at the just-right level of challenge, he will be successful. And he will want to do it over and over again, because getting it right is naturally rewarding. In this way, the therapist taps into what Ayres called the child's *inner drive,* his natural motivation for growth.

Many children with sensory processing problems avoid following their inner drive. They have been pressured to do things they cannot do. As a result, they feel inadequate. Their inner drive is in neutral, and they may hesitate or refuse to take physical risks. It is the OT's job to entice them to participate in activities that will stretch their abilities. This is done through the use of fantasy and a focus on fun. By engaging the child's imagination, the therapist gets him to respond to a series of elaborate physical challenges. To perform these tasks, the child must coordinate input from several senses at once. With each success, he masters a new level of sensory integration without his conscious awareness. He doesn't know he's rebuilding his brain. He doesn't even know he's working. He just thinks he's playing with an unusually lively grown-up!

In this entertaining, emotionally safe place, the child feels free to push himself beyond his perceived limits. He learns to trust the therapist to help him succeed and to accept him if he fails. And success *is* the reward. With repeated accomplishment, the child begins to believe in himself, to feel confident and competent. This leads to enthusiastic, self-conscious–free involvement in physical play, which is exactly what his brain needs in order to make the neural connections that will improve his sensory processing.

This state of optimal alertness, focused attention, and pure enjoyment is what psychologist Mihaly Csikszentmihalyi calls "flow." In his studies of optimal experiences, he found that when the mind is fully absorbed in an activity, physical and mental performance becomes enhanced. Captivated by the pure pleasure of the act itself, the person forgets about whether he is failing or succeeding. Csikszentmihalyi was quoted in the *New York Times* as saying, "People seem to concentrate best when the demands on them are a bit greater than usual and they are able to give more than usual. If there is too little demand on them, people are bored. If there is too much for them to handle, they get anxious. Flow occurs in that delicate zone between boredom and anxiety."

Good sensory integration treatment takes place in that zone. A skilled OT can get a child to perform activities just beyond his former limits, then the pure joy of success maximizes his motivation to continue. The child gains a new sense of empowerment and self-control that is exhilarating, a hallmark characteristic of "flow" experiences. And, just as Ayres suspected, the brain quiets down when it is in a state of flow—that is, contrary to the expectation that challenging tasks might increase cortical arousal, there is actually a lessening of activation when the challenge is in the just-right range. Optimal experiences occur when the brain is working at peak efficiency. Inasmuch as sensory integration treatment activities are inducing flow, they are improving brain functioning.

Over time, the child becomes more adept at responding to the environment. He learns to use sensory information to direct and organize his behavior. Parents and teachers may notice less sensory defensiveness, improved attention, more purposeful, cooperative behavior, less irritability and explosiveness, and improved physical coordination. It is the assumption of occupational therapists—although it cannot be proven—that these changes are the outward evidence of internal changes in the organization of the child's nervous system.

YES, BUT DOES IT WORK?

By no means is sensory integration treatment a quick fix. There is nothing magical about it, and some parents don't want to invest the time (at least 6–12 months) and money that is required. "I don't trust them," one mother told Karen S. about her 5-year-old son's occupational and physical therapists. She was taking him to therapy three times a week and paying over $2,000 a month for his treatment. "You see all that money going out," she said. "And our doctor says he's just immature.

Not many people even believe in sensory integration." Her point is well taken. It's hard to put your faith and your money in a treatment that may or may not be effective.

While many parents and clinicians have reported dramatic improvements in some kids' behavior following sensory integration therapy, what has caused those changes is unclear. Occupational therapy is a relatively young discipline without a solid scientific foundation, and many of the available treatment outcome studies fail to meet the rigorous standards of scientific methodology. Currently, a growing number of researchers are focusing on basic questions such as how to reliably identify and classify children with sensory processing problems, how to define sensory integration treatment, and how to select reasonable treatment outcome measures. Until these questions are answered, we will not have clear guidelines about when to recommend occupational therapy for sensory processing problems or what to expect from it.

Nevertheless, the anecdotal support for its usefulness is strong. Many children appear to experience significant improvement in their sensory processing capabilities in response to treatment. Others continue to have processing irregularities but learn to cope more effectively with the difficulties. There is also much to be gained by seeing a child through the eyes of a professional who understands the impact of sensory processing on behavior. An OT can teach you to recognize and respond to the sensory challenges that may be preventing your child from being successful at home and at school. She can show you how to improve his "sensory diet" in ways that will encourage healthy development on a daily basis.

A "DIET" THAT MAKES SENSE

Occupational therapists refer to our patterns of sensory intake as our sensory diet. And in the same way that we are what we eat, *we live what we sense*. The bits and pieces of sensation that enter our body through sensory receptors are the fragments of perception that construct our emotions, thoughts, and, ultimately, our actions. By controlling what we take in through our senses, we can influence how we feel, what we think, and how we behave.

We all are happier and more productive when we get the sensory nutrients that we need. People who exercise regularly will often comment that they just don't feel right if they miss a workout, and, in fact, research has consistently demonstrated the positive effects of exercise on mental as well as physical health. Remember the last time you took a quiet walk in the woods or a midnight stroll on the beach? How about the last time you danced yourself silly? Compare those memories to the last time you spent the day cooped up in the house watching TV and eating junk food. Which left you feeling exhilarated? Peaceful? Grumpy? Lethargic?

The impact of daily sensory experience on your child is probably even more extreme. For her, a healthy sensory diet is as essential as rest and nutrition. It affects her general mood, level of arousal, ability to monitor and modulate her behavior, and, as a result, it influences the likelihood that she will obey your requests rather than resist them. Paying attention to your child's sensory diet is an example of what author Ross Greene calls a "front-end strategy" in *The Explosive Child*. It is an attempt to prevent, rather than react to, a problem. And an ounce of prevention is worth a lot, if you can avoid the hassles of dealing with a problem on the "back end."

Too many of us leave our kids to their own devices—that is, within reason, we let them occupy themselves in whatever way they choose. And it is a delight to watch young children absorbed in the world of play and creativity or to see older children immerse themselves in a hobby, a sport, or a passion. In fact, we see it as a mark of maturity when they stop asking, "What can I do?" and start entertaining themselves. They are following their inner drive, and they are energized and organized by the sensations they are taking in. However, the child with sensory processing problems may not consume a balanced sensory diet when left to her own choices. It is too easy for her to avoid active play that is threatening or uncomfortable (like tactile exploration or games that require more complicated motor planning) and to overindulge in passive play that is compelling but ultimately disorganizing (like TV or computer games). Just as you would not let her eat chocolate cake three times a day, you must also set limits and provide healthy alternatives to her sensory preferences.

An OT can help you plan a balanced sensory diet for your child based on her particular needs. However, if your child is not working with an OT, you can do this yourself. You will want to consider your child's age and specific sensory sensitivities as you plan for her. If you structure her sensory diet when she is younger, she will learn to do many of these things for herself as she grows older. And you may find that *your* sensory diet improves as you pay closer attention to hers.

When Karen S. and her husband came to understand that Evan's passive, sedentary lifestyle was part of his problem, they began planning more family activities focused on play and physical exploration. They got up off the couch and started spending more time outdoors. They went on flashlight walks at night, puddle stomps in the rain, and bike rides all over town. Evan responded well to these experiences, and so did they! "He's going to save all of our lives," Karen's husband said one day as they headed out the door for a hike in the woods.

If your family is like ours, you don't have a lot of time to redesign your daily routine. But if you can find a few tried-and-true methods of regulating sensory input that appeal to your child, you can use them over and over again in different situations. Here are some ideas that work particularly well with preschoolers and elementary-age children. You will find other ideas in many of the resources listed in Appendix B.

MOVEMENT AND BALANCE

Jumping: Jumping provides pressure to the joints and muscles and input to the sensors in the inner ear. Small exercise trampolines are invaluable aids that can be purchased at your local sports store. Large bouncy balls with handles are also a good investment. In addition to bouncing up and down around the house, your child can lie across the top of the ball while reading or putting puzzles together. The motion and pressure to his abdominal muscles can calm and organize him. Hopscotch and jump rope are two jumping games that kids enjoy.

Swinging: Some children find swinging to be calming. This is particularly true if the swing is pliable and hugs the body, like a string hammock or a swing made out of an inner tube. Lying flat on a swing provides pressure to the abdominal muscles and gives the child a different orientation to gravity. Your child may prefer twirling around and around rather than swinging up and down. Spin slowly—not quickly—and follow your child's lead in determining when he's had enough. Never force your child to do something he is afraid to do. He may require that the swing be low to the ground if he experiences gravitational insecurity.

Some parents have hung a swing in their basement; others have rigged up a tire swing on a tree branch or constructed a jungle gym in their backyard. Karen S. and her husband built a fort for Evan that has five different kinds of swings, a rope ladder, a firefighter's pole, and a slide. Karen G. used to walk Ben to a school playground or city park so that he could spin on a tire swing to his heart's (and brain's) content.

Pushing/Pulling: Heavy work such as pushing, pulling, lifting, and carrying can get your child's system in gear. Playing games that involve pushing or pulling each other along the floor in large boxes, arm or leg wrestling, or "Row, Row, Row Your Boat" (sitting on the floor, pushing and pulling each other) provides this kind of input. Pull-ups on a bar, push-ups against the wall, pillow fights, and pushing a big ball along the floor are also helpful. Many household chores require heavy work: moving furniture, carrying groceries, sweeping, scrubbing, raking, and washing the car. By giving your child a job, you're accomplishing several goals simultaneously.

Sitting in a Bean Bag Chair: A bean bag chair can be calming or alerting, depending on how it is used. Being surrounded by the deep pressure of the chair is comforting to many children. It is often a good place for a child to "chill out." In contrast, he can play games in which he throws himself into or against the giant bean bag, or piles the chair on top of himself, which alerts his system and gets him moving.

Rocking: Rocking chairs provide movement that can be calming or arousing, depending on the degree. Children with modulation difficulties, in particular, are likely to rock too hard and overstimulate themselves. Sitting on a big ball (with feet flat on the floor) provides children with a rocking sensation that is more easily controlled.

Working on a Move'N'Sit Cushion: Move'N'Sit cushions are available from occupational therapy catalogs. They are designed to allow some movement to the child while he is seated. Some teachers keep one in their classroom, and we have seen several children who have benefited from using it there. One third-grader recently said to Karen S.,

"Thanks for the cushion! It keeps me from falling out of my chair." They are also helpful for getting children to sit through homework or dinner.

TOUCH

Swaddling: Children who crave deep pressure like being swaddled. Rolling your child up in a blanket ("making a burrito") can be very calming. Of course, you want to keep his head outside of the blanket. To intensify the pressure, roll a big ball over him slowly while he is swaddled. Some children also respond well to mummy-style sleeping bags or lying in bed with piles of pillows surrounding them.

Weighted Blankets and Weighted Vests: Weighted blankets and vests are also available from occupational therapy catalogs, but they can be made at home inexpensively. Fill up pockets sewn securely into a blanket or vest with sand, beans, or rice. The weighted blanket is effective as an aid to relaxation. The weighted vest is most useful at homework time or when a child is engaging in a task that is likely to be frustrating or disorganizing. You can also drape a sand-, bean-, or rice-filled "snake" (made from an athletic sock) across your child's shoulders when he is concentrating on written work.

Bear Hugs: Again, take your cues from your child. Most children with sensory processing problems crave deep pressure. Bear hugs are a good way of providing this. Remember, though: never surprise your child by hugging him unexpectedly, or you are likely to set off his fight-or-flight alarms.

Massage: Nighttime massages are a good way to calm your child before bed. Some children like light touch, but most prefer deep pressure touch: back scratching, firm back rubs, or even a session with an electric massager.

Textured Play: Provide your child with a variety of textured materials to play with—sand, clay, shaving cream, rice, and beans are just a few examples. Finger painting, digging in the dirt, helping with planting, kneading bread dough, playing with fiddle toys, and running her fingers through beans, rice, or pasta are just a few of the tactile experiences she will benefit from if she is gradually desensitized to their effect on her nervous system.

A small sandbox for the backyard is a worthwhile investment. Karen G. remembers taking Ben to the beach as a preschooler and watching him roll in the warm sand, never tiring of its soft, grainy texture. It was a remarkably calming experience for him. Even now, at age 15, he loves to dig a large hole in the sand and have others bury him up to his neck. Other children are threatened by the texture of sand. Know your child!

Clothing: Respect your child's clothing preferences. Most children with tactile defensiveness cannot tolerate labels, seams on their socks, or rough materials such as denim or wool. You can easily remove labels, and you can now buy seamless socks and tagless T-shirts. Sweatpants are a gift to many of these children. If your child cannot tolerate long sleeves, let him wear short sleeves year-round. If you can be flexible, he will be a happier, more comfortable person, and the two of you will have one less battle to fight.

Hair Washing and Hair Brushing: For children who are tactile defensive, the head is often the most sensitive area, and perceived threat to it generates the most frequent and intense battles. This makes daily hygiene a challenge. Some sensory solutions for hair washing include (1) preparing your child with a head massage (if he finds this kind of touch relaxing); (2) lying your child flat in the tub with just enough water to cover the back of his head. In this position, he does not have to lean backward (which creates gravitational insecurity), nor does he feel water trickling down his face (which creates a defensive reaction to the light touch sensation); (3) using a handheld shower nozzle for greater water pressure (decreasing the light touch sensation) and greater accuracy in directing the water spray. If hair brushing is too uncomfortable, consider a short haircut that eliminates the need for brushing. Use antitangle spray. Encourage your child to take over this aspect of caring for himself early—he is less likely to feel attacked by the hairbrush if he is controlling it.

Toothbrushing: This task of daily hygiene has to be done, and it has to be done properly to be effective. In order to accommodate the child with gravitational insecurity, hold his chin from behind to decrease the extent to which his head wobbles around. Try brushes of varying hardness and ask him which amount of pressure feels good. Some kids tolerate the deep pressure of an electric toothbrush better than the light touch of a handheld brush. Others like to use a Nuk™ brush (a rubber brush for massaging the gums) before the toothbrush. Again, it is better for him to control the toothbrush. Prepare him for this task by allowing him to jump on the trampoline or run his hands through water or bang on a drum. If it helps, let him listen to music through headphones to keep himself calm.

VOLUME: UP OR DOWN?

As children get older, they become aware of and articulate about their need for modulated sensory input. They become better architects of their own environments and know when to increase or decrease sensory intensity. When they are younger, however, they rely on their parents to create a comfortable sensory environment for them. In order to do this, watch your child carefully and tune in to what sorts of input he seeks and how he uses it to soothe or excite himself.

Hideaways: The child with sensory modulation difficulties needs calming experiences. Set up a small space such as a tent or a cardboard box large enough for her to fit inside. Fill it with lots of pillows and her favorite music and books. Allow her to go into this sensory shelter when she needs to recover from too much sensory assault. This is particularly helpful to some children during the transition from school to home.

Lighting, Colors, Smells, Sounds: Think about the lighting, colors, smells, and sounds in your child's room. Are they soothing or stimulating? Does he relax when he spends time in his room or remain agitated? Should he have a heavy blanket or a down quilt on his bed? What kinds of sheets will he find most comfortable? Is there too much visual clutter? Is the lighting too bright? Are there annoying smells (fresh paint, carpet backing) or sounds (clocks ticking, fans whirring) that keep him awake or disturbed?

Relaxation: Children can be taught to relax in any number of ways. Slow, deep breathing in which they visualize their lungs filling with air like a big balloon is one simple method. Slow, rhythmic rocking while listening to music is another possibility. With a bit of practice, you can teach your child to relax from head to toe by tensing, then releasing related groups of muscles (i.e., face, shoulders, arms, stomach, buttocks, legs). See Appendix B for resources that describe relaxation programs for children. Swinging, hanging upside down, swaddling, and deep pressure massage are other activities that are calming to most children.

TEACH YOUR CHILD TO KNOW HIMSELF

By raising your child's awareness of his sensory diet, you are teaching him to tune in to his body and to recognize and respect his sensory needs. If he can become an observer of his own reactions to sensory input, he can learn to seek out situations that are comfortable and avoid situations that are likely to be overwhelming. As he gets older, these are the kinds of independent coping skills he will need.

Mike's mother, Teresa, signed him up for group piano lessons when he was 6. However, she and Mike quickly discovered that the noise generated by the other students in the class was unbearable for him. The kids would turn the volume on their electronic keyboards up too high, or they would hold one key down, creating a high, piercing reverberation. Despite Teresa's attempts to help Mike cope—by buying him earplugs, holding her hands over his ears, and asking the teacher to turn down the volume on all of the keyboards—he was miserable. "All he could do was flop around," Teresa said. "It was too painful. He finally decided to opt out." She didn't see this as a failure experience, though. "The most amazing thing," she said, "was his ability to articulate his feelings and figure out what to do about it."

Teaching your child to use language to describe his experience and to guide his behavior is the key to self-regulation. If he can talk rather than react, he can use all the powers of his thinking brain to cope with his sensory discomfort. Language allows him to plan ahead for challenging situations, to check out the accuracy of his perceptions when he feels himself getting into trouble, and to generate solutions to problems as they arise. Here are a few things that you can do to encourage him to use language to cope with his sensory sensitivities:

- Talk through the steps of a challenging task or situation ahead of time. (He talks, you listen.) For example, before he goes to a friend's house, talk about how he will handle the noise, the food, the rough-and-tumble play. Help him identify the body cues that will indicate that his system is getting overloaded. Rehearse words that he can use to tell his friend how he is feeling.

- Role-play how to ask for help if problems arise. (Switch roles so that you can model giving and receiving help.) Pretend to be your child and say, "This noise is hurting my ears. I need to go outside on the porch for a few minutes." Or, "Mrs. Jones, I need to call my parents. May I use your phone?" Then pretend to be the helpful grown-up and say, "Billy, you look upset. Is there something I can do to help you?" Or, "Why are you holding your hands over your ears, Billy? Are you okay?"

- Allow him to talk himself through the steps of a problem as a way of keeping himself focused on the solution. If this self-talk is disturbing to others, ask him to whisper. During homework, don't complain or ridicule him if he talks to himself as he does his work (i.e., "Okay. Let's see. Where is my pencil? I don't see my pencil. Oh, there it is. Now, first I have to add these two numbers. 25 + 35 = hmmm, that would be 60. Now I have to multiply by 3. That would be—no, don't tell me—that would be 60, 120, 180. That's odd. That was the answer to the last problem. Oh well. Now, next I have to . . .").

- Rather than reminding him of what he needs to do in a given situation, ask him to say out loud what needs to happen. After breakfast, say, "What should you be doing right now?" Or, when he is packing his book bag, say, "What should be in your book bag? Tell yourself what you need, then look to see if it is in there." Or, if he is overstimulated, say, "Tell me what you can do to calm yourself right now."

TEACH YOUR CHILD TO ACCEPT HIMSELF

Our children take their cues from us. The better we understand them, the better able they will be to understand and accept themselves. Teresa laments that it took her five years to figure out what was going on with Mike. "If I had known about sensory integration," she said, "or if I'd had a pediatrician who understood, we might have known within the first forty-eight hours that Mike had these problems." His severe difficulties nursing, sleeping, and quieting down were all early clues that she recognizes as sensory processing problems now. "I feel that he has made phenomenal progress," she said recently. "But no other kids or parents should have to go through the torture of this."

Helping your child know himself and teaching him to come to terms with the ways in which his sensory processing problems affect his behavior are the most important things you can do to ease his frustrations. Remember: he takes his cues from you. Show him by example how to accept and respect himself.

- Get to know your child's sensory sensitivities. The more you understand about his sensory needs, the better prepared you will be to help him through the day. Don't sit in the waiting room or run errands while he is in his occupational therapy session. Observe. Take notes. Try to figure out what they are doing. And by all means, tell your child's therapist about the problems he is having at home and at school. Ask for her advice and practical suggestions. Learn as much from her as you can.
- Tune in to your own sensory needs. Pay attention to what is alerting and calming for you, then you can begin to develop a framework for understanding your child's sensory needs and reactions.
- In any situation, be willing to ask yourself: *Is there a sensory piece to this problem?* No matter how sure you are that this is not a sensory integration moment, just ask yourself the question. No matter how tired or fed up you are, no matter how inappropriate or unacceptable the behavior is, just raise the question.
- Respect your child as a unique individual. There is no one else like him on the planet. Literally. Don't criticize him for being different. As much as possible (and on many days it will not seem possible), honor his individuality. When Evan came home from second grade with the class award for uniqueness, Karen S. had to agree that it was well earned. Although it struck her as a backhanded compliment, Evan was proud of his award. It felt like an honest recognition of who he was, and he knew he deserved it. Find a way to sincerely celebrate who your child is.

• Emphasize his likability factor—that is, accentuate the positive. Ayres said it best: "The child with a sensory integrative problem who is accepted and supported by his parents is the one who can make a go of it in life." The others, she feared, are likely to lose faith in themselves. Finding a way to genuinely like your child, even at his most difficult, is perhaps the greatest investment you can make in his future.

||||||||||||||||||||||||||||||||||||||||||||||||||||||||||||||||||||||||||||||

CHAPTER SEVEN

There's No Place Like Home

*I don't have a problem with noise anymore. I'd be fine if you
people would just stop talking so loud.*

—BEN,
at age 13

*I love you so much that I want to kiss you,
but I know that I can't.*

—EVAN'S SISTER,
at age 6

HOME, SWEET HOME

Home is where we seek refuge from the demands of the outside world.
It is where we shed our public image, kick off our shoes, and relax. It is
where we are applauded for our accomplishments and chastised for
our mistakes, where we feel known, accepted, and appreciated. It's where
we first learn to love and be loved. The toddler peeks out from behind
his mother's skirt and ventures forth to explore the world, checking
back to make sure she is still there when he needs reassurance. Similarly, as the older child moves away from the comfort and security of
home, she needs to know that her family awaits her return. Home is
where things need to feel right, or everything feels wrong.

The foundation of your child's identity—her feelings about herself
and her ability to relate to others—is laid in the context of her relationship with you and the rest of your family. Research has repeatedly
demonstrated that positive family interactions, from parent–infant attachment to parent–teen communication patterns, are critical to healthy child

development. This is especially true for children who have developmental hurdles to jump. If your child has sensory processing problems, she is going to need more support, more patience, and more understanding from her family. She is high maintenance, and your job is to do what you can to keep her from falling apart.

In order to do this, you must accept her as she is, not as you wish she would be. You must give up your vision of the child you were hoping for, the one who would be so much easier to raise. Why is this step so crucial? Because our children want to please us, and they are keenly aware of the ways in which they fail to do so. Karen S. recalls an excruciating moment when Evan put it on the line. "I think that you're the perfect mom for me," he told her. "Am I the perfect boy for you?" At that moment, she realized that she was still clinging to an ideal vision of her son, and he knew it, too. He needed reassurance that his mom understood his struggles and accepted them, that her love was not contingent on whether he would continue to be a high-maintenance kid. And it wasn't just her love and devotion that he was asking about but also her ability to enjoy and celebrate him just as he was.

For the child with sensory processing problems, home can be a battleground, a minefield of misunderstanding, a combat zone where she feels constantly challenged and threatened by the people she loves and needs the most—her family. Some days, the entire household is on edge, confused and disheartened by the mismatch between her needs and everyone else's. It is one thing to acknowledge that a child's experience of the world differs from that of other family members; it is quite another to know how to make peace with those differences. And the larger the family, the more complicated the negotiations become. "Nobody taught me how to do this!" beleaguered parents complain to us. "Why don't these kids come with instructions?" Indeed.

In this chapter we explore ways in which you can keep your home from becoming a battleground. By practicing "sense-able" parenting, turning down the emotional heat in the family, planning ahead, showing empathy to siblings, protecting your marriage, and making peace with your extended family, you can prevent sensory processing problems from throwing your household off balance. You can make your home the safe haven you want it to be for all of the members of your family, including yourself.

SENSE-ABLE PARENTING

Positive parenting skills are essential in any family. They are absolutely crucial when a child has sensory integration difficulties. The child who is poorly regulated needs a home that is well regulated. He needs parents who are patient, predictable, and pragmatic. He needs a calm atmosphere where he can take shelter from the sensory storms that blow in so quickly, so forcefully. He needs siblings who cut him a lot of slack. He also needs coaching, because home is the place where he must learn to confront and overcome the challenges of living with sensory processing problems.

You have undoubtedly read many parenting books before picking up this one, and you have probably found some of them helpful and others less so. We have nothing new to say about good parenting. The formula is fixed: LOTS OF LOVING ATTENTION AND PRAISE + CLEAR AND REASONABLE EXPECTATIONS + PREDICTABLE CONSEQUENCES FOR MIS-BEHAVIOR = POSITIVE PARENTING. If you add to this formula the sensory analysis that we describe in this book, you will be well prepared for most parenting dilemmas. By taking into account *who your child is, where he is,* and *what is expected of him,* you will be able to prevent many problems before they occur and plan a reasonable response to those that take you by surprise.

THE SENSORY LENS: WHO? WHERE? WHAT?

Let's look at how the sensory lens described in Chapter Four can alter the parenting decisions you make. At a large family gathering when Evan was 5, his grandmother served a fish casserole redolent of shrimp, crab, and salmon. As her father prepared to say grace, Karen looked over to see Evan out of his seat, squirming about under the table. She asked him to get up off the floor. He refused. "We're waiting for you," she said. Annoyed that he was already "acting up," her first instinct was to give him an ultimatum, and, if necessary, make him leave the room. Instead, she looked at the situation through a sensory lens. There was Evan, with his poorly modulated sense of smell (*who he is*), being asked to sit politely (*what is expected of him*) in a chair placed directly in front of the smelly fish casserole *(where he is)*. He couldn't do it! Quickly, Karen moved the casserole to the other end of the table, explaining to her family that Evan couldn't tolerate the smell. Then she asked him to sit in his chair. He did so without complaint. On the ride home, Karen and Evan talked about the importance of using words when a smell, sound, or touch is bothering him.

FIRST THINGS FIRST

The most powerful tool that you possess as a parent is your relationship with your child. The more you nurture and protect this connection, the more goodwill there will be between the two of you. This is important because you're going to need to draw on that goodwill when the going gets tough. Stanley Greenspan, a well-known child psychiatrist, suggests that parents make a special effort to spend positive time with a child in anticipation of the demands that they are going to place on him. He recommends that any time a parent is about to increase expectations (i.e., begin toilet training, add a new household chore, raise a grade on a report card), he should also increase fun time with that child. It's easy to remember: greater expectations require greater involvement.

Try to set aside special time each day to spend with your child. We know that this is difficult given the other responsibilities and stresses in your life, so it doesn't have to be a lot of time. Just a little bit, as often as you can do it, will build up the store of goodwill between you and your child. During this time, let your child choose the activity while you give him your undivided attention. He is the boss of the play. If he is young, get down on the floor and play with him. Comment on what is happening, but do not criticize, correct, or try to teach. Play options that include a range of sensory experiences are great. Sand, clay, shaving cream, finger paints, bouncy balls, swings, and other good sensory materials will make this play time even more valuable. But remember, your child gets to choose. If he wants to play with his action figures rather than his bouncy ball, do it! Stay involved and show interest in his play without controlling it (this is no small feat for many of us). Just describe what he is doing and follow his lead. These comments about what your child is doing, called descriptive comments, enhance the quality of the attention you are giving your child. Here is an example of descriptive play between a boy and his father:

JOHNNY (age 5): "Let's play with trucks." Starts taking out his construction vehicles.

DAD: "Okay." Looks expectantly at Johnny.

JOHNNY: "You take these." Hands dad the dump truck and a backhoe.

DAD: "I have the dump truck and the backhoe. You have the cement mixer." [**descriptive comment**]

JOHNNY: Starts to move the cement mixer across the floor, making truck noises.

DAD: Moves his truck along the floor, making truck noises.

JOHNNY: Pretends to mix cement.

DAD: "The truck is mixing cement." [**descriptive comment**]

JOHNNY: Drives the cement truck over to the backhoe, making truck noises. Dumps the cement out.

DAD: "The cement truck is dumping a big pile of fresh cement." [**descriptive comment**] Moves the backhoe into position, making construction vehicle noises, and pretends to pick up the cement with the backhoe. "Wow, what a tough job, picking up all that cement!"

Even though kids as old as age 10 or 11 love to see their parents on the floor pretending to be someone or something they are not, you are more likely to be playing sports or a board game with your older child. Still, it is your interest in the activity, your undivided attention, and your willingness to let your child be in charge that are important. For teenagers, talk time is as important as playtime. Although talk time is more likely to happen spontaneously than in a planned fashion, the principles are the same. Follow your child's lead, be a good listener, offer emotional support, and refrain from directing, criticizing, or teaching.

TAKE A BOW

Praising your child is another way to increase his self-esteem. Child development experts suggest that the ratio of praise to criticism in conversation with young children should be very high, perhaps ten to one. We believe that this ratio may need to be even higher for the child with sensory integration difficulties. Assaulted by his surroundings, betrayed by his body, and criticized by those who misunderstand him, he needs a large reserve of goodwill just to get through the day! "There is no good side to sensory integration problems," Ben insists. "It's like you're being shot!" Your child needs a lot of praise to counterbalance the negative experiences that come from living with this hidden disability.

In order for praise to be effective in changing behavior, it should be specific and it must be genuine. Saying, "You're such a good kid," out of the blue, for no apparent reason, is positive; but it isn't as helpful as saying, "Thanks for taking out the recycling," after your child has finished his chores. In the first instance, he doesn't know why he is being praised, so he doesn't know what he can do to continue being praised. It may also be hard for him to own the good feelings that go along with the compliment. In the second example, he knows what he's done to earn the pat on the back. General praise, such as, "You've got a good head on your shoulders" or "You're a very talented musician," enhances a child's self-worth, but eventually feels empty if not accompanied by more specific praise.

It is especially important to find opportunities to praise your child for managing his sensory needs appropriately. Say, "I'm glad you told me that the seams of your socks are bothering you. Now we can help your feet feel more comfortable." Or, "You had a good idea when you bounced on your ball before starting your homework." One way of teaching him to use words to communicate his sensory needs is to describe with words what he is doing to regulate his behavior successfully. Praising him for his efforts will encourage him to continue trying to identify sensory solutions. It will also call his attention to the many little successes that he experiences but perhaps doesn't notice throughout the day. Often children do not know, until it is pointed out to them, what they are doing right. (However, they know very well what they are doing wrong.)

LET GO OF THE LITTLE THINGS

Another way to emphasize the positive in your relationship with your child is to deemphasize the negative by letting go of the little things. "I don't struggle anymore if I know John can't handle something," said Diane, the mother of a 5-year-old with sensory modulation difficulties. "I make other arrangements. Recognizing this has been most helpful." She was sitting in Karen G.'s office on a snowy winter day describing how her understanding of John's sensory processing difficulties had reduced the tension in her family. Before she knew that he had sensory processing problems, her insistence that he follow her directions sometimes led to full-blown temper tantrums in which she was hit or bitten. Now her understanding of him has shifted, and she doesn't get drawn into as many battles. For example, when John refused to wear a shirt because it was "too sleeve-y," Diane accepted his reality and helped him think of a solution. By avoiding a power struggle, she taught him that he could exercise some control over a threatening situation. It was a beginning lesson for John in how to express the emotions that get stirred by his sensory sensitivities.

Like many parents we have worked with, Diane has learned to ease up on some of her expectations. "I've learned to weigh things," she said. "To balance how hard something is for John against how important it is that he do it. It's amazing how much we ask our children to do that really isn't that important!" We wholeheartedly endorse her philosophy. It reminds us of the advice once given to Karen S. by an older friend: *You don't have to attend every argument to which you are invited.* We would add, *Please don't.* Every day, there are many opportunities to get locked in a power struggle with your child, but what will be lost is the goodwill you have invested in your relationship. Let go of the little things. Learn to live with annoying but acceptable behaviors.

What, you might ask, are the little things? Here are just a few examples. Let your child wear the same pair of sweatpants every day. Allow her to sleep on the floor instead of in a bed. Buy a down vest instead of a bulky winter coat. Permit her to stand when she is eating or lie down while she is doing homework. Resist neighborhood pressure to sign her up for soccer. Plan holiday gatherings that are small and well structured. Buy a larger hot water heater so that she can take extra-long hot

showers to relax. Do not expect her to tolerate foods that send her diving under the table. Tune out her noisemaking.

When a child struggles every day to manage the sensory challenges
of school, peers, and the larger culture, he needs a home that offers
respite. "If I didn't have parents who understood sensory integration
and made accommodations for me," said Ben recently, "I'd probably
jump out a window."

TURN DOWN THE EMOTIONAL HEAT

By the time most children with sensory processing problems arrive in
our offices, the emotional temperature in their families is uncomfort-
ably high. There is an explosive quality to their daily interactions. Tem-
pers flare, and they may lash out at one another over seemingly
insignificant disagreements. As parents have described it to us, "Everything is a struggle." Family therapists call this level of emotional reactivity *expressed emotion*, and it has been shown to be a powerful
influence on recovery from mental illness—that is, the lower the levels
of expressed emotion in a family, the better the chances that a chronically ill patient will not relapse. These results suggest that reducing the
overall level of emotional stress in a family helps sensitive family members manage their own vulnerabilities.

There are a couple of reasons why the expression of emotion can be
so intense in families with children who have sensory processing problems. First, these children have more difficulty managing their own
emotions than do children born with more efficient regulatory systems
and more mellow temperaments. When describing John, Diane said,
"He has so much input coming in, he short-circuits. He can't think
properly. His thinking becomes more of a reaction than a thought process." Second, because these children can be difficult to manage, they
generate higher levels of frustration in their parents. More frustration
leads to more emotional reactivity. And, the emotional heat increases
as the number of people in the family increases—siblings, cousins,
grandparents, aunts, and uncles can all add to the level of emotional
stress in the family. More than one parent of a sensory-challenged
child has said to us, "He was really meant to be an only child."

Learning to regulate emotional arousal is a critical developmental task. And home is where children receive their primary training in how to manage their emotions. These skills develop gradually, with maturation and experience.

Karen G. recalls her first interview with David, the highly verbal fifth-grader with significant motor planning problems and sensory defensiveness whom you met in Chapter Three. "I feel angry all the time," he said. He went on to describe the high level of irritability he experiences throughout the day. Sometimes he understands the source of the irritation—feeling different in gym class because of his motor sequencing difficulties or being overwhelmed by the noise in the cafeteria, for example. At other times he just breaks down, suddenly emotionally overwhelmed without knowing why. He told Karen that he uses up a lot of energy trying not to lash out at people.

David is an only child in a single-parent family, and his mother has spent years educating herself about dysfunctional sensory integration, so he is fortunate to come home to an environment that has been tailored to meet his needs. He sheds most of his clothes, plays music he finds soothing, and takes extremely long showers before beginning his homework. There are no siblings whose needs have to be met and no family interactions to negotiate other than his relationship with his very accommodating mother.

The level of emotionality that David describes is not unusual in children with poor sensory regulation. On several occasions Ben has said to Karen G., "I have an anger management problem." Coming from a child who has never been in trouble at school for verbal or physical aggression, this is a statement about Ben's subjective, internal experience. Although he has learned to control his emotional reactivity in public places, he still *feels* angry or irritable more often than he would like. At home, where he can let down his guard, he is more likely to explode impulsively in response to being irritated. When this happens, he has learned that certain kinds of sensory input, such as jumping on his trampoline or listening to music with a heavy beat, help to calm him.

Because your child's sensory sensitivities can interfere with his ability to regulate his emotions, he may need more support, for a longer period of time, in more carefully constructed ways than other children his age. Reducing the level of emotional intensity in your household and showing your child how to be aware of and in charge of his own emotions are critical components of your parenting job. Over time, he'll need less external emotional control as he develops his own strategies for internal control.

Diane still struggles with knowing when to make decisions for John, when to run interference for him, and when to let him learn by doing. She described a situation in which he surprised her by making his own decisions about how to regulate his reaction to a sensory threat. "We were in Mexico," she recalled. "And there were a number of wild, very loud, barking dogs. In the past, John would have spun out of control in response to this noise. But I watched him talk himself all the way up the hill away from those dogs. He was saying things I had taught him, like, 'It's important not to run from dogs' and 'It's just some barking dogs.' It was clearly his ability to talk to himself all the way up that hill that kept him calm."

CHANGE YOUR THOUGHTS: YOUR FEELINGS WILL FOLLOW

How do you reduce the emotional intensity in your home? Begin by changing the way you think when your child refuses to do something you've asked him to do or when he responds to you in a provocative manner. In these situations, most of us find ourselves thinking things like *Why can't he ever do what I ask him to do?* or *He is so difficult!* or *I'm tired of doing so much for this child and getting so little back.* These negative thoughts arouse anger, impatience, and a sense of hopelessness. Altering these thoughts can dampen, rather than fuel, the emotional heat in your house. Extensive research has demonstrated that our thoughts affect our moods. By controlling what we think, we can change the way we feel.

It is a revelation—and it stirs an emotional revolution—when you recognize that although your thoughts, opinions, and beliefs about your child come unbidden initially, they are not solid or absolute. They are, after all, *your* thoughts and *you* can change them. You can think of your child as a troublemaker or a "bad seed" or a spoiled brat or an oddball, or you can think of him as a person who is trying his best and failing. You can choose a position of curiosity rather than criticism. When he misbehaves, you can ask yourself, *What might be creating a sensory challenge for my child right now?* and *How can I make this task easier for him?*

Children learn to control their emotions by watching their parents. If you can view each negative event discretely, rather than thinking *It's always going to be this way!* and if you can attribute the problem to your child's sensory challenges rather than to willful disobedience, you're more likely to remain calm. And calm is what your child needs. We're not proposing that this is easy to do. It takes willpower and practice. But if you can learn to stop, take a deep breath, and count to ten when you're frustrated or angry, your child will learn to do the same. If he hears you saying things that make the problem smaller rather than bigger, he'll learn to do so as well.

Parents of children with sensory processing problems often complain to us that it takes their children longer to develop emotion regulation skills than their same-age peers. That may be the case; however, it's possible that they actually have the same skills as their friends. Because they experience the world as more assaultive, they're more easily overwhelmed, making it harder to use the skills that they have. At age 12, Ben was invited to a sleep-over with lots of other boys and he opted out. "I don't think I'll go," he told Karen. "It's not my thing." Later, at age 15, feeling he had developed the skills to handle the sensory chaos of a sleep-over, he made a different choice.

Stick with it! Parents often hold a secret number in their head, the age at which they believe their child will reach a developmental milestone or achieve a particular degree of behavioral or emotional control. They manage to be patient until that age arrives, then they crash. These feelings of frustration and disappointment are understandable. They're a natural reaction to a thought—*My child should not be having this problem anymore!*—that is chosen. If you change the thought—*This challenge is bigger than I realized,* or *I wonder if there is a sensory piece to this puzzle that I haven't yet identified* or *I'm really tired today and I'm having a hard time managing things*—your feelings will begin to shift as well.

CHILL-OUT BEFORE TIME-OUT

One of the most valuable tools you can use to turn down the heat is the chill-out. Unlike a time-out, which is a response to misbehavior or outright defiance, a chill-out is an opportunity for your child to calm herself before a problem escalates. It is an exercise in self-regulation. Whereas a time-out is imposed by an adult for a specified amount of time, a chill-out is generally taken voluntarily (or can be suggested by an adult) and lasts until the child feels calm and ready to move on. Unlike a time-out, in which your child's activities are curtailed (he cannot play computer games or read a book), in a chill-out he can do whatever he wants (within reason) to calm himself. As you can see, learning to take chill-outs requires a certain amount of self-awareness. Your child must learn to recognize when he is becoming angry or agitated and be able to chill out before he explodes.

Parents need chill-outs, too. For you, this might be as simple as going into another room and counting to ten or taking a few deep breaths. For your child, a chill-out might involve a reduction in sensory input (reducing the noise level, turning out the lights, taking "shelter," going to her room) or an increase in stimulation that helps her regain self-control (rocking, sucking, swinging). Let your child judge when she is calm enough to end the chill-out.

Ben has learned to give himself chill-outs. For example, when someone talks too close to his face, it sets off an internal trigger that, as he says, makes him feel like somebody he's not. "Even when they're being nice to me," he explains, "if they're in my face, it sets off that trigger." When asked what he needs at these times, he replies, "Give me space—just sitting in my room—leaving me alone helps." At other times, he jumps on his trampoline, listens to music, or takes a hot shower to calm himself.

By taking a chill-out yourself, you show your child how effective it can be. Removing yourself from an escalating interaction, not talking, and taking a deep breath reduces the emotional tension in the room. By calming yourself, you teach your child a lesson in self-regulation. The art of a chill-out, of course, is taking it or suggesting it to your child before things get out of hand. It helps if you suggest it in a neutral, nonjudgmental voice so that it doesn't feel like a punishment. Planning for chill-outs when things are calm—and even practicing them—can be very helpful in getting your child to take one when it is needed.

PLAN AHEAD

All children need structure, and the importance of planning ahead and sticking to a routine cannot be overemphasized for the child with poor sensory regulation. Again, the formula is simple: the more structure you build into your home life, the fewer battles you will have with your child. Why? Because children with sensory processing problems often feel internally disorganized; consequently, they are more dependent on external organization. The predictability of a set routine will help your child feel more secure and better organized. Morning charts, bedtime charts, homework schedules, and chore lists reduce the number of verbal reminders you have to give him. You can say, "Go do your bedtime chart," instead of barking out a sequence of commands: "Put on your pajamas. Wash your face. Have you brushed your teeth yet? Don't forget to go to the bathroom. And put those dirty clothes in the hamper!" This barrage of reminders, perhaps delivered in an increasingly loud and irritated voice, creates tension. Your child may feel the urge to strike back, especially if he is sensitive to the sound of your voice or to the tasks of washing his face and brushing his teeth. Remember: less nagging → less resistance → lower emotional heat in the family. A bedtime chart for a second-grader might look like this:

	Mon.	Tues.	Wed.	Thurs.	Fri.	Sat.	Sun.
Pack Backpack							
Put on Pajamas							
Brush Teeth							
Wash Face							
Put Dirty Clothes Away							
Lay Out Clothes for Morning							

For the younger child, or for a child who has difficulty reading, the chart can be constructed using pictures instead of words. Checking off the tasks for the older child or getting a sticker at the bottom of the page for the younger child is generally sufficient reward. The primary purpose of the chart is to organize the child's bedtime behavior and encourage independence, so in many ways it is self-reinforcing. However, if necessary, the chart can be connected to a reward system.

After-school schedules serve a similar purpose. It is tempting to give kids some downtime after the school day, but some children fall apart without firm structure in the afternoon. Karen S. recalls that Evan used to come home from school wound tight as a top. He would come in the house loud, hungry, crabby, and whiny—and things would go downhill from there. Karen knew that he needed to unwind, but the way he chose to spend his time—playing computer games or watching TV—made him more testy and argumentative, not less. So she planned out his afternoon with designated activities that provided the range of sensory input she knew he needed. More than one visitor to her kitchen raised an eyebrow at the schedule posted on the refrigerator:

2:45 Snack

3:00 Play outside: bike, scooter, fort

3:30 Begin homework

4:30 Computer game (only if you finished homework): can earn one sticker for stopping when time is up

5:00 Reading, drawing, playing in room

5:30 Clean up room: can earn one sticker for doing a good job

6:00 Dinner

6:30 Family game (if homework is done and room is clean)

7:00 Bath, brush teeth, put on pajamas: can earn one sticker if no arguing

7:30 Bedtime story

8:00 Lights out

Truthfully, Karen felt like a bit of a control freak saying exactly when Evan was expected to ride his bike or read a book. But Evan didn't resist. He embraced the structure and worked for the stickers. His behavior improved. The emotional heat decreased. It worked.

Transitions and sudden changes in routine are frequently difficult for the child with sensory processing problems. A timer may be helpful in moving him from one activity to another. By telling him that he has to stop playing on the computer when the timer sounds, you make his world more predictable and seemingly less arbitrary. You also take yourself out of the mix—it is the clock reminding him of the limit, not you. As a result, he is more likely to experience this as an opportunity for self-control rather than as an instance of other-control (which he is likely to resist). A word of warning, however: For the child with auditory sensitivities, a timer with an audible tick can be more irritating than helpful. A silent timer or a sand timer would work better for him.

ANALYZE PROBLEMS THROUGH A SENSORY LENS

Planning ahead also means preparing your child for difficult tasks by providing her with helpful sensory experiences beforehand. For example, before asking your child to start her homework, build in a sensory experience that is alerting and organizing, such as swinging or bouncing. The more difficult the task is from a sensory perspective, the more she needs time to prepare herself, and, ideally, a sensory setup before beginning. Letting her know what's coming next can make the difference between a cooperative interaction and a hostile one. "When you just come up and hug me," Ben once told his mother, "I have a problem with that. If you ask me first, that's fine." The best way to prepare your child for trouble spots at home is to do a thorough sensory analysis of your daily family routines and sensory diet.

Begin by making careful observations of her behavior. What does she do when she is stressed? What kinds of activities appear to be calming for her? Which ones are disorganizing? Which periods of the day are most difficult for her? Is it possible to plan positive sensory experiences for those times of the day?

Think about the sensory characteristic of your family environment. Is your family loud and chaotic? Are some members of the family rough or boisterous? Is someone learning to play the violin/the tuba/the flute? Is the television/radio/computer game always on? Is there a lot of visual clutter in your home? Is there ample space, or are you on top of one another? Do you have access to the outdoors or a playground?

Finally, identify daily tasks that present sensory challenges for your child. To do this effectively, keep a diary for a week or two. You might want to organize your diary as follows:

DAILY DIARY

Day:
Time of Day:
Problem Incident:

Sensory Characteristics of the Environment:

Sensory Characteristics of the Task:

Child's Response:

Parent's Response:

Recovery (how long it took and how it was accomplished):

Sensory Analysis of the Problem:

Sense-able Solution:

Let's look at an example. Ella is an 8-year-old girl whose father takes her to school every day. As soon as he tells her to put on her coat, she starts complaining. She dawdles, resists, and sometimes completely refuses to go to school. However, she loves school, and her father can't figure out why she hangs back like this when it is time to leave the house. They are frequently late due to Ella's resistance. An analysis of this problem in her father's diary would look like this:

DAILY DIARY

Day: Monday, September 24
Time of Day: Morning
Incident: Ella began arguing as soon as we got ready to leave the house. As we moved toward the back door, she became increasingly irritable and whiny, and she finally refused to go down the back stairs to the

alley. She pulled her hand loose from mine and started running around the house. I chased her until I caught her.

Sensory Characteristics of the Environment: The back stairs are very steep with open slats. They let out onto the back alley where a large generator for the building next door periodically makes a loud, grating noise.

Sensory Characteristics of the Task: Ella had to walk down the stairs, managing her balance and the visual input from the open staircase. Once in the alley, she had to manage her fear of the large, grating noise from the generator.

Child's Response: Resistance, refusal, oppositional behavior

Parent's Response: Frustration, yelling, saying unkind things

Recovery: As I got louder and angrier, Ella became more out of control. She screamed, "I hate you," and turned into a "wet noodle," collapsing onto the floor, refusing to walk. I told her she was going to lose her video privileges for the day, which had no effect on her. I finally had to pick her up and carry her screaming down the stairs and into the car. It wasn't until she was safely in the car that she actually calmed down.

Sensory Analysis of the Problem: Ella has difficulty with balance and heights. Stairs she can see through have always frightened her because she feels as if she is going to fall through them. Ella also has extreme auditory sensitivity—loud noises are frightening and disorganizing for her.

Sense-able Solution: Allow Ella to hold onto my hand on one side and the stair rail on the other. Teach her to look straight ahead, rather than down, to increase her sense of stability. Provide Ella with a Walkman so that she can play one of her favorite tapes. This will help with the transition from house to car and will also protect against her fear of sudden loud noises in the alley. Try to be patient and reassuring, rather than critical and demanding.

This solution worked very well for Ella and her father. It was simply a matter of identifying the triggers and preparing Ella in advance for the sensory challenge of walking down the stairs and through the alley.

TIME-OUT AND OTHER CONSEQUENCES

Creating a safe, healthy, balanced environment for your child is challenging. Even when you plan ahead for his needs and find ways to accommodate them, there will be days that feel all wrong. There will be times when he is out of sorts, no matter how you have attempted to control his world. If he behaves in ways that are unsafe or otherwise unacceptable, you will need to respond with a consequence.

As parents, we all draw the line between acceptable and unacceptable behavior at different places in the sand. What is important is that your child knows that there is a line he should not cross, and that it does not waver. If he crosses it, no matter how overloaded or out of sorts he is feeling, he must accept the consequences of his actions. This outer limit—this boundary between what will and will not be tolerated—is crucial to the development of self-control. A poorly regulated child needs particular help in determining where that boundary lies.

In *The Explosive Child*, Ross Greene writes, "Consequences can be effective if a child is in a state of mind to appreciate their meaning, but they don't work nearly so well if a child is not able to maintain such a state of mind." It is especially difficult for the child with sensory processing problems to maintain such a state of mind. If you find yourself in a situation where things have gotten out of hand and a consequence must be applied, remember that your purpose is not to punish but to teach. Your goal is to change his behavior in the future. Research indicates that this is more likely to happen if the consequences are reasonable, immediate, consistent in severity with the offense, and have a clearly defined end point. Keep the following principles in mind, as well:

- A time-out is more likely to be successful if the sensory conditions of the time-out are consistent with your child's sensory sensitivities. (If he has to sit in an uncomfortable chair, he's not going to cooperate.)
- Consequences that deprive a child of sensory experiences that are comforting work against what you are trying to accomplish. (Don't take away his music if that is what he uses to soothe himself. Don't take away recess from a child who needs to jump and swing to get her brain working properly.)

- Many children with sensory processing difficulties are sensitive to noise. Don't yell! Stay calm and use the softest possible voice you can muster.

- Do not force your child to stand close, maintain eye contact, or stop fidgeting while you reprimand him. It is likely that he is working hard to make this highly emotionally charged encounter tolerable enough to take in what you are saying. Look closely: he's barely holding it together. Don't push.

- Don't expect your child to take a consequence gracefully. Since you are working on teaching your child emotion regulation, it is reasonable to expect a certain degree of self-control. Temper tantrums, cursing, or physical violence are not acceptable responses to consequences. However, muttering under his breath, moaning that it's "not fair," or complaining that his sister always gets away with the same violation can be ignored. Take some deep breaths and focus on modeling emotional self-control yourself.

- Children who feel like they have little control over themselves often respond better to gaining something for good behavior than they do to losing something for bad behavior. A system of management in which they earn privileges is often more effective than one that punishes them by taking privileges away. For example, you can make tickets that say "ten minutes of video game time" and award them to your child when he achieves a goal you've set for him (i.e., speaking kindly to his brother, using words to express frustration, completing his homework, etc.). These tickets can be cashed in whenever he wants "screen" time. This gives him a greater sense of control over the outcome and avoids the explosive reaction some kids experience when a privilege is taken away from them.

- Allow your child to choose her own consequence for negative behavior. Research indicates that children frequently give themselves harsher consequences than adults give for the same offense, so you needn't worry that she will let herself off easy. This alternative allows her to experience self-control and helps her internalize the notion of consequences.

SHOW EMPATHY TO SIBLINGS

It is always difficult to create a family environment in which everyone's needs are met. It becomes even more complicated when one child in the family has special needs, especially when those needs are hidden, as is frequently the case with sensory processing problems. Normal sibling rivalries can be exacerbated by the challenge of dealing with a poorly regulated brother or sister, and your other children may be unwilling to accommodate a difficult sibling. The incompatibility of your child's sensory sensitivities with the needs, habits, and personalities of everyone else in the family can create tension and raise the emotional heat at home.

Karen G. is confronted with this dilemma in her house every day. Ben is extremely sensitive to noise, particularly at high pitches. Kate, his sister, loves to sing and frequently sings her way through the day in a high soprano voice that feels like fingernails on a chalkboard to Ben. In closed spaces at home or in the car, the sound of her voice is a trigger that sets Ben off. Because he has told her that her voice bothers him, he feels like she is deliberately tormenting him when she sings, and he quickly becomes furious with her. As she sees it, she "can't do anything around him."

With needs on opposite ends of the sensory continuum, these two clash on a regular basis. Ben needs space, while Kate likes to be close. Ben craves deep pressure, unlike Kate, who loves light, feathery touch. Ben hates riding a bicycle, going on roller coasters, and being in high places. Kate loves bicycles, daredevil roller coasters, and mountain hikes. These differences in their sensory preferences make it hard for them to enjoy being together. Their differences also lead to misunderstandings, hurt feelings, and resentment.

"I understand," Kate says when her mother tries to explain Ben's needs to her, "but it's hard for me. He gets angry really fast. He hates it when I get close to him in any sort of way. And when I hug him, he pushes me away."

Kate is a very perceptive, empathic girl. In her circle of friends, she can always be counted on to speak up for the underdog, but with her brother, she runs out of generosity quickly. "I want to be able to act like he's regular," she confesses. "I don't want to treat him differently. I know it's really hard for him, but it's hard for me, too, because I have to deal with him."

Your other children may think that you let their sibling get away with things they can't get away with. Or they may accuse you of indulging his preferences in order to avoid a sensory integration crisis. Don't let their judgments put you on the defensive. They may be right. Fair doesn't necessarily mean equal—and there's no reason to pretend that you treat your children equally. It's practically impossible (and usually not advisable) to do so. There is good reason to make every attempt to treat them fairly by acknowledging and addressing their individual needs and desires. Your other children can understand this principle, even if they don't always like it.

If your child is going to weekly occupational therapy sessions, his younger siblings may feel left out of all the fun. Evan's sister spent eighteen months of her preschool life wondering why she never got a turn to play with Rebecca. At the end of every one of Evan's sessions, she quickly took off her shoes and headed for the mats and swings in the OT clinic while Karen S. paid the bill. More than once, she had to be carried to the car, shoeless and crying, because she wouldn't leave on her own.

Be aware that your other children may unwittingly become targets of their sibling's frustrations. The child who is poorly regulated may be extremely controlling and overreactive in his interactions at home. He is less likely to yield to the requests of others or to empathize with their point of view. Sibling play, which can be highly charged emotionally under the best circumstances, can quickly become volatile. This emotional intensity is very difficult for the poorly regulated child to manage, and the interaction between siblings can spin out of control.

"It happens so quickly," a mother told Karen S. "One minute they're playing nicely, and the next they're at each other's throats." She knew it was normal for her children to argue with each other, but she was bothered by the lack of empathy her 7-year-old son showed for his little sister when she got hurt or upset. "Whenever she cries, he just sits there with his hands over his ears," she said. "He hates the sound of her crying. I understand that, but it worries me that he shows no concern for her at all."

"What kinds of thoughts run through your mind at those times?" Karen asked her.

"I don't know," she mused. "I guess I start thinking that he's going to grow up to be a person who only thinks about himself, someone cold and uncaring. I don't want him to be like that."

"Does he show concern for his sister in other situations?" Karen asked.

"Oh sure," she said. "They actually get along very well most of the time, but that's because she usually does what *he* wants to do. He's delightful when things go his way. But when she's upset, he can't see past his own discomfort to acknowledge hers."

"Let's think about it this way," Karen suggested. "If your sister was upset about something and she communicated her distress by slapping you in the face repeatedly, how empathic would you feel toward her?"

"Not very," she allowed.

"Exactly," Karen agreed. "If we're being attacked, it's natural for us to feel defensive. Your daughter's crying is painful for your son. It feels like an attack. So, it's probably not reasonable for you to expect him to respond empathically *at that moment*. After she has quieted down, then you can help him find ways to communicate his concern. But they both need time to recover first."

This look at sibling conflict through a sensory lens examines *who the child is* (a boy with auditory sensitivities), *where he is* (in a room with a loud, crying person), and *what is being expected of him* (to think about his sister's feelings). It assumes that he would do well if he could—that is, he would show empathy for his sister if he were not under attack. It makes accommodations (wait until his sister has quieted down) and provides support (help him communicate his concern). It addresses his mother's concern (that he learn to be a caring person) and it respects his needs (to feel respected and accepted). It also communicates two messages to his sister (her crying is painful to him *and* he cares about her). Too often, siblings only get the first message—your brother has special needs—without the second. In this example, the sister's emotional needs were acknowledged as well. If you want to improve your children's relationships with each other and turn down the emotional heat between siblings, try these suggestions:

- Be sensitive to the needs of all your children. Make every effort to treat them fairly, rather than equally, and give to each according to her needs.
- Help your other children understand their sibling's sensory difficulties. Encourage empathy by explaining—and having him explain to them—how he experiences the world differently from them.
- Acknowledge that life is not fair, and empathize with your children when they are treated badly by their sibling. Emphasize that they are not to blame for his emotional reactivity.
- Help your children take responsibility for explaining their needs to each other and for showing and requesting mutual respect regarding their differences.
- Be aware that siblings will exploit each other's vulnerabilities when they are angry. All siblings know how to "go for the jugular." Children with poor sensory regulation are particularly vulnerable to this sort of exploitation. Do not tolerate provocation.
- Keep the expression of emotional intensity in your house low. When sibling interactions deteriorate, tension rises. You can help by staying calm. Take a chill-out if you need one.
- Provide rewards and incentives for cooperation between siblings.

MIND YOUR MARRIAGE

Family therapists have long understood the importance of a healthy marriage and a strong, unified alliance between parents. Research has documented the connections between parents' satisfaction with their marriage and the health and happiness of all other members of the family. On the flip side, when parents fuss and fight with each other, their children are at much greater risk of developing all sorts of problems. This is especially true if those children have other problems to begin with. For a child with poor self-regulation skills, marital discord—especially hostile, unresolved conflict between parents—is potentially very damaging. Besides being more vulnerable to the ill effects of marital conflict, the sensory sensitive child is also acutely aware that he contributes to that conflict! Thus develops a negative cycle that raises the emotional temperature in the entire household.

It is not unusual for parents of a child with sensory integration difficulties to disagree about how to handle him. They may interpret his behavior differently. Maybe one parent has been talking to professionals and collecting advice while the other has been hoping he'll just grow out of it. Or they may understand the problem in similar ways but disagree about the solution. Even parents with a strong relationship can find themselves snapping at one another when they are overwhelmed by confusion, anxiety, and frustration. As the emotional temperature in the family rises, the child is even more likely to spin out of control. Before long, an escalating spiral of negative emotions has everyone feeling agitated, alienated, and defeated.

Resolving your conflicts constructively and presenting a unified parental response to your child's challenging behavior is critical to the health of your family and the success of your child. Keep some of the following ideas in mind:

- Make your marriage a priority. Find time to go out, be with friends, and enjoy yourselves. There was a good reason why you married each other in the first place. Return to those pleasurable activities that brought you together.
- Talk about your child frequently. Share your worries and fears. Even if you don't agree, make sure you each understand the other's perception of the problems he is experiencing.
- Both of you should have ongoing contact with the members of your child's treatment team. Take turns driving your child to OT and therapy appointments. When possible, both of you should attend school conferences. In this way, you'll both be equally informed about your child's difficulties. This also keeps the burden of caring for him from falling on only one person.
- Support each other in your efforts to teach and discipline your child. Even if you disagree with your spouse about a particular situation, try not to say so in front of your kids. If you must speak up, adopt a respectful, problem-solving attitude. Letting it slide is probably less damaging than raising the emotional tension in the house.
- Do a sensory analysis when you're planning ahead or trying to reach a joint decision about a particularly difficult situation.

MAKE PEACE WITH YOUR EXTENDED FAMILY

"I feel like a stranger in the family," Ben said when he was asked about how sensory integration has affected his relationships with his grandparents, aunts, uncles, and cousins. He went on to tell about a recent incident during a large family function when one of his aunts, very happy to see him, came up and hugged him. Later she apologized, saying that she knew he didn't like hugs but that she had done it impulsively because she was so glad to see him. "I like that," Ben said. "If other parents could tell their relatives about this, it would help."

Extended family relationships are often difficult. The Thanksgiving example in Chapter Four gives just a hint of the many ways in which the child with sensory integration problems struggles with, and contributes to, tensions in the extended family. In our offices, parents list numerous complaints about their family members.

"My mother just doesn't get it," says one exhausted mother of a difficult boy. "She keeps saying if I would just discipline him properly I wouldn't have this problem."

"I know my sisters don't want to take him for the weekend even though they're always willing to watch each other's kids," says another. "He spins out of control when he's with his cousins . . . it's almost as if they're trying to get him going."

"I hate always looking like the bad mother," complains a third.

The feelings generated by these interactions with extended family members range from anger to self-doubt to embarrassment. Judgments— real or perceived—can feed and fuel marital conflict regarding how to handle your child. Your parents and your spouse's parents may feel inadequate themselves when they can't manage your child effectively. These feelings affect their relationship with you and with your child. These guidelines may help you avoid some of these pitfalls:

- Help your family understand your child. Share what you've learned about his sensory integration difficulties. This will take patience and repetition. These are not concepts with which people are generally familiar, and it may take time for the ideas to sink in.
- Teach those members of your family who spend a lot of time with

your child how to do the sensory analysis described in this book. Do it with them.

- Help them plan ahead for your child by telling them how they can accommodate his sensory needs. Remember: they want to feel successful with him, too.
- Do not take criticism of your child to heart. Instead, help other family members understand his behavior through a sensory lens.
- Celebrate your child's successes with them.
- Thank them when they make an effort to understand your child's difficulties. Let them know how much you—and he—appreciate it.

|||||||||||||||||||||||||||||||||||||||||||||||||||||||||||||||||||||||||||||||||||||||||

CHAPTER EIGHT

Surviving and Thriving at School

It's a good thing all my teachers like me so much.
They give me second chances.

—EVAN,
at age 9

I feel really irritable after school because
I've been sitting for so long.

—BEN,
at age 15

OST PARENTS feel a mixture of apprehension, excitement, hope, and misgiving when they send a child off to school for the first time. After all, school is not home. When your child steps into a classroom, he must manage himself without your protection or guidance. You will not be there to wipe his nose, dry his tears, lead him by the arm, or pat him on the back. He'll have to learn to make it on his own.

School is your child's nine-to-five job, and what a job it is! The list of skills required is extensive and they constantly change. Assignments are mandatory and cannot be negotiated. Supervisors evaluate his performance daily and insist on steady improvement. Coworkers can be difficult to get along with. The workday is long, with few breaks, and compensation is minimal. He did not apply for this job, nor can he legally resign from it, but he can go on strike and stop producing if he gets discouraged.

Your child's teacher wants him to succeed. She wants him to feel competent and confident and to enjoy learning. She wants him to get along with the other children. And, of course, she wants him to master the academic skills he will need to become an independent learner. But she needs your help in order to make these things happen.

Research shows that students whose parents get involved in their education earn higher grades and test scores, develop better social skills, and are much more likely to graduate from high school and go on to college. An active collaboration between home and school is even more critical when a child has sensory processing problems. As one father of a third-grader said, "My son's teacher knows that he's bright, but she also knows that he's a pain in the butt. He has to work harder than other kids to conform to the rules, but she doesn't see, know, or appreciate that about him." He added, "It's up to us to educate her about him and pave his way. We can't afford to let it turn negative."

BEING THERE: A CHALLENGE IN AND OF ITSELF

School is a potential nightmare for the child with sensory processing problems. While you may accommodate his sensory needs at home, his teacher probably doesn't even recognize the barrage of sensory assault that he faces at school. She doesn't understand why he is having difficulty coping with the class routine when everyone else seems to be doing just fine. But a look through a sensory lens quickly reveals what might be making it difficult for him to cope with the sensory demands of being at school.

Look back at the lists of sensory processing difficulties described in Chapter Two and consider your child's school experience from a sensory point of view. Once you have his sensory vulnerabilities in mind, think about the school environment. Fluorescent lights buzz overhead, electrifying the room with the glare of artificial light. Colorful visual displays punctuate the walls, shelves, and bulletin boards, clamoring for students' attention. Classmates move around the room, crowding, bumping, and touching one another unexpectedly, grabbing things out of each other's hands, and pulling on each other's clothing. The temperature in the building may be poorly regulated. The pungent smells of a freshly mopped floor, a sweaty gymnasium, or the day's lunch permeate the air. The acoustics of tiled floors and concrete walls are harsh, and there is the constant din of voices in the lunchroom, in the hallways, and on the playground. School is an intense sensory experience!

Consider the demands placed on your child. He must dismiss thoughts, emotions, and physical sensations that are not relevant to his schoolwork. He must sit at a desk for long periods of time and get up only when granted permission. He must keep himself and his belongings organized. On demand, he must be able to switch from working independently to working in a small or large group. He must get along with a wide variety of people. He must move quickly and cheerfully from one activity to another. He must follow rules, keep quiet, respond to multiple directions, delay gratification, accept consequences, and manage his frustration in socially acceptable ways.

When you look through the sensory lens, you can see that the sensory challenges of school are continuous, with many opportunities for failure, frustration, and misunderstanding throughout the day. In *Raising Your Spirited Child*, Mary Sheedy Kurcinka points out, "Kids who are constantly forced to adapt become exhausted and frustrated and as a result act out, or give up." When a child is regularly called upon to adapt to the sensory characteristics of his surroundings, the amount of effort involved in *just being there* is enormous. If his attempts to cope are misunderstood, he may withdraw, melt down, or tune out.

From the teacher's point of view, a child with sensory processing problems can be hard to teach. He may be less flexible and more easily frustrated than other students. He may not do what he knows how to do when his thinking brain is not getting solid, reliable information from his lower brain. Consequently, his behavior may seem erratic. Because he may not respond to rewards and punishments that work for other kids, his teacher could mistakenly get the impression that he is not motivated to do well. She may find it difficult to identify the sensory situations that trigger his defensive reactions, and she may miss the behavioral warning signals that forecast trouble. This may leave the teacher feeling disrespected and your child feeling misunderstood—a situation in which it is very difficult for learning to take place.

"A downward spiral can get started," one parent said. "It's hard for my child to jump through the hoops at school. She gets in trouble, which affects her performance, her teacher's evaluation of her, and, ultimately, her opinion of herself." He went on to explain, "It's really a parent–student–teacher problem. We have to be involved in monitoring what's going on, but our daughter has to be involved, too, in determining what she can and can't do. And the teacher has to cut her a little slack by realizing that there are things she is trying to do that are hard for her."

Your child's teacher has a great deal to offer your child. She is knowledgeable about how children learn. She understands the art of teaching, and she uses strategies and activities that make learning come alive. But she does not know your child as well as you do. She does not know how his needs might interfere with his behavior in the classroom. By forming an alliance with her and teaching her to see your child through a sensory lens, you will be helping her succeed at her job. As a result, your child will be much more likely to succeed at his.

Of course, there are many reasons why a child can have difficulty learning. In this chapter, we only focus on the sensory challenges that you, your child, and his teacher may face as he moves from preschool to elementary and middle school. Our approach is simple: use a sensory lens to identify his needs and to accommodate them. However, many children with sensory processing problems have other conditions that affect their learning and behavior. If this is the case for your child, you will need to look through a kaleidoscope of lenses to fully understand his educational needs and to determine what kinds of resources he needs to support his learning.

GETTING A HEAD START: THE PRESCHOOL SETTING

The 3-year-old enters preschool barely toilet trained and with all the unsocialized energy of a puppy. She is accustomed to the safety and security of home, where she is the center of the universe and the rules are fashioned with her in mind. School is different: the rules don't bend; the teacher pays attention to her only some of the time; and there are lots of kids tumbling around. While she is thinking about how to get enough snack and stay on the swing as long as she wants to, the teacher will be seeing to it that she is developing the academic, behavioral, and social skills she'll need for kindergarten at age 5.

These skills include learning to count, to recognize shapes and colors, and to use a pencil and scissors. They also include being able to soothe herself when she is upset, use words to express her feelings, take turns, follow directions, and control her body. In addition, she will need to be able to share toys, play cooperatively, and join a group without being disruptive.

This is a tall order for a young child, especially if she is struggling with hidden sensory difficulties. As we've noted, the whole sensory carnival of school can jangle the very fiber of her being. How do you help your child have a positive preschool experience?

First, choose the preschool carefully. Before enrolling, visit several classrooms. Does the physical environment match your child's sensory needs? If you've never seen her in a school setting before, it will be difficult to know exactly what she is going to need. Pick a school that *feels right* for your child. Then arrange a meeting with her soon-to-be teacher. Tell the teacher about your child—her personality, her likes and dislikes, her strengths, and her sensory weaknesses. It is unlikely that the teacher will know about or be trained to deal with sensory processing problems. You have important information that she needs. The better she understands your child's sensory sensitivities, the better prepared she will be to make this first school experience enjoyable.

No matter how well prepared you and the teacher may be, sensory-based problems will develop that you didn't anticipate. When this happens, visit the classroom and observe what's going on. Watch closely to see whether there may be a sensory mismatch between your child and her classroom situation. Look through the sensory lens we first described in Chapter Four.

Think about who she is. What kind of sensory processing problems does she have? (In fact, this may be the first time you ask yourself this question. Many parents do not actually discover their child's sensory processing problems before she starts having trouble in school.)

Think about where she is. Tune in to the sensory characteristics of the classroom.

Think about what she is being expected to do. What are the sensory and motor demands of the tasks that are causing her trouble?

Once you have answered these questions, you and the teacher can begin to generate some solutions to the problem. For example, Marcus was a preschooler who was having difficulty keeping his hands and feet to himself during group time. He danced and did cartwheels while everyone else was finding a place in the circle. Once seated, he was all arms and legs, bumping the children next to him with his elbows and feet, touching their heads with his hands, and flopping over and lying across their laps. His teacher complained that he was causing a commotion and disturbing the other children. She told his mother that he didn't seem to learn from his mistakes, because he would come back from a time-out and do the same thing all over again.

Who he is: Marcus is a child with a poorly regulated sense of movement and body position. He has modulation difficulties in the proprioceptive system.

Where he is: At circle time, Marcus was asked to sit on the floor, in the midst of other children who frequently jostled each other and competed for spots next to their favorite classmates. There was no clearly designated place for each child to sit.

What is expected: Several times a day, the children were expected to sit upright on the floor, close to one another, with legs crossed for approximately twenty minutes. During this time, they were expected to listen and follow verbal directions.

Sensory Analysis: Sitting on the floor in a spot with no visual or tactile boundaries (unlike sitting in a chair) was hard for Marcus because of his poor sense of body position. Difficulty judging personal space and low muscle strength/poor posture (related to an underreactive proprioceptive system) caused him to flop over onto his neighbors.

Sense-able Solution: Rather than making Marcus sit apart from the group in time-out, his teacher decided to provide him with a visual boundary for his physical space. She gave him a cushion to put on the floor that marked his spot in the circle. She also gave him a pillow to hold in his lap or a squeeze toy to hold in his hands so that he would not feel the need to touch others. These visual, tactile, and proprioceptive cues helped Marcus define his body map, know where he was in space, and stay within his personal boundaries.

Another child, Thomas, was having difficulty getting along with the kids in his classroom. He told his parents that he didn't like the other children, and, in fact, he spent most of his time on the computer, with a teacher, or in solitary play. "He wants to be in total control," his mother said. "He can't tolerate unexpected touch and he doesn't want too much noise or commotion." She recognized that Thomas's extreme difficulties with sensory modulation were preventing him from making friends. He had been in trouble several times for yelling, hitting, choking, and pouring chocolate milk on his classmates.

The typical response to such seemingly aggressive behavior might be discipline, but all too often disciplinary measures don't teach appropriate behavior. What this boy needed was help. Looking at Thomas's behavior through a sensory lens reveals that he responds defensively (and inappropriately) to the tactile, auditory, and visual overstimulation of being in a classroom full of children. When he feels threatened, he withdraws or lashes out. Either way, his sensory needs interfere with his behavior. A sense-able solution would be for his teacher, parent, or therapist to coach him in the appropriate words to use when he is accidentally bumped or touched. Thomas also needs a sensory shelter in the classroom where he can retreat when he is feeling overwhelmed by the noise and activity. Finally, he needs structured, closely supervised play experiences with a few select peers (perhaps a social skills group with the school counselor) to learn that friends can be fun.

Marcus and Thomas are different in the way their sensory difficulties are expressed, but the analysis applied to their behavior is the same. Once you learn to look through a sensory lens, you can examine any situation from a sensory perspective. If you have trouble identifying the problem, slow down, look the situation over carefully, and listen to what your child is telling you about his experience. If you have difficulty generating sensory-based solutions, consult with your child's OT or refer to the books and other materials describing sensory adaptations in the classroom listed in Appendix B.

MAKING THE GRADE:
THE ELEMENTARY SCHOOL SETTING

Elementary school ups the ante at your child's job. Each year, the demands increase. By third grade, she is expected to have mastered basic reading, writing, and arithmetic skills. Her work assignments have become more complex, and she must keep herself organized, manage her time wisely, and begin to develop independent study habits. Now she is expected to follow the routines of the classroom without a great deal of assistance. She must control her emotions, attention, and behavior in accordance with the demands of her surroundings. It goes without saying that she must be able to read the environment accurately in order to judge the appropriateness of her behavior: *Is this a time when I should talk or keep my comments to myself? Is this a place where I can run around, or do I need to sit still? Is this a person with whom I can be funny, or do I need to be serious?* At this age, her friends expect her to curb her aggressive impulses and manage anger and frustration without lashing out. Increasingly, she will share and compare her grades and accomplishments with other kids, and if she comes up short, she may feel inadequate and struggle to fit in.

Every child needs a teacher who respects individual differences and believes in preventing problems rather than reacting to them. In your child's case, this would be a teacher who pays attention to the sensory characteristics of the classroom and modifies the sensory demands of the work. How do you find this teacher? With enough information, the principal is in the best position to identify the teacher who will be the best match for your child, so we suggest that you write a letter to the principal describing your child's strengths and sensory weaknesses. Do this early in the summer before your child is assigned to a class. Ask for a teacher who is willing to learn about sensory challenges in the classroom, and make it clear that you will work closely with her to address your child's needs.

You may be reluctant to describe your child's problems. If you're like most parents, you may worry that she will be labeled in a negative way. Or you may worry that you will be seen as a demanding or overprotective parent, and you don't want to risk making matters worse for your child by being the squeaky wheel. You may feel uncomfortable or self-conscious because you don't really know what to say. These worries are understandable, but our experience tells us that they are mostly unfounded. An active, supportive partnership with the teacher, one in which you and she work together as allies, is the key to your child's academic success.

If you can introduce your child to her teacher before the first day of class, that is ideal; however, if this is not possible, at least take her on a tour of the building. Familiarity and structure are critical elements of success for your child. Talk about how she is going to get to school, and rehearse that routine beforehand. If you have flexibility in your own schedule, plan to walk her into class to help her get settled for the first few days, until she is familiar with the routine. And don't be late! Your child needs a calm beginning to her day. Decrease the number of after-school activities for at least the first month of the school year. Be mindful of her level of fatigue and frustration, and give her a lot of time at home for rest and relaxation. She's going to need it, and so are you.

Make a point of meeting with the teacher within the first couple of weeks. Try not to be intimidated by the hustle and bustle of a busy elementary school. You are there to help the teacher anticipate and solve problems that might arise for your child in the classroom. She will be grateful for your input if you acknowledge her expertise and show respect for the many demands on her time. Keep in mind that she is balancing the needs and coordinating the instruction of more than twenty individuals in the classroom. If you explain how you use a sensory lens to analyze and respond to your child's behavior at home, she will be able to apply this way of thinking to the sensory-based problems your child may experience at school.

SENSORY SOLUTIONS IN THE CLASSROOM

Let's revisit Jorge, the first-grader we met in Chapter Three who was having so much difficulty getting his work done. A sensory analysis of Jorge's classroom situation would look like this:

Who he is: Jorge has problems with balance and movement that interfere with motor planning. He has trouble sitting in a chair without falling off. He frequently bumps into people and things, and it takes him a very long time to complete tasks requiring sequenced motor activity and to follow multiple directions. His poor sense of balance makes it hard for him to copy things from the board onto his paper. His impaired sense of personal space causes him to intrude upon others, which they sometimes interpret as aggression.

Where he is: The classroom is very crowded; therefore, Jorge's teachers want the students to stay in their seats. They assign a lot of independent seat work that must be copied off the boards at the front and sides of the classroom. The desks are arranged very close together, so the kids have to move between rows carefully, stepping over each other's backpacks, coats, and books when they move around the room.

What is expected: As is true in most first-grade classrooms, a lot of the work emphasizes sequenced motor activities such as cutting, pasting, and assembling objects. The teachers write the morning assignments on the blackboard, then expect the children to progress independently from one task to the other. When the children line up for lunch and the bathroom, they must stand extremely close to one another due to the space constraints in the room. This requires good balance and a well-defined body map.

Sensory Analysis: Motor planning confusion often limited Jorge's ability to complete his assignments within a reasonable period of time. In addition, he lost his place each time he looked back and forth between his desktop and the blackboard. While this task would be a developmental stretch for many first-graders, it was beyond Jorge's capabilities. Finally, his difficulties with balance caused him to bump into children and things as he moved around the room.

Sense-able Solution: Jorge's teachers gave him desktop copies of the morning work that was written on the blackboard. The work was arranged with one assignment on each page. Rather than looking up and down from board to desk, Jorge just had to turn the page when he finished each task in order to find the next assignment. He was allowed extra time to complete his assignments, but his teachers encouraged him to work steadily by tracking his progress on a star chart (for which he was rewarded at home if he completed his work in a given amount of time). Jorge's desk was moved so that he no longer sat in the middle of this crowded classroom. Also, he was allowed to stand at the front of the line when the class left the room so that he was less likely to bump or accidentally push his classmates. At other times, he was asked to hold the door open for the other children, then join the end of the line as the "caboose."

To help your child's teacher see the situation through a sensory lens, ask her what she is already doing with him that works. Then talk about some steps she may be able to take that would make the classroom more comfortable, the work demands more reasonable, and her relationship with your child more secure. You may want to refer to Chapter Six, where we discuss sensory diet activities, or Appendix B, where we list several excellent resources for teachers who want to know more about classroom adaptations that accommodate sensory processing problems.

TEACHING SELF-AWARENESS

Once your child feels secure in the classroom and you know that his teacher is aware of his sensory needs, you can begin to teach him some ways to keep himself on track at school. First, he can learn to keep an eye on his own behavior—that is, he can watch himself and notice when he is "on" (doing what he is supposed to be doing) and when he is "off" (not doing what he is supposed to be doing). This is called self-monitoring, and it is a helpful method of increasing your child's self-awareness and self-control. Have your child's teacher tape an index card to his desktop where he can make a simple mark whenever he notices that he is "on" or "off." His teacher can cue him to mark the card at regular intervals. Together, you and he can set a goal to increase his number of "ons" and decrease his "offs." Reaching this goal may or may not be linked to a reward. Usually elementary-age kids can be trusted to monitor their behavior accurately, but stress the importance of honesty in his self-observations.

Next, remind him about his sensory diet. By paying attention to *what goes in* to his brain (his sensory diet) and *what comes out* (his behavior), he can learn to use sensory input to turn himself "on" or "off" as needed. With a short mental list of sensory strategies to keep himself on track in the classroom, he may be able to prevent some problems from occurring. Or he may be able to pull back from a problem before it gets out of hand.

Two occupational therapists, Mary Sue Williams and Sherry Shellenberger, have developed a method of teaching sensory regulation skills to children. Their program, described in *How Does Your Engine Run?*, shows children how their senses affect their readiness to learn. As we know, our level of arousal can be raised or lowered by input from our seven senses. Usually, this is an unconscious process, a self-correcting cycle that operates outside of our awareness. But Williams and Shellenberger have put together a series of activities that teach children how to tune in to their level of arousal, or what they call "engine speed" (which can be high, low, or just right). Children can learn to deliberately adjust their speeds by seeking out calming or alerting input from their senses.

Karen S. taught this program to first- and second-graders in the elementary school where she works—and it was an eye-opening experience! These children were not identified as having any particular sensory processing problems; they were just typical 6-, 7-, and 8-year-olds. Over an eight-week period, they became good observers of their levels of arousal. They could tell whether their "engines" were running high, low, or just right. However, it was hard for them to consciously control their "engine speeds." With reminders from their teacher and hands-on demonstrations of sensory diet activities (like sitting on a therapy ball, holding a soft stuffed animal, clapping hands, pulling putty, eating crunchy foods, listening to music), they could regulate themselves. But they needed a lot of direction, encouragement, and reminders from the adults in the room.

This type of approach to self-regulation was unfamiliar to the children. Usually, an adult just tells them—politely at first, then forcefully—to sit still or pay attention or get quiet. And they just do it (if they can). They were not accustomed (and neither were the teachers) to thinking about *how to use their bodies* to control their behavior. How wonderful it would be if adults actually taught children how to control themselves by showing them how to use their eyes, ears, nose, mouth, and bodies to organize their behavior. Then they might know *how to be calm* rather than just *how to act calm*. Instead, we offer carrots to entice children to settle down and we threaten sticks to force the point. For most kids, that works, but for the child with poor sensory regulation, it often doesn't. He needs to be taught how to control himself.

Children can learn to tune in to their engine speeds, if adults will remind them of the connection between their senses and their behavior. Older children are better observers of their own behavior than younger children, which is why elementary school is a good time to begin teaching this process. They can readily identify the feelings of *just right* (when they are able to pay attention to their work), *too high* (when they are loud and agitated), and *too low* (when they are spacey and lethargic). They can understand the conceptual relationship between sensory experiences and attention and arousal. They also see the connection between cause and effect (i.e., *If I listen to music, I will calm down; If I eat a pretzel, I will perk up*) more clearly than younger children do.

Depending on the particular situation, many of the activities suggested by Williams and Shellenberger can be calming (settling to an overaroused child) or alerting (energizing to an underaroused child). Below is a list of techniques based upon Williams's and Shellenberger's work that we have found effective:

Use your mouth
- Eat something hard, crunchy, chewy, sour, or sweet (alerting or calming).
- Drink from a straw (calming).
- Take slow, deep breaths (calming).
- Chew on a toothpick, straw, or other hard object (alerting).
- Drink a carbonated drink (alerting).

Move your body
- Sit on a therapy ball (calming or alerting).
- Shake your head from side to side (alerting).
- Roll your neck in a circular motion (calming).
- Swing on a swing set (calming).
- Jump up and down (alerting).
- Dance (alerting).
- Tap your foot (alerting).
- Stretch (alerting).
- Lean back in your chair (alerting).

Reach out and touch
- Hold "hand fidgets" (putty, squishy ball, stuffed animals, paper clip; alerting or calming).
- Rub arms and legs vigorously/gently (alerting or calming).
- Take a shower or bath (calming or alerting).
- Hold a stuffed animal or pillow (calming).

- Twist your hair (calming).
- Wash your face with cold or hot water (alerting).

Look
- Dim or brighten lights (calming or alerting).
- Clear work space of all distractions (calming).
- Watch a lava lamp (calming).
- Watch a fish tank (calming).

Listen
- Talk to yourself (calming or alerting).
- Listen to classical music (calming).
- Wear earplugs to block out environmental noise (calming).
- Use headphones to muffle classroom noise (calming).
- Turn on "white noise" machine (calming).
- Listen to loud music with an uneven beat (alerting).

RECRUITING A SUPPORT TEAM

Despite your best wishes, the teacher's best intentions, and your child's best efforts, you may find that he continues to struggle in the classroom. As we've mentioned, it is not unusual for sensory processing problems to coexist with other conditions that affect learning, such as language difficulties, motor skill problems, attention deficits, or social/emotional problems. Frequently these difficulties are identified and diagnosed during the early elementary school years. If you are concerned *at all* that your child may have academic or emotional difficulties in addition to his sensory processing problems, talk to his teacher.

In every school district, there are procedures that parents can follow to request educational evaluation and support for children who need it. How does this work? Generally, either a parent or a teacher requests a meeting to discuss the child's difficulties. A team of school-based experts is called together to evaluate the problem from several perspectives. Depending on the nature of the difficulties, this team may include any of the following people: the classroom teacher, the school counselor, a learning disabilities specialist, an audiologist, an occupational therapist, an educational psychologist, a behavior specialist, a speech/language therapist, and a school administrator. The purpose of these team meetings is to determine the child's strengths and weaknesses, identify situations that need to be avoided or altered, and decide what kinds of supervision, assistance, or intervention might be helpful.

This sounds a lot like the sensory analysis that we have been discussing—that is, the members of the team will be looking at who your child is, where he is, and what is being expected of him. The main difference, of course, is that they will be looking through an educational lens. As the parent member of the team, one of your responsibilities will be to introduce the sensory lens to the school personnel and to educate them about your child's sensory needs. If an OT is on the team, she can help you do this. Other members of the team are responsible for identifying specific academic or behavioral problems that might be interfering with your child's learning. All pieces of the puzzle must be taken into account.

The team will develop a comprehensive plan to help your child be more successful. Be sure to include some strategies that will improve the sensory climate in the classroom and reduce or alter the sensory demands being placed on your child. Good teaching that respects his individuality and provides the just-right challenge can actually improve his ability to organize and regulate himself in the classroom. Success at the just-right level will reinforce his efforts and encourage him to take future risks. This emphasis on prevention is a much more constructive approach than focusing on punitive or remedial reactions to failure experiences. Here are a few general ideas about how various members of your team can contribute to this preventive problem-solving approach:

- Ask your child's OT to consult with the teacher about how to arrange the classroom and modify task demands to accommodate your child's needs.
- Ask the behavior specialist or educational psychologist to set up a functional behavior program that takes into account your child's sensory integration difficulties.
- Ask the school counselor to develop a classroom intervention to explain sensory processing problems to your child's classmates.

- Ask the classroom teacher to allow your child to monitor his own behavior and make adjustments in his "sensory diet" as needed.
- Give the teacher your support and hands-on assistance whenever possible.

Keep records of your meetings. Ask for copies of evaluations, goals, strategies, and any reports that might document your child's problems and progress. Use these records to evaluate the effectiveness of the educational strategies that are being implemented. If the plan is not working, insist on a different plan. Regular communication between yourself and the members of the team will help your child tremendously because it will cut down on miscommunication between home and school. He needs well-informed, well-coordinated help, not excuse making or finger shaking. Keep everyone on the same team.

Although you are bound to have disagreements and disappointments with people at your child's school, do not talk to your child about them. When you are at odds with school personnel, you unwittingly set up a loyalty conflict for your child. He cannot fully and enthusiastically engage in the learning process, because it may seem like a betrayal of his devotion to you. In addition, he may use your displeasure with the school as justification for not persevering in the face of his own frustrations.

Of course, there are many things that you can do at home that will help your child and his teacher in their work together. Here are a few ideas:

HELPING FROM HOME

Promote a school-ready attitude at home.

Make sure your child gets sufficient rest. The importance of a good night's sleep cannot be overestimated! Establish a bedtime routine, and stick to it.

Help him pack up his schoolwork and supplies for the next day before he goes to bed. This prevents the rapid rise in emotional heat that comes when you're rushing or running late in the morning. Don't do this for him. Instead, encourage him to do it himself.

Help him sort out his backpack, notebooks, and desk on a weekly basis. Establish this habit so that he learns to take responsibility for managing his own clutter. For a disorganized child, less visual clutter means less mental confusion.

Make sure that he has comfortable clothing. Take him with you when you go shopping so that he can "feel" the clothes. Forget about style. Focus on comfort. If there is a school dress code, do what you can to accommodate his sensitivities within the guidelines.

Avoid overscheduling. Less is more for the sensory-sensitive child. Keep his life as simple and as predictable as possible. When a busy day can't be avoided, plan ahead to reduce stress as much as possible. Let him know ahead of time what the day's schedule is going to include.

Communicate a steady attitude at school.

Always show respect and empathy for your child's teacher. Emphasize solutions rather than problems. Tell her what she does that works well for your child. (Of course, this is easy when things are going well, more difficult when there are problems.)

Respecting the teacher doesn't mean you will always agree with her. But agree when you can. Search for common ground.

When problems arise repeatedly and no ready solution presents itself, there is a tendency for parents and teachers to blame one another. Don't go there. Stay calm. Avoid tension between home and school so that your child doesn't feel caught in the middle.

Giving up is not an option. You are teaching your child to persevere in the face of difficulty. Set the same goal for yourself.

A mother recently called Karen S. to talk about her third-grader. His resistance to doing his homework was creating such uproar that his whole family was out of control, yelling at and arguing with one another every afternoon. "This is destroying our family," she said. "And I'm at the end of my rope." Third-grade homework—a few math problems, a spelling list, an occasional book report—was destroying a family. It sounds unlikely, but it can happen so easily, especially when a child is coping with a hidden disability like poor sensory processing. These parents were not bad parents, and this boy was not a bad kid, but they were so focused on a problem that they didn't know how to fix that they had lost their bearings.

Many parents complain about the homework hour. Here are a few suggestions that may help you and your child stay on course with homework assignments:

HANDLING HOMEWORK
Set the scene.
Do homework in the same place every day. Choose a location that is light, quiet, spacious, and relatively free of distractions. Lying on the floor works better than sitting at the table for some kids. Sitting in a beanbag or on a ball works better than sitting in a straight-back chair for others.
Do homework at the same time each day. Most kids need some time after school to relax, unwind, and "get the wiggles out" before starting their homework. A schedule helps avoid procrastination. Fit it in with a regular dinnertime and bedtime.
Have all necessary materials available and organized.
Do something alerting and organizing before getting started (i.e., eating, jumping on a trampoline).
Getting started is the hardest part of doing homework! Help your child by sitting with him and coaching him through the first few problems, then gradually withdraw your attention. This

is much more likely to be successful than insisting that he do it alone from the beginning.

Supervise the work.

Write out a "to do" list and a plan of action that numbers assignments in the order in which they will be done. Your child can cross items off the list as they are completed.

Too many problems on a page can be overwhelming, especially for a child with visual discrimination problems. Give him a piece of paper or cardboard that he can use to cover the problems he is not working on at the moment.

Make a homework-planning calendar for big projects. Break down the big assignment into smaller parts with individual deadlines. (Don't be taken by surprise the night before the science project is due.)

Make sure your child understands each assignment before he gets started. If he cannot explain it to you, he does not understand it himself. Encourage him to call a friend for help if he can't figure it out himself.

Check back at regular intervals to make sure the work is being done correctly. This prevents the frustration of extensive corrections at the end of the assignment.

If your child has difficulty with handwriting and can't type on a computer keyboard yet, let him dictate his longer written assignments to you while you type them into the computer.

Be available for help. Encourage him to ask questions.

If he gets frustrated and begins to resist doing the work, take a short break. Engage him in some calming sensory activities (i.e., deep pressure, swinging).

Check his work for accuracy and completion.

Praise him for all steps in the right direction. Emphasize effort over end product (i.e., "I can see that you're really trying").

If turning in assignments is a problem, set up a chart for your child to monitor how often he turns in his work to his teacher. This can be tied to an end-of-the-week reward.

Another option is to set up a homework check-out and check-in with his teacher, in which she needs to initial his assignment notebook to confirm that he has his assignments written down properly and the necessary materials in his backpack. Then you initial the page at home when he completes the assigned work.

Walk the walk.

Show interest in his assignments. Talk about how they relate to real life.

When he gets frustrated, stay calm. Keep the emotional intensity low.

Ask to see his completed assignments once they have been graded. Display his work.

Show him that you enjoy learning by reading and searching out answers to life problems in books, on the web, at the library, and so on.

Ask his teachers for suggestions about how you might help with homework and for regular feedback regarding how he is progressing.

WALKING THE HALLS:
THE MIDDLE SCHOOL SETTING

Middle school is exactly what its name connotes: it is in the middle between elementary and high school. Your child is also in the middle developmentally, traveling from childhood to adolescence. This is a time of rapid biological, cognitive, and social change that tends to be challenging even for the most well-regulated child. She is expected to function much more independently, and middle school is designed to move her along on this journey toward increased autonomy. At times, both you and she will be reluctant travelers.

Demands increase. You no longer walk your child to her homeroom in the morning or clean out her desk once a week or bake cupcakes for the class party. Often you don't even have the opportunity to meet all of her teachers! A less intimate, more business-like environment replaces the nurturing atmosphere of elementary school, and your child may miss the support she received from her elementary school teachers. She now has a locker and a combination lock, which she must visit several times a day to collect the books, assignments, and supplies that she needs. Every forty-five minutes or so, the bell rings and she has to make her way through the crowded halls to her next class. In class, she must focus her attention for longer periods of time, take notes on what is being discussed, and work at a faster pace. She is also expected to hand in assignments on time and produce work that is neat, free of careless mistakes, and well organized.

Despite the fact that these expectations are extremely challenging for many children, parents and teachers often have the mistaken notion that middle-schoolers should receive less hands-on assistance with day-to-day tasks. "I'm not going to help her organize her backpack," parents say to us. "She should be able to do that on her own by now."

The social demands of middle school are daunting. (Let's face it, would you like to return to that period of your life?) Middle-schoolers are large and boisterous, and, in case you haven't noticed, smelly. Ben describes this element of middle school life especially well. "The makeup and perfume are horrible," he says. "I hate coarse smells that have texture to them—they tingle in your nostrils and just won't go away."

Preadolescents hang out in groups, and they are unforgiving of children who are different in any way. Kids who don't conform are ignored, rejected, or treated cruelly. The school lunchroom is the site of much ribbing, taunting, and joking. Sexual attraction sparks, and the already disjointed conversations among kids become riddled with double meanings.

Getting Support in Middle School

In order to help your child succeed in this new environment, get to know some of the important adults at the school. Decide who is the best "point" person: the one who will arrange and monitor the sensory-based interventions that your child needs. If your child has other learning problems that make her eligible for special education assistance, she will have an individualized education plan (IEP). In that case, her resource teacher is likely to be your point person. If she does not have an IEP (and sensory processing problems, in and of themselves, usually do not necessitate an IEP), ask the school counselor, social worker, or assistant principal to coordinate your child's support at school. Again, take the lead in recruiting a support team that will work to prevent sensory-based problems.

Let's look at the kinds of support your team might consider. The following IEP was developed for David, one of the children we described in Chapter Three. It was especially designed to accommodate his motor planning difficulties, sensory defensiveness, disorganization, and social problems—and, as a result, it includes many modifications that can be made in the middle-school setting. You can request these same kinds of modifications even if your child does not have an IEP.

Issue	Concern	Modification
Knowledge of dyspraxia	School personnel are unfamiliar with the disorder.	All staff in contact with student will study the information packet.
Stairs—safety/use	Amount/steepness of stairs; crowds/proximity, closeness; noise level; pace; loss of balance.	Adult supervision on stairs. Emergency evacuation plan via elevator.
Lockers/lock	Proximity/spacing. Weak fine-motor skills cause difficulty with lock/combination.	Location of locker at end of row. Extra key/combination with resource staff.

Issue	Concern	Modification
	Weak organization/ space within locker.	Develop organization system for locker. Extra time—arrive early.
Lunch	Noise level/pitch/ echo; proximity/ crowds; seating; lunch line; carrying tray.	Quiet lunch with counselor; assigned seating on the perimeter of the lunchroom; stand at beginning/end of lunch line.
Classroom	Noise; proximity/peers, seating; anxiety, stress; inability to keep up with work due to writing difficulties; processing/ sequencing difficulties.	Give early warning for changes in routines. Have a quiet place. Use stress survival bag— earplugs, stress ball, gum, tape recorder with headphones; access to computer, word processor for typing instead of writing
Study/organizational skills	Poor organizational skills; poor note-taking skills related to writing difficulty.	Daily check-in/check-out; assignment notebook with prewritten dates and subjects. Sealable plastic bags to organize materials by subject in locker; checklist for each bag so that student can check himself.

Issue	Concern	Modification
		Textbook stored within each classroom and a set to remain at home. Checklist of tasks to complete within given time frame in class. Allow student to listen vs. taking notes (very strong auditory/visual memory).
Seating	Movement/space; furniture height; sensory issues (lighting glare, "traditional" posture difficult to maintain for long periods); slide-in type of desk may be challenging.	Seat at perimeter, near instructor; face instructor; leave space for minor movement; desk/table with separate chair.
Music	Noise level; sensitivity to high pitches.	Avoid high-pitched sounds.
Testing	Noise level; proximity/crowds; seating; inability to consistently transfer correct response from booklet to answer key bubble.	Untimed tests; separate testing site. Break down test into smaller components. Mark answers in test booklet instead of on computer card, or give oral response to proctor. Use computer for written tasks.

Issue	Concern	Modification
Written language	Fine-motor difficulties; editing/organizational difficulties; note taking.	Use of computer/laptop; verbal/oral response when appropriate; extra time to complete written work. Provide him with copies of other students' notes. Modify "craft" assignments.
Physical education	Weaker gross motor skills; sensory concerns with PE uniform; locker, changing/time frame; proximity, crowds, echo; combination lock.	Consistent consult with PE/modifications to PE classes. Needs direct guidance for independent PT (physical therapy) program. Alternative uniform— cotton, same color/style. Key lock and spare key with PE teacher.
Stress; anxiety; poor peer relations	Overwhelmed at times by sensory input; difficulty reading nonverbal social cues; inappropriate verbalization at times.	Establish quiet place; make counseling services available.

As you can see, these modifications address many of David's sensory processing problems by taking into account *who he is, where he is,* and *what he is being asked to do* throughout the school day. They are very good examples of preventive problem solving. However, David's IEP does not include any mention of his strengths. This is a mistake, because he has considerable talent that could be used to his advantage. For example, his math abilities fall in the gifted range (in fact, he has been placed in an advanced math class); he demonstrates tremendous creativity in the area of science; and he has excellent dramatic abilities and a great sense of humor. He could be assigned the job of tutoring kids who are having trouble in math. He could earn extra time in the science lab by helping the teacher clean and maintain the equipment. He could be given center-stage in drama productions or put in charge of designing a catchy slogan to publicize a school project.

Focusing on what psychologists Robert Brooks and Sam Goldstein, authors of *Raising Resilient Children*, call "islands of competence" would maximize David's opportunities for success and build upon his considerable talents. It would also provide him with a position of leadership and prestige in the middle school social scene, where he often feels awkward and out of place. Too often, school is a place where kids feel like their failures rather than their successes are displayed. David would be likely to enjoy school a great deal more if he knew that his strengths were recognized and highlighted as much as his weaknesses were.

WHEN IT'S STILL NOT WORKING

Sometimes the mismatch between a child and his school is so profound that you may find yourself thinking about changing schools. This is never an easy decision, and it should be considered very carefully. As we have said repeatedly in this book, sensory-based problems always arise from a combination of factors; therefore, the solutions to those problems must take into account the child's individual characteristics *(who he is)*, the environment *(where he is)*, and the demands of the task *(what is being expected of him)*. If he is not experiencing reasonable success at school, even with the kinds of modifications that we have described in this chapter, you may want to move him to another school where he will receive better support services.

Jorge's parents made this difficult decision when it became obvious that he could not adapt to the overcrowded situation at his school. Even though his teachers made a number of helpful modifications, the classes were still too large and the occupational resources were too sparse for Jorge to succeed in that setting. His parents chose to move to another school district where they thought his needs could be better met. This was not a magic solution—it never is! But they now feel that he is in a school where he will get the right combination of accommodation to his sensory needs and recognition of his brighter-than-average capabilities—that is, he is now in a place where his parents hope that he can both survive and thrive.

Another mother of a sensory-sensitive child found herself in a desperate situation, and she chose a more extreme solution. "When my son, Cody, was little," she said, "the common opinion in our family was that he'd grow up to be a delinquent. That sounds harsh, I know, but he absolutely would not do anything anyone told him." She recalled nightly battles over bathing, washing his hair, and doing homework. By the time he was in fifth grade, he was running away from school on a regular basis. "I knew his teachers couldn't keep him in school when he didn't want to be there," she said. "Frankly, neither could I." In an effort to preserve Cody's self-esteem and restore family peace, she decided to home-school him. "It was a tough decision," she admitted, "especially since so many people made negative judgments about me and about him. But, I just couldn't continue to let him fail over and over. It was tearing our family apart."

After several years of home-schooling, Cody decided he wanted to try public high school. With considerable trepidation, his parents agreed to send him. "I was nervous at first, but it's worked out okay," his mother reported. "He gets up and goes without a fuss, and so far he's holding his own academically." She's not sure what made the difference for Cody—neurological maturation, more control over his own life, or a large dose of tender, loving care—but she's confident that she made the right decision for him.

This family's story is unusual, to be sure. His mother took a risk when she withdrew him from school—her difficult-to-manage 11-year-old could have dropped out completely at that point and never graduated. But perhaps because she shielded him from failure, he eventually found a way to embrace success. Every parent/child/school situation is different. Although another parent might not have made the same decision Cody's mom did, her clear-headed commitment to his emotional well-being was the key to figuring out what he needed. Their struggles have not ended, but their connection with each other remains intact.

The relationship between home and school is a complicated one that is often filled with tension and anxiety. You want your child to succeed at school, but you also want her to feel good about herself and the world in which she lives. Life is harder for her than it is for other kids, and she needs to feel that you are on her side, no matter what. You want her to leave school with a diploma *and* the confidence that she can solve the problems life will bring her way.

Your child's sense of self-esteem comes from feeling secure at home and competent away from home. School is her job, and it is essential that she learn to do this job as well as she possibly can. She is learning more there than facts—she is learning how to be successful. Your job is to nurture, support, and challenge her to succeed. To make this happen, you must work together with your child and her teachers to make school a just-right challenge that is within her reach.

‖‖

CHAPTER NINE

Twenty-First-Century Kid Culture: The World of Peers

For my son, two is company, three is a crowd.

— Diane,
mother of 7-year-old John

I am not going to be the only kid in this town who doesn't play baseball.

— Ben,
at age 10

"MY BIGGEST worry is the social thing," Cynthia, the mother of 6-year-old Brad, said to Karen G. "It happens the same way every time. At first kids like him because he's cute and very engaging, and he likes all the things they like. But then something always goes sour and they refuse to play with him again." She went on, "One kid even made a play date to come to our house. Then, as we were walking home from school, the boy suddenly stopped dead in his tracks and said, 'I'm going home.' Brad was devastated. He had no idea what had gone wrong, and, frankly, neither did I. But I see this same scenario in some form or another played out again and again with him." She paused, then added, "I'm worried that he'll never have friends."

This mother's worries are familiar to us. From very early on, sensory processing problems can interfere with a child's friendships. "A friend is someone who you like and who is fun," Evan once said. "He agrees to do what you want to do even though he doesn't want to do it. And the same thing goes for you." Even a quick look through our sensory lens makes it clear that this seemingly simple exchange is likely to be challenging for children with sensory processing problems.

THE SENSORY ANALYSIS

Think about the challenges these children face in the world of peers. Children with sensory defensiveness experience noise as louder, scrapes as more painful, and tumbling and jostling as more threatening than other kids do. Children with discrimination difficulties may not enjoy assembling pirate ships, building models, or making jewelry. Motor planning problems might interfere with a child's ability to swim, ride a bicycle, jump rope, or play hopscotch. For these kids, playing sports can be exhausting rather than exhilarating. Living inside a body that feels out of control may cause the child with sensory processing difficulties to try to control everything around her, including her playmates. This inflexibility and resistance to going with the flow makes it hard to keep friends.

Think about where kids go when they are with their friends. The playground is chaotic. Children run, climb, shriek, chase, and bump into each other; the older they get, the more daring their play. When they are playing inside, they practically sit on top of each other looking at flashing screens, sharing toys, or hiding in a tent or makeshift fort. Younger brothers and sisters intrude, stepping on feet, pulling on clothes, grabbing playthings, and crying loudly. At a friend's house there are unfamiliar smells, foods, and noises. Older kids may be invited to join their friends at an arcade, bowling alley, skating rink, or shopping mall—all places that assault the senses.

When friends get together, what do they do? Play is the ultimate sensory processing exercise. Childhood games require the integration of sensory input (especially balance and movement) with fine- and gross-motor output: swinging, playing catch, riding a scooter, and skate boarding, to name only a few. Play requires organization, body control, and the ability to translate ideas into actions. In games, children must follow the action and respond to the words and movements of other kids. In free play, children have to negotiate, compromise, and take turns. This is how they come to learn about themselves and their relationships with other people and the world around them.

There are three basic types of play, and two of them pose particular challenges for the child with sensory processing problems. Exploratory play entices the child to delve into the sensations of the world. Manipulative play investigates how things work: how they are assembled, how they move, and how they can change. Imaginative play, the easiest type for children with sensory difficulties, encourages the child to take on a new identity or place himself in an unfamiliar circumstance. Let's use our own imaginations for a moment. Pretend that you are a child with tactile defensiveness. Would digging in a sandbox be fun for you? How about playing dress-up or finger painting? If you had tactile discrimination problems, would you enjoy building with small interlocking blocks, drawing, or playing Twister? If you had trouble with your sense of balance, would you want to ride a bike, be on the swim team, or learn to in-line skate? A child's play options can be severely limited by poor sensory processing. Mike from Chapter Six used to hide, rather than play, when he went to friends' houses because the noise and unfamiliarity overwhelmed him. "It certainly didn't make him popular," his mom recalls.

TO MAKE A FRIEND, YOU HAVE TO BE ONE

We are social creatures. We live, work, and play in groups. As adults, we use one another as communal yardsticks, gauging our weight, wisdom, wealth, and other measurements of self-worth against one another. Our relationships often define us: daughter/son, wife/husband, mother/father, teacher, neighbor, friend. We turn to these relationships for guidance, protection, comfort, and companionship. And those of us with solid social connections weather the ups and downs of life better than those who live a more isolated existence.

Babies are fascinated by the human face, and for good reason. They quickly learn that a smile and a gurgle in the direction of a face will usually lead to a show of affection or some pretty good entertainment. Thus begins the social metamorphosis from *me* to *we*. Over time, children must learn to consider the wants and needs of others, to care about their feelings, to give way to their wishes. They must be taught to notice other people, speak politely, wait their turn, and share their cookies. They must surrender the urge to grab, scream, hit, and do only what they want to do. And in time, they come to appreciate the balance between give and take, now and later, yours and mine.

This process of socialization is gradual. With a great deal of coaching, correction, and sometimes coercion, children learn the rules of society, including how to be a friend. This training begins early, but it usually isn't until preschool that children find their first real friend. And what a joy it is to have that one special friend to romp and giggle and explore with!

In the freewheeling fantasy world of the preschooler, everyone is a potential friend and foe. A playmate becomes an imaginary enemy. The line between real and pretend is crossed repeatedly, as is the boundary between laughter and tears and love and hate. As children's interests shift from solitary to cooperative play, they face the challenge of learning to share and take turns, to control aggressive impulses, and to apologize for transgressions. With practice and supervision, they begin to figure out the implicit and explicit rules of friendship, but this takes time.

In today's kid culture, the play of our childhood memories— unstructured antics in the backyards, garages, and tree houses of the neighborhood—has been replaced with a tight schedule of weekly camps, classes, and lessons. A not-unusual assortment of possible preschool activities in Karen S.'s small town includes soccer, roller hockey, t-ball, tae kwon do, swimming, gymnastics, ballet, reading readiness, foreign-language classes, kinder-music, Suzuki violin lessons, ceramics, and art lessons. In these group activities, children must react to the world in a prescribed manner and do what everyone else is doing. They are not playing. They are being instructed. Before they are ready, they must learn how to be a part of a group, take turns, and follow detailed directions. As hard as these expectations may be for many children to meet, they are nearly impossible for the child with sensory processing problems.

"We signed our son up for kiddy gymnastics just before his third birthday," Stephen's mother, Kathy, said. "We thought it would be fun." Instead, she found that it was an almost insurmountable challenge to keep Stephen on task. He wanted to run freely from activity to activity, but he was expected to practice specific drills in a particular sequence. "All I did was chase him around the gym saying, 'Go this way, not that way. Do this, not that. Go over the bar, not under. You can't jump on the trampoline right now.' On and on and on."

"I bargained with Stephen and promised him treats if he would follow directions. I threatened to take those treats away when he refused to stand like a pelican during group time, or when he galloped around the circle while the other children sat quietly waiting for the teacher. I never imagined that he *couldn't* follow the directions. All of the little girls dressed in their leotards and tutus could stand in line while they waited for their turn to do a flip on the bar. Why couldn't Stephen?"

Kathy got a phone call from the instructor complaining about Stephen's disruptive behavior during class. "She suggested that we come to class ten minutes late, after group time was finished," she recalled. "I felt sick. He was there to learn, but he wasn't welcome because he didn't already know how to be there." Because he couldn't sit on his bottom in the middle of a loud, cluttered gymnasium full of things to jump, climb, swing, and bounce on, he was excluded from the group. Why would we expect any 3-year-old to be able to do this? While many can rise to the challenge, others can't. The child with sensory processing problems will find it nearly impossible to meet these kinds of group expectations without a great deal of preparation and support. To make matters worse, parents with the more active, less regulated kids are often left out of group discussions and excluded from plans for informal play groups.

Thomas, the preschooler we met in Chapter Seven, has had sensory processing problems since infancy: sleeping problems, eating problems, and extreme tactile and auditory sensitivity. "He can be so demanding and controlling at times we just want to scream!" his mother told Karen S. "He seems so intense and emotional and overbearing that it drains all our emotional resources."

"What are your greatest concerns about Thomas?" Karen asked her.

"They're mostly social," she replied. "It breaks my heart to think his sensory integration difficulties have caused poor peer relationships. He feels safest when he is alone, playing on the computer, watching TV, or with us."

His teachers say that Thomas usually chooses classroom activities that don't require social interaction. Overwhelmed by the sensory demands of getting along with a roomful of 4-year-olds, he resorts to aggression (fight) and withdrawal (flight) when other kids come near, two primitive responses that are unlikely to win him many friends.

"When he comes home every day, we ask who he played with, and he'll mention one of his teachers," his mother told Karen. "Poor thing! We can tell he wants to have friends, but it is such a challenge." She sighed, "Our deepest desire is that he learn to interact with his peers."

CAN TOMMY COME OUT TO PLAY?

Thomas's parents want him to develop good social relationships. How can they help him? They understand that he is aggressive not because he is a bully but because he is unable to regulate the sensory/emotional arousal that gets turned too high by the chaos of preschool play. This recognition is a good starting place for sense-able problem solving.

Thomas is likely to do better in a one-on-one situation than in a large group. A structured play date with a well-chosen companion might be the perfect opportunity for him to begin to develop some social skills. His parents need to think of a sensory comfortable place where he can practice spending time with a friend. For Thomas, home might not be the best choice, because he hasn't yet learned to share his possessions with other children. "He has to have things just perfect," his mother told Karen. "If a toy gets knocked over or moved, he goes nuts." It wouldn't be wise to invite a friend into his neatly arranged bedroom and expect things to go well. They will also want to avoid situations that might degenerate into the sort of free-for-all, rough-and-tumble play that many boys his age enjoy. Perhaps allowing Thomas and his friend to choose between a picnic at the park, a trip to the library, or a walk to the ice cream store would be a good starting place.

Preschool play dates are a good idea for all children. They are even more useful for the sensory-sensitive child who is having difficulty getting along with peers. Is your child like Thomas? Would a play date at home be a bad idea, or is home the place where he feels safest? Orchestrate the details of his play dates so that you control the sensory elements of the situation. That way, your child's sensitivities are less likely to interfere with his attempts to be friendly. Ask him whom he would like to invite. If he can't state a preference, make your own choice based on your observations of the children he knows. Plan the play date carefully, keeping your child's sensory diet in mind. Take advantage of the amount of control you can exercise over the situation at this age. These guidelines will help you plan for success:

- Keep it short. Children with sensory processing difficulties can keep themselves together for only so long. Know your child's limits. You might even talk with him beforehand about how he can let you know when he is ready for his friend to leave. Try to end the play date *before* there is a problem, not after.
- Find out if there are any toys he is unwilling to share. Put these away in a safe place.
- Talk about good host behavior: sharing, cooperation, and polite language.
- Practice game-playing skills: taking turns, making choices, following rules.
- Plan activities with your child's sensory needs in mind. For example, if you know that swinging is calming for him, include a trip to the playground.
- Stay nearby and step in if the play starts to get out of hand. Your child is not yet prepared to handle conflict well. Don't let him get overloaded.
- If a problem arises, stay calm. Do not blame either child. Try to redirect the play to a sensory-safe alternative. If things really break down, reassure them that there will be other chances to play together.
- If your child is invited to someone else's house, talk beforehand about good guest behavior: following directions, asking before touching, polite language.
- Go along the first few times your child is invited away from home.
- Consider talking to the parents of your child's friends about her sensory difficulties. If they understand that your child has difficulty with loud noises or manipulative play, they can help make

the play date more successful. Similarly, if your child sometimes lashes out when friends get too boisterous, sharing this information might help these other parents address any difficulties that arise between your child and her friend.

THE (DREADED) BIRTHDAY PARTY

We have yet to meet a parent of a child with sensory processing problems who looks forward to birthday parties. Karen G. still remembers getting a call to come retrieve Ben from a party when he was 3 years old. When she walked into the house, she was accosted by the sight and sounds of fifteen very loud 3- and 4-year-olds crowding around a clown who was holding a bunch of balloons above their heads. The children jumped up and down, grabbing for the balloons and screaming loudly as they crashed into each other. All the while, the clown was turning a noisemaker and grinning wildly. It was a nightmarish scene.

Karen was directed to the kitchen, where she found Ben sitting on a teenager's lap with his hands clasped over his ears and tears streaming down his face. The girl said that she wasn't really sure what had happened except that Ben had suddenly started crying hysterically, run into the bathroom, and thrown up. Now he was asking to go home. Karen knew Ben hadn't gotten sick in reaction to the party food, since they hadn't even served the cake and ice cream yet. Concerned that he was ill, she watched him closely for the rest of the day. Much to her surprise, he seemed just fine once they got home. He couldn't tell her what had upset him at the party. It was not until several years later, when she began to understand his sensory processing problems, that Karen realized that Ben had been physiologically overwhelmed that day.

Many similar stories could be told about other birthday celebrations. There are parties at roller-skating rinks, ice-skating domes, inside play scapes, video arcades, movie theaters, gymnasiums, swimming pools, and baseball parks. There are parties with no particular plan, just a roving rumble of kids. There are parties with horses and llamas. There are sleep-overs and camp-outs. There is always the cake, which everyone crowds around. There are the presents, which every child wants to see and hold. There are the little hats with the elastic band under the chin and the piñata with its rain of candy. And, always, the noise, noise, noise. Do the sensory analysis on all of that and watch your sense-o-meter soar.

What is going on here? Today's birthday party is a spectacle, an entertainment extravaganza, a big event. Whatever happened to simple? What about the tried-and-true guideline of inviting only as many children as your child's age? Simple and small almost always work well as a party formula, but big events are a sensory train wreck waiting to happen. We urge you, as a parent of a child with sensory processing problems, to resist the trend toward spectacle when you are planning your own child's birthday celebrations. When he is invited to someone else's extravaganza, think seriously and plan carefully about how to make it a good experience for him. Keep these ideas in mind:

- Make deliberate choices about which parties he attends by comparing his sensory vulnerabilities to the sensory demands of the party. It's okay to decline.
- Stay with him. At most parties, parents are permitted, or even encouraged, to stay.
- Plan ahead of time what you will do if he gets overwhelmed. Tell him the plan.
- Do not make judgments. If he needs some sensory relief, don't force him to participate.
- Be prepared to leave early. It's better to go home when he is still feeling good than to leave after he has fallen apart.
- Be aware of your own feelings. If you are embarrassed or ashamed of your child in front of the other parents, it may cause you to react to him negatively rather than supportively. Remind yourself that he is undoubtedly doing the best he can.

CULTURE SHOCK

Birthday parties are just one example of the many experiences your child will want to have that need to be carefully analyzed and controlled. Indeed, you must become the gatekeeper to the entire twenty-first-century kid culture. You will find yourself saying no more often than other parents, because too many typical children's activities assault and overwhelm the sensory-sensitive child. You and your child are not going to be able to just go along with what everyone else is doing. Together, you're going to have to define your own brand of fun.

Many of today's children consume a sensory diet dominated by video games, commercial TV, computer software, music videos, and movies. With only a few exceptions, these products are programmed and promoted by big-money entrepreneurs and marketing executives, not by people who have kids' best interests at heart. They're certainly not developed by sensory integration experts! These predominantly visual experiences capitalize on fast-paced, fragmented graphic displays, over-whelming images, and compelling auditory scores. Frequently, they draw children away from other activities that are more physical. Sitting in front of their screens, barely aware of the world around them, kids' touch, movement, and balance senses are almost totally ignored, while their brains are overpowered by visual and auditory input.

When they do turn off their video toys and go outside, children are likely to be involved in structured group activities rather than old-fashioned play. It's hard to find many children who have regular opportunities to dig in the dirt, run through the woods, splash around in a stream, build a tree fort, chase fireflies, collect bugs, hang upside down, or play hide-and-seek. This is the kind of play that would allow them to respond to their bodies and seek out the sensorimotor experiences that they crave without fear of failure. But most kids don't spend their time playing like this. For the child with sensory processing problems, this lack of freewheeling exploration of the outside world is a tremendous loss.

BOYS WILL BE BOYS AND GIRLS WILL BE GIRLS

When children do have the opportunity to hang out with the neighborhood kids, those with sensory processing problems often feel left out. As they get older, children's friendships change. Kids join together in groups and no longer think of everyone as a friend. Instead, they tend to identify with children who have similar interests, and they may have trouble joining a group of kids who are not their usual companions. Often the groups break out according to gender. As one second-grader explained to his mother, "Sometimes I have that playground problem. You know, when I can't find anyone to play with." He described the scene: the boys who play football, chase, and superheroes on the one side, and the girls pursuing their own activities on the other. This boy, who was athletically awkward and socially self-conscious, couldn't always find a group to fit into. "I'm not really a group person," he said. "And I'm too sensitive."

Outside play during the elementary school years becomes more organized, governed by rules and playground customs. Four square, jump rope, soccer, and basketball are common activities on the school playground. Children begin to compare their bodily strengths and weaknesses, testing their physical agility and muscular might. Those who run the fastest, jump the farthest, or hang on the monkey bars the longest are the ones who get noticed. Those who hang back or stay on the periphery of the fun, like the child with sensory processing problems, start to feel different and may not know how to join in.

We met John and his mother, Diane, in Chapter Seven. Diane told Karen G. that she wrestled daily with questions about how to help her son spend time with peers. "I don't feel all that comfortable signing him up for organized sports yet," she said. "All the kids are starting to sign up for soccer and basketball." She paused. "But I just think it's going to be too hard for John. I think he needs something more structured." Instead, she decided to enroll him in a kids' bowling league because it required less teamwork and she could stay with him during the games.

Even this carefully chosen activity is difficult for John. "He's ready to leave early, before the other kids," Diane said. "He gets overwhelmed, so he'll start going to the bathroom a lot. He picks the bathroom all the way at the other end of the bowling alley. I finally realized that he does this because he needs to give himself a break." John's method of coping with the sensory overload was causing problems for the other kids, however, because the game got held up while he was in the bathroom. "They get impatient and start yelling, 'Where's John?'" Diane said.

"But this is still a positive step," Karen pointed out. "He is taking care of his needs by leaving the situation rather than lashing out at the other kids or making himself a nuisance in some way."

Diane recognized that this was an achievement worthy of recognition, and she agreed that John should be congratulated for this degree of self-control. At the same time, she and Karen searched for a way to make bowling less stressful for him so that he could be a more active member of the group (which was the point of being there, after all). Perhaps he should only stay for one game or try wearing earplugs to mute the noise or gradually shorten his bathroom break so that he wouldn't keep the other kids waiting.

Finding something your child wants to do with other kids may tax your creativity. So many of the choices require sensorimotor agility: from organized sports to playing catch to riding a scooter to climbing a tree; from dance lessons to climbing on a jungle gym; from making arts and crafts projects to playing tag. Most kids like play that is sensory rich and motor challenging—that's what makes it fun. For the child with sensory processing problems, that's what makes it *not* fun. "Boring," he might say. *Terrifying* is what he means.

IT'S ONLY A GAME

Organized sports have become an important part of family life in America. They involve children in safe, well-supervised activities, promote friendships, and introduce parents to other adults who have children of the same age and similar interests. Belonging to the local soccer team has meaning for you as well as for him. "Soccer mom" is practically a recognized occupation in many communities! In these ways, sports bind a community together. You spend a lot of time with the families of your child's teammates, and you want them to like him, even if he's not headed for the World Cup. You don't want him to get a reputation for behaving badly on the field. Likewise, you don't want him to be left out of the camaraderie of the team. As adults, we are no less vulnerable to the sting of embarrassment than our children. Though we hate to admit it, from time to time we all feel that our children's successes and failures reflect on us as parents—even on the soccer field.

If you're trying to decide whether organized sports would be fun for your child, do a basic sensory analysis. What are your child's sensory vulnerabilities? What are his motor weaknesses? What are the sensory demands of the sport you are considering? Can your child tolerate groups (football) or does he need an individual sport (tennis)? Does he do better with more structure (tae kwon do) or less (soccer)? Is the sport played in a large, echoing gym (basketball) or outside on an open field (baseball) or in a swimming pool? Does it involve physical contact with other players? If you answer these questions carefully, you will be more likely to choose an activity that your child will enjoy.

Some children may resist the very notion of being physically active. As we have said, many children with sensory processing problems do not enjoy movement. Still, your child needs a balanced sensory diet, which includes some form of regular physical activity. Karen S. has faced this dilemma with Evan. Left to his own devices, he would choose reading as a sport. He never goes outside on his own, but he will ride bikes and roll down hills and get dirty if he's with a friend. He tried t-ball for a season because his best friend signed up, but he didn't enjoy it. Now he won't even go along as a spectator at his friend's baseball games. "How come everybody thinks that baseball is a boy thing?" he complained recently. "I'm a boy, and I don't like it!"

Help your child find a physical outlet that will play to his strengths. He needs to feel skillful and respected in the world of his peers. Find a way to let him shine. We have counseled some children into chess clubs instead of soccer teams, because they could flourish on the chessboard in a way they never would on the soccer field. However, if your child *wants* to play a particular sport, he will work at mastering the skills he needs. By the same token, no matter what his motivation for playing a sport, he will eventually leave it if he does not feel successful. After all, how many of us willingly place ourselves in situations where we feel destined to fail? We don't, nor should we. Do not force your child to stick with an athletic activity if he can't master it. Help him find a way to leave the team with dignity and goodwill. It's only a game.

Karen G. watched this drama unfold in Ben's life. Ben has great difficulty tolerating noise and close physical contact. He also has trouble planning and remembering sequences of movements (such as dribbling a basketball or hitting a baseball). To make matters worse, he has an instinctive flinch reaction that causes him to draw back quickly any-time a ball comes at him. Nevertheless, from the time he was a very lit-tle boy, he has loved watching, playing, and talking about sports—an interest that binds him intimately to his father.

At age 7, he asked to sign up for a basketball team. Karen and her husband were concerned that playing basketball would be difficult for him, but they soon realized that motor skills were only part of Ben's problem on the court. The bumping and crowding around the basket, the spatial relationships among players running back and forth, and the noise in the gym confused him and contributed to his mediocre performance on the team. He continued to play, season after season, even though his skills remained weak. Karen and her husband talked to him each year about stopping, but he was determined to keep play-ing. He worked on his strengths and developed a good shot from the three-point line, far away from the hustle-bustle under the basket. He also tried to get rid of his flinch reflex by asking his dad to throw balls at him in the backyard. Nevertheless, all through fourth, fifth, and sixth grades he felt disrespected and underappreciated by his team mem-bers. Karen wondered whether he should be allowed to play since he seemed so demoralized at times. In the end, though, she let him make the decision each year. Finally, at age 15, Ben has come into his own on the basketball court. At five feet ten inches tall, and having over-come his flinch reflex, he has become a valuable forward on the Park District basketball team.

How did he do it? "I just started dealing with the bumping and push-ing under the basket," Ben told Karen. "I said to myself, 'I love this game, and the only way for me to play is to manage being in the mid-dle of all these people.' I stuck with it because I knew I had to. Dad's a huge fan. Friends were criticizing me, saying I couldn't play. I needed to do it. If I didn't, I was a failure to myself." He went on to say that his determination to overcome his weakness on the court had made it pos-sible for him to learn not to take the criticism personally. "You have to use it to your advantage," he said.

Ben's experience with baseball was different. He signed up for a team in fourth grade, right after his family moved to a community where baseball was big. He had never played the game before, but he was not about to be left out. Try as he might, he had trouble connecting with the ball. Every time he got up to bat, he looked like he was standing at the plate for the first time. Nothing went smoothly for him. In contrast to his teammates, who all came to the game with good motor memories and automatic motor sequencing, Ben had to think consciously about each step in the motor sequence: where to plant his feet, how to hold the bat, when to shift his weight, where to place his swing. Invariably, he swung too late. Karen suggested that he give up baseball. "Mom," he exclaimed, "I'm not going to be the only kid in this town who doesn't play baseball!" Despite his steely determination to succeed and several years of perseverance, he just could not consistently connect with that ball. In the spring of his thirteenth year he surprised his parents when he announced, "I don't think I'm going to play baseball this year." Older and more sure of himself, he seemed content with this decision—primarily, Karen believes, because he made it himself.

Organized sports present children with hurdles other than the physical ones. There are also mental and social challenges associated with participating in a competitive group activity. For the child with sensory processing problems, learning to be a good sport and finding a way to be an asset to his team are goals that might be beyond his reach. He may feel like a loser in many daily situations; therefore, tolerating defeat on the playing field may be more than he can handle. Also, he struggles to fit in at school, in the neighborhood, in his family—he doesn't want to feel like the weak link on the baseball team, too. Cutting up in the dugout could be his way of making a place for himself on the team, but it won't be well received by the coach. For these reasons, an individual sport may be a better choice for some kids.

FINDING A BUDDY

Not all children need a lot of friends, but everyone needs a buddy or two. Research indicates that the best protection against teasing in elementary school is not ignoring it or responding to it but finding a friend. Children who are paired up with at least one friend are less likely to be teased, and they seem to handle it better when they are. If your child has difficulty making friends, she needs your help both at school and at home. Cliques form as early as third or fourth grade—and the membership rules for being "in" or "out" are unspoken and elusive. The normal round of acceptance/rejection that most children experience from time to time is especially stressful for the child who already feels different or out of sorts.

At school, the counselor or social worker may be able to help by including your child in a friendship group. At the school where Karen S. works, a teacher arranged to eat lunch with a popular student and a girl who frequently got in trouble in class. That afternoon, the popular student said to the teacher, "I never knew Mandy was so interesting." Your child's teacher may be able to "buddy up" your child with a socially desirable peer and give her an opportunity to show off her strengths. For example, she may assign her to be a peer tutor or make her an art consultant on another student's book report or give her a shared responsibility with a socially savvy child.

At home, you can still influence your child's social life, particularly in the elementary school years. You may find that she and her friends begin to develop different interests and skills that make it hard for them to spend time together. This happened to Evan and Carl, a friend he had known since he was 2. Carl was an astonishingly gifted athlete from early on. As he and Evan got older, the difference in their physical abilities became an impediment to their friendship. As 5-year-olds, they were on the same soccer team, but they could have been on different planets when they were on the field. At age 6, Carl was winning kids' bike races and playing roller hockey. Evan still had training wheels on his bike.

Karen realized she needed to intervene one day when Carl was visiting and he and Evan couldn't find anything to do. Carl kept asking to go outside. Evan kept insisting that they draw. After Carl went home, Karen talked to Evan about their argument.

"But I don't like to go outside!" Evan complained. "It's not fun for me."

"I know that," Karen said. "But that's how Carl feels about drawing. He's not good at it, so it's not fun for him."

"He doesn't like to draw?" Evan asked, incredulous. In that egocentric way that children have, he had assumed that his friend enjoyed what he enjoyed.

From then on, Karen and Carl's mom worked to find common ground for the boys. Evan invited Carl on an elaborate dinosaur hunt that involved being outside but didn't require physical agility. Carl invited Evan to go with him to a water park, a place where Evan could have fun without being a great swimmer. For a few years, they spent less time together, but now, at age 9, they have reconnected. They both like rock climbing, computers, and being silly. Here are some things you can do to help your child find a buddy at home:

- Continue to encourage play dates.
- Volunteer in your child's class so that you get to know the kids and their parents. The more involved you are in your child's world, the easier it will be to figure out who might be a good buddy for her.
- Same-age cousins or your friends' same-age children can become important sources of social support. Develop these relationships.
- Plan high-interest activities (keeping the sensory lens in mind) and invite a classmate along. High-interest activities increase the likelihood that your child will be seen as a fun companion.
- Get your child involved in activities that capitalize on her strengths. She is more likely to make friends under these circumstances.

TEACHING YOUR CHILD HOW TO BE A FRIEND

Children who easily make and keep friends are usually good at interpreting social cues, regulating their own emotions, controlling their behavior, and responding empathically to others. James, a 7-year-old boy with poor sensory processing, has trouble in all of these areas. "I noticed that things weren't quite right with James when he was in his first preschool," his mother said. "He seemed to withdraw or become aggressive with other kids out of fear. He was especially fearful of kids who couldn't talk yet, because they were so unpredictable." He seemed to want to have friends, but he didn't know how to connect. "He still struggles a lot," she said. "He can't figure out how to get involved in other kids' play."

James has trouble reading other kids and understanding their intentions, particularly when they don't explain themselves with words. This makes him anxious, which causes him to withdraw or become aggressive—two defensive behavioral responses. He also lacks the social skills to know *how* to get involved in other kids' play. This combination of social deficits makes it hard for him to feel comfortable around other children.

Many of the children we see with sensory integration difficulties also lack social skills. They may have a nonverbal learning disability—an inability to read and respond to the nonverbal cues that are a critical element of social interaction. Others may behave impulsively, or they may be irritable or explosive when their sensory sensitivities have been aroused. Their difficulties regulating their behavior and emotions make it unpleasant for others to be around them at times. Ben once said, "People make judgments about me—they say, 'Why are you so overreactive?' That bothers me."

Children can be taught the basic skills of social interaction; however, research on the effectiveness of social skills training indicates that lessons learned in a therapist's office rarely generalize to the real world. A child may be able to provide appropriate social responses with the adult who is coaching him but then be unable to respond appropriately in the classroom or on the playground. In the emotional heat of the moment, it's hard for him to do what he knows. He needs support and reminders from nearby adults.

The child with sensory processing problems must learn to analyze social situations using the sensory lens. Only he can determine what he can handle and what he can't, when he should stay and when he should leave, and how he can feel more comfortable in a particular situation. As a parent, you can help him plan ahead and rehearse potential scenarios. You can highlight the friendship skills that he already has. You can step in and coach him when you see him having a problem with a friend, but eventually (usually around fourth or fifth grade) he will have to learn to make it on his own.

Keep in mind that your child learns about social interaction at home first, and those lessons begin before you realize it. He listens and watches as you talk about your co-workers, make decisions with your spouse, entertain your friends, handle your road rage, show kindness to strangers, and certainly he is fully tuned in to how you deal with him. Loving, respectful experiences with you teach him how the social world works and show him how to get along with others. Here are some things you can say and do at home that will help your child have the skills he needs to be a good friend away from home:

- Provide a wide range of friendship possibilities. Seek out opportunities for you and your child to meet new people.
- Bring your child along when you spend time with your friends.
- Be a good model by making your child's friends feel welcome in your home.
- Get to know the parents of his friends. Ask for their assistance in planning and monitoring the time your kids spend together. Explain your rules and agree on some guidelines for appropriate activities.
- Teach your child to stop, look, and listen when he is uncertain about how to behave in a social situation.
- Teach him the body cues that indicate when he is getting upset with a friend. Encourage him to monitor his own level of arousal. Is his "engine" too high? Is he "on" or "off"? Make adjustments if necessary by engaging in a calming activity.
- Help him figure out what the problem is. Write it down for emphasis.
- Generate a list of possible solutions, including wild and far-fetched ideas. Predict the consequences of each solution. Evaluate each idea to determine if it is a good one.
- Show him how to tune in to his friend's feelings. Choose the solution that will maximize good feelings for everyone involved.
- After he tries a solution, help him evaluate how well it worked. Focus on whether his solution made the problem "bigger" or "smaller."

THE MIDDLE SCHOOL SCENE

The early adolescent social scene is difficult for all children. Many kids lose touch with their childhood buddies when they move up to middle school. At this competitive, insecure stage, kids typically identify themselves and each other by who they hang out with. They say, "He's a jock . . . geek . . . band member . . . skate boarder . . ." Who a child hangs out with is often determined by his looks, athletic ability, academic performance, social class, race, and personal interests. A child who can't find a place in these rigid social strata—one who is more "out" than "in"—may be tested, excluded, or bullied. He may become isolated and lonely, just at the time when he most needs a friend to help him figure out who he is and whether he's okay.

All children feel vulnerable to social rejection during this phase, but the child with sensory processing problems may feel it even more keenly. He may not look like the other kids—he may be unkempt due to sensitivity to hygiene routines; he may not conform to the current fashion code due to discomfort with clothes; and he may wear the same uncool clothes over and over again. He may be athletically clumsy, academically weak, or socially awkward. He may not be able to figure out the nuances of budding sexual attraction, and he may not be comfortable with the kinds of physical touching (holding hands, kissing, whispering, leaning and/or lying on one another) that comes with that territory. It may be hard to find others who share his interests, and he may have a hard time enjoying the sights, sounds, and smells of typical hangouts like the mall, a basketball gym, movie theater, skating rink, or teen center. Parties—large crowds of kids chattering and moving around, loud music booming, strobe lights flashing, the mingling smells of incense, perfume, food—may be unpleasant experiences for him, even though he wants desperately to be a part of the scene.

Karen G. recently learned firsthand about the sensory challenges of eighth-grade life as a volunteer at Ben's middle school "lock-in" (an event in which children are "locked into" the school for a giant sleep-over). She and her husband wondered whether signing the permission form for this all-nighter was wise. After all, not so many years ago, a sleep-over with too many kids would send Ben reeling. When they asked him about the lock-in, they discovered that Ben had his own reservations about subjecting himself to twelve moonlight hours of martial arts, dancing, arts and crafts, jousting, and general adolescent mayhem. The group social demands would be tough, and the potential for sensory overload would be high. But because he didn't want to miss what his classmates considered to be the highlight of the eighth-grade year, he decided he would rather be locked in than left out. So they gave their permission, and Karen signed up as a volunteer for the midnight to 2 A.M. shift.

When she arrived that night, the kids seemed to be enjoying themselves. They were scattered throughout the building, divided into various activities that were finishing up before the dance that would start at midnight. Contrary to Karen's expectations, the scene was orderly and controlled. The sounds of voices and laughter echoed through the hallways but no louder than on a typical school day—in fact, maybe quieter since the fifth-, sixth-, and seventh-graders were home sleeping. Then the dance began. In the darkened gym, strobe lights bounced off the walls and techno music echoed loudly. The bass was turned so high that the room literally vibrated, and it was impossible to hear anyone speak. Karen looked for Ben, her old anxieties rising to the surface. "How is he managing this?" she wondered. She couldn't imagine how he could tolerate the noise when she could barely stand there without clasping her hands over her ears.

Kids were clustered in tight groups all around the gym. Dancers lunged this way and that, elbows and knees flying, everyone in everyone else's space. Periodically, someone would skid across the slick floor, tripping or bumping into other dancers. Karen worried about Ben's discomfort with close physical proximity, but as the evening progressed she was struck by the way in which he moved in and out of the dance. At times, he was in the middle of the action; at others, he was on the edge of the crowd. A few times, he left the room entirely. In this way—perhaps consciously, perhaps not—he regulated his exposure to the sensory commotion.

When the dance ended and the music stopped, the silence was so intense that Karen felt like she could reach out and touch it. She was struck again by how assaultive the whole experience must have been for Ben. Yet, when she asked him to rate the lock-in on a scale of one to ten (with one being awful and ten being great), he gave it a seven-and-a-half. His experience had been no better or worse than that of most of the other kids there. With relief, Karen realized that Ben had reached a degree of neurological, emotional, and behavioral maturity that had allowed him to enjoy participating in an important social event that would have sent him over the edge several years earlier.

The desire to belong to a group and to go along with what everyone else is doing is strongest during the adolescent years. It is possible that Ben decided to go to the lock-in because he knew that he had arrived at a point in his life where he could handle the sensory aspects of the situation; however, it is just as likely that he wanted to be with his friends whether he could handle it or not. There is always a sensory price to pay for conformity to twenty-first-century kid culture. Remind your adolescent to think about the sensory characteristics of his environment and to be aware of his reactions to them. He must learn to avoid situations that are likely to overwhelm him and agree with you on a backup plan for how to safely leave a scene if it is too hard to handle. Help him think of ways to spend time with his friends that won't overload his ability to regulate himself. More than other kids, he must learn to take charge of his own experience rather than follow the crowd.

STEP BACK AS THEY STEP OUT

Your child's adolescence is a time when you must step back and begin to let her find her own way. As all parents of teenagers learn, there is a fine art to knowing when to offer advice, when to put your foot down, and when to let your child make her own decisions. It is especially hard to figure out when and how to let go of a sensory-sensitive child who has needed extra support and supervision through a roller-coaster childhood. You hope that by the time your child reaches adolescence she will be strong enough to stand on her own two feet. And yet you can't help but wonder if you have done enough to help her understand her sensory needs, regulate her emotions, and control her behavior.

Contrary to popular myth—and to what they may tell you in the heat of the moment—kids between the ages of 12 and 16 still consider their parents to be the most important people in their lives. More than their friends, most adolescents think of their parents as the first people they would go to if they were in trouble. Despite his bravado, your teenager continues to need your support and guidance. He is testing his own strengths and weaknesses, growing into his adult body, defining his identity, and exploring his place in the world, but he can still learn a great deal about himself and his possibilities from you. Take every opportunity to continue the dialogue with your child about who he is, where he is, and how he can succeed!

||||||||||||||||||||||||||||||||||||||||||||||||||||||||||||||||||||||||||||

CHAPTER TEN

Making Sense of Sensory Integration:
What We Know and What We Don't

I feel that we would all be lost in knowing how to cope if we
didn't understand what sensory integration means.

—SARA,
mother of an 8-year-old boy

Will he always be this way?

—NANCY,
mother of a 5-year-old boy

YOU PICKED up this book because you are looking for answers. You want to know how to make your child's life more pleasant, how to reduce stress in your family, how to ease the daily struggles. You want to know why you are having so much trouble moving through the day, and, more importantly, you want to know what to do about it. The sensory-based approach that we have described has probably addressed many of your concerns, but it may have raised some questions, too. How do you decide where to go to address your child's complicated needs? Who should you listen to and what should you believe? While you are willing to do almost anything for your child, you don't want to spend hundreds of dollars and endless hours on a wild goose chase. You don't want to lose precious time running in the wrong direction.

Now that you have read this book, you probably have a good sense of whether your child has sensory processing problems. You know how to use a sensory lens to analyze situations in which she is having trouble, and you have some good ideas about how to prevent sensory break-down. Still, you may wonder if you should be doing more. All sorts of treatment suggestions are being discussed in the media and on the Internet. People talk about auditory training, "brushing," and vision therapies. What are these things? Would they be helpful? What about medication or counseling? You probably have reservations about all of these treatments, especially since none of the experts seem to be able to say, *Do this. We know it works!*

We understand your confusion about how to choose the best treatment for your child, and we share many of your reservations. In this chapter, we use a scientific lens to address some of the questions parents frequently ask us about dysfunctional sensory integration. These are the best answers we can offer given the current state of research, but there is no magic here. There is no single thing that you can do to "fix" your child's problems. We hope that many of the ideas we have offered in this book will be helpful. But remember: there is no substitute for your love, understanding, patience, and creativity—and the willingness to believe that your child is doing the best that she can.

If dysfunctional sensory integration is not a diagnosis, what is it?

Current understandings of sensory processing are inexact, so you may find that different professionals talk about dysfunctional sensory integration in different ways. This is because specific, technical definitions of sensory integration vary from one researcher to another. Parents often complain that these differing definitions are confusing. They sometimes seem to encompass everything! Children with sensory processing difficulties display a broad range of behaviors that don't fall neatly into a single category. Whether these behaviors are parts of the same problem or comprise different problems in different children is still unclear. This confusion has led to the criticism that dysfunctional sensory integration is just a wastebasket category for what is otherwise inexplicable behavior.

To establish dysfunctional sensory integration as a scientifically sound diagnosis, researchers would have to agree on their definitions and terms. They would then have to demonstrate that children with this problem display a cluster of observable behaviors that can be consistently and reliably identified. Finally, this cluster of bahaviors would have to be demonstrably different from the clusters of behaviors that define other disorders. Until this sort of scientific progress is made, it will remain difficult to talk about sensory processing problems without confusion.

Nevertheless, we find the theory of sensory processing to be an extremely useful explanatory concept. Looking through the sensory lens allows us to understand many puzzling problems that some children experience. In this book, we have tried to impart an understanding of what it feels like to be a child with sensory processing problems. That knowledge allows you to respond empathically and effectively to the behaviors that compromise and complicate your child's daily functioning.

How many children have these problems?

Studies of sensory integration have not surveyed enough children to determine the percentage of the population that struggles with these difficulties. In fact, inconsistencies in definition and disputes regarding subtypes of the problem have made it difficult to design such studies. Some occupational therapists estimate that 10 to 20 percent of all children experience sensory processing problems; however, the number for whom these problems interfere with daily living is undoubtedly smaller. In a large sample of 3- to 6-year-old Chinese children; the prevalence of mild sensory processing difficulties was 28 percent, while the prevalence of severe problems was 9 percent.

Increasingly, researchers are looking at the association between sensory processing difficulties and childhood psychiatric diagnoses such as developmental disabilities, attention deficit hyperactivity disorder, oppositional defiant disorder, anxiety disorders, and autistic spectrum disorders. In order to diagnose and treat these children more effectively, we need to better understand the relationship between these disorders and sensory processing problems.

What causes sensory processing problems? Are they genetic?

Nobody knows the answer to this question, and any theorizing about possible causes is pure conjecture. Although it is normal to be curious about how your child came to be who she is, it really is not helpful to focus your thoughts on the "what ifs." It is much more productive to think about the "what nows" and help her know and accept her particular strengths and weaknesses.

What is the relationship between sensory processing problems and attention deficit hyperactivity disorder (ADHD)?

OT researchers are just beginning to address this question. Studies show that some children diagnosed with attention deficit hyperactivity disorder demonstrate a variety of sensory processing problems, including weaknesses in vestibular processing and motor planning, sensory defensiveness, and modulation difficulties. A significant subset of ADHD children have sensory modulation deficits that distinguish them from a normally developing group of children. In some ADHD children, a relationship has been found between aggressive behavior, sensation seeking, and tactile sensitivity, suggesting that subgroups of ADHD symptoms may be related to certain types of sensory modulation difficulties. Also, ADHD children who complain consistently about not feeling well have been shown to be sensitive to movement.

While ADHD and dysfunctional sensory integration are not the same, some interesting connections are emerging. Further research is needed on the relationship between sensory modulation difficulties and ADHD symptoms. It is possible that children who have a combination of ADHD and sensory modulation deficits would benefit from occupational therapy in addition to medication and behavioral treatment.

What is the relationship between sensory processing difficulties and learning disabilities?

Defining the exact relationship between sensory processing and academic achievement would require careful study of the correlations between sensory processing problems and the various types of learning disabilities, and these studies have not yet been done. However, it is reasonable to suggest that the percentage of children with both sensory processing problems and learning difficulties is extremely high, if you define learning in the broadest sense. Since poor sensory regulation affects a child's perceptions of the world and her organization of those perceptions into appropriate motor responses, her learning will undoubtedly be affected. If she has visual discrimination problems that make it difficult for her to tell one shape from another, she is likely to have trouble recognizing the letters of the alphabet and learning how to read and write. Auditory discrimination problems will make it difficult for her to differentiate the sounds of the letters and to grasp phonetic concepts.

Other types of sensory processing problems are less likely to interfere directly with academic learning. However, they may have a significant impact on a student's behavior, which could directly interfere with her academic performance. For example, tactile defensiveness may cause avoidance of hands-on classroom activities or explosive behavior or distractibility. Both a sensory and an educational lens is necessary to understand how sensory processing problems affect a child's learning.

What is the relationship between sensory processing difficulties and pervasive developmental disorders such as autism and Asperger's syndrome?

Children with a diagnosis of autism or Asperger's syndrome typically experience significant sensory processing problems. In fact, dysfunctional sensory processing is one of the defining characteristics of these disorders. Although all children with pervasive developmental disorders have sensory processing difficulties, the reverse is not true. All children with sensory processing difficulties *do not* have a pervasive developmental disorder. In fact, most of the children you have met in this book do not have a pervasive developmental disorder.

I want help for my child, but I don't know if we need to see a professional. How do I know if her sensory processing problems are extreme enough to require professional treatment?

Whether your child's sensory processing difficulties require professional intervention depends on the extent to which they interfere with her daily functioning. Think about the frequency, duration, and intensity of your child's problems. Do they interfere with her success at home, school, or elsewhere in the community? Do they interfere with healthy development? Are they causing secondary problems, such as anxiety about school performance or social difficulty with friends? If the answer to any of these questions is yes, then it is time to seek professional help.

A professional who understands the theory of sensory integration can determine how far outside the normal range your child's sensory functioning falls. This information may help you make a decision about treatment. Research indicates that children with sensory processing difficulties severe enough to interfere with daily functioning can be reliably distinguished from children without these difficulties based on their parents' responses to questions on a sensory profile. Furthermore, children with sensory processing problems have different physiological responses to sensory stimulation in laboratory settings. These physiological findings suggest underlying biological differences. In the future, we may have a better understanding of the relationship between these physiological differences and the emotional and behavioral differences that we can observe. Currently, we can only speculate about these connections.

Will my child outgrow her sensory processing problems?

We would need longitudinal data on the outcome of sensory processing problems in order to predict the futures of these children. Longitudinal studies follow groups of individuals with particular characteristics over time to determine how they develop and change. No such studies have been done on children with sensory processing problems. However, brain research reveals that neurological development continues well into adulthood. Because we know that experience affects brain development, it is reasonable to assume that "just-right" experiences like the ones described in this book can improve your child's neurological functioning over time. Whether these changes will be substantial enough to completely free her of sensory dysfunction is unclear.

Children whose difficulties with sensory processing go unrecognized are less likely to "outgrow" them. Their experiences are frequently characterized by failure and misunderstanding and can lead to poor self-esteem. If these children don't learn strategies for coping with their social, emotional, and behavioral difficulties, their problems are likely to become more complicated over time. These complications further reduce the likelihood that the situation will improve "naturally."

Our experiences with our own sons and our clients have led us to believe that a combination of factors is necessary for success. Neurological growth and development, supportive, structured home and school environments, and multiple opportunities to master a range of challenging sensorimotor experiences all contribute to improved functioning. A team of professionals who understand your child's needs can design growth-enhancing experiences that will teach her to understand and help herself.

Why has my child's psychologist/psychiatrist never mentioned sensory integration as an explanation for my child's problems?

Most psychologists/psychiatrists do not look at children's behavior through a sensory lens. Many of them do not know about sensory processing difficulties, and others may consider sensory symptoms to be secondary to a psychiatric disorder. Psychologists and psychiatrists look at children through the professional lens with which they are most familiar. Since many children with sensory processing problems also exhibit behaviors consistent with psychiatric diagnoses (although the "fit" may not be perfect), they are likely to be viewed through a DSM-IV lens rather than a sensory one.

We believe that understanding your child's strengths and weaknesses and knowing how to deal with them is more important than coming up with the "right" diagnosis; therefore, it is most helpful to look at your child through a kaleidoscope of lenses. The best, most effective treatment is likely to be multidisciplinary, drawing on the expertise of a psychologist or psychiatrist, an occupational therapist, and a learning specialist. Finding the right professional to spearhead this effort can be difficult, since many health care providers are poorly informed about dysfunctional sensory integration.

Seek out professionals who understand and treat children with sensory processing problems. If you are already working with a therapist who does not know about sensory processing problems, explain what you have learned and ask if he is willing to do some reading or consult with a colleague who understands these problems. If you can find the help you need in a single setting, such as a children's hospital or a child specialty clinic, it will be easier for your team of professionals to coordinate their treatment efforts. However, it is not critical that they be in the same place as long as they are willing to consult with one another to create a coordinated treatment plan.

Does sensory integration therapy really work?

As we explained in Chapter Six, sensory integration therapy covers a broad range of activities used by occupational therapists to treat children who have sensory processing problems. The OT chooses a program of activities based on a careful analysis of a child's specific problems and a set of goals designed to improve her everyday functioning. For example, a child who throws tantrums over tooth brushing might be gradually introduced to sensory experiences designed to increase her tolerance for the oral and vestibular sensations associated with tooth brushing. Or a child who has motor planning problems is challenged to make her way through an obstacle course that requires the integration of vestibular, proprioceptive, and tactile input.

Ayres believed that sensory integration treatment would improve a child's academic functioning; thus, since the 1980s, researchers have tried to document a positive relationship between sensory integration treatment and the remediation of learning disabilities. They have been unable to do so. Instead, educators have concluded that the direct teaching of particular skills (such as reading and writing) is much more effective than sensory integration treatment in improving the school performance of learning-disabled children. These research findings have led to the premature rejection of sensory integration treatment outside of the field of occupational therapy.

Indeed, much of the research on dysfunctional sensory integration has been poorly constructed and is seriously flawed. However, OTs are trained as clinicians rather than researchers, and they have been ill equipped as a profession to respond to the criticisms of these studies. As a result, general skepticism remains in the fields of pediatrics, psychology, psychiatry, and education about the usefulness of sensory integration theory and treatment. Therefore, parents of children with sensory processing difficulties often run into resistance from mental health and educational professionals when they try to discuss sensory processing problems. If you encounter this skepticism, you will need to educate the professionals you are working with about the usefulness of the sensory lens for understanding your child's behavior. We have provided many resources throughout this book and in the appendixes to help you.

While the science and art of sensory integration treatment continues to evolve, it remains a popular choice for parents of children with sensory processing difficulties. Many of these parents have not found parent–child therapy with a therapist unfamiliar with sensory problems to be helpful enough. When behavior therapy fails, medication is frequently recommended to control symptoms such as hyperactivity and emotional reactivity. Many parents are reluctant to medicate a child or find that the medications are less helpful than they had hoped.

In a professional article recently published by OTs entitled, "Parental Hopes for Therapy Outcomes: Children with Sensory Modulation Disorders," parents described their hopes for how therapy would benefit their child. Their therapeutic goals for their child included (1) improved social participation and acceptance, (2) better self-regulation skills, and (3) increased feelings of self-worth and competence. These same parents hoped that therapy would provide them with (1) emotional support and (2) strategies to use at home with their child. Almost without exception, the parents we have worked with over the years have reported that occupational therapy has helped them tremendously by changing their understanding of their child. This new understanding leads them to approach the tasks of daily living in a manner that makes family interactions less combative and more cooperative.

According to Lucy Miller, a renowned OT researcher, the question *Does sensory integration work?* is naive. The more appropriate question is, *What effects are evident for a specific group of individuals receiving a specifically defined intervention compared to another intervention?* The current research on sensory integration treatment is not nearly well designed enough to answer this question. However, increased collaboration between occupational therapists, educators, and mental health professionals should lead to a clearer understanding of sensory processing, its many manifestations, and what can be done to help children with sensory processing problems.

What is "brushing?" Does it work?
"Brushing" is a shorthand way of describing a therapeutic technique developed by two OTs, Julia and Patricia Wilbarger, to help adults and children who have sensory sensitivities. The Wilbarger protocol is based on the assumption that certain types of sensory experiences—specifically deep pressure, proprioception (joint compression), and vestibular input—will reduce sensory defensiveness. Brushing is only one component of the program, and it is not meant to be delivered in isolation. The protocol consists of three parts. First, the child and parent are taught to recognize sensory defensiveness and understand its impact on daily life. Second, a sensory diet is developed for the child that integrates sensory-rich activities into her routines at home and at school. Third, the parent is taught to follow a program involving the application of a brushing technique that consists of using a stiff surgical brush applied to the child's skin in a particular manner.

Although scientific support for the relationship between certain types of sensation and adaptation to and modulation of environmental input is growing, the Wilbarger protocol itself has not been studied in a systematic scientific manner. As a result, there is no evidence supporting either the effectiveness or lack of effectiveness of this approach.

Will vision training help my child?
Vision training consists of a series of exercises that are designed to improve the integration of the visual and vestibular systems so that children can better track things visually. Visual tracking is critical to many daily tasks, including following the words on a page while reading, finding our way around obstacles, and playing sports. Although sensory integration therapy also addresses visual/vestibular deficits, proponents of visual tracking therapy, which is provided by developmental optometrists, believe that a more concentrated approach to visual tracking deficits is sometimes necessary. We are not aware of any research documenting the positive effects of vision training.

Will auditory integrative training (AIT) help my child?
Auditory integration training was originally based on the observation that the auditory and vestibular systems work together. The French physician Tomatis who developed this technique assumed that particu-

lar patterns of high-frequency sounds could have a beneficial effect on individuals with sensory processing difficulties. Although this program is available in the United States in its pure form, an alternative therapeutic listening program developed by Sheila Frick is more commonly used. This program combines auditory stimulation with standard sensory integration treatment. According to Frick, the use of appropriately modified music in conjunction with sensory integration techniques enhances the benefits of both. It may be that these repeated exposures to the music work as a gradual desensitization to auditory input. Although several case studies have suggested that AIT may be useful, there are no group outcome studies that demonstrate its effectiveness.

How can I best help my child?

Raising children, no matter who they are, is a journey with many bumps in the road and occasional false turns along the way. The good news is that children are amazingly resilient and they naturally gravitate toward healthy growth and better functioning. We know that neurological development continues beyond childhood and that experience plays a significant role both in shaping your child's mind and determining who she becomes. As adults, we choose areas of life that maximize our strengths and minimize our weaknesses. We find friends, lovers, and colleagues who appreciate us for what we have to offer rather than deride us for our limitations. You can choose experiences and situations for your child that will encourage growth. Help her combat her limitations and celebrate her strengths. It is these strengths that will carry her into a joyful, productive adulthood.

||||||||||||||||||||||||||||||||||||||||||||||||||||||||||||||||||||||||||||

Turning Around:
A Look at Two Boys

*You can say, "He had some problems,
but he worked them out."*

—EVAN,
at age 9

I want you to tell parents that it's going to get better.

—BEN,
at age 15

EVAN: MY RELUCTANT HERO

Does every mother's heart ache when she sees her son from a distance?
I stand on our front porch on a warm spring day and watch Evan scurry
toward a friend's car in the driveway. He hunches his shoulders forward
like a little old man, then skips, leaps, keels to the right, then hops
again, head down, arms bent and close to his sides. I feel a tug at my
heart. No other child I know moves through space like that.

I wave good-bye. He doesn't notice. His mind is on the Game Boy™
his friend is playing in the backseat. Long ago we banned video games
at our house because of their aftermath: irritability, sassiness, outright
defiance. So Evan has learned to edit himself when asking if he can
play with friends whose parents are not so restrictive. He'll say, "I really
want to go to Jeff's house, but it isn't *just* because of Game Boy. Jeff is a
lot of fun to play with, too." "Uh-huh," I say.

As I watch the three of them drive away, I wonder how Jeff and his mother will react to Evan. Will they think he's funny or awkward? Will they find his preoccupation with Game Boy rude? Will they be amused by his cartoon-dominated conversation, or will they find it odd? Will they invite him back again?

I tell myself that everything will be fine, and it will be. Evan loves going to other kids' houses, and he tries very hard to be a good guest. He'll hold it together until he comes home. But as soon as he walks in the door, I'll see the effects of too much noise, too much rough play, too many choices of things to do, and too much Game Boy or TV. He'll be tired, glassy-eyed, and brittle. He will snap at his sister, balk at my directions, and argue about the simplest things. Like a snake that's been handled roughly, he'll be full of venom.

We've come to expect this, and we've learned to accommodate it, somewhat. But when he's in this agitated state, it's not easy to avoid his bite. For me, this emotional edginess remains the hardest part of living with Evan's sensory sensitivities—and yet, I'm coming to believe it's the part he'll always need the most help with.

Since we first took Evan to Rebecca four years ago, he has changed dramatically from a boy who hated school to a boy who sees himself as smart and capable, from a kid who could barely scratch out his name to an undeniably talented artist. No longer at the constant mercy of the pull of gravity, he enjoys riding a bike, scaling a climbing wall, and jumping off a diving board. Most days now, he offers no more resistance to getting dressed, taking a bath, washing his hair, or brushing his teeth than any other 9-year-old boy does.

He still asks us to lie down with him at night for protection against the shadowy figures he conjures so easily in the dark but also for the pure physical pleasure of cuddling under the covers. With lights out and his favorite threadbare blanket under his cheek, he asks me to scratch his back (with firm touch, not light). He also (barely) tolerates an occasional kiss on the ear and practically purrs when I wrap him in my arms. He recently explained, "It used to feel bad when you hugged me, but now it feels like all the love in the universe is coming to me. I love hugs."

He has learned to tie his shoes, buckle his seat belt, hit a softball, and follow elaborate sequences of visual directions to build Lego™

star fighters, pirate ships, and castles. He swims and plays chess, tennis, and badminton. He has gone from rolling on the floor at that first pre-school parents' breakfast to singing, dancing, and acting in school plays. He is no longer "out of sync," as Carol Kranowitz calls it. He's in a groove. Of course, this metamorphosis hasn't been simple or smooth. It hasn't been constant or complete. It's been trial and error. It's been bumpy.

After eighteen months of weekly sessions with Evan, Rebecca suggested that he take a break from therapy. His fine-motor skills had vastly improved, his postural difficulties and bilateral coordination problems had decreased significantly, and tactile defensiveness was no longer interfering with his daily life. Rebecca noticed that he was not as enthusiastic about the therapy activities as he had been. Tasks that provided a great deal of proprioceptive, vestibular, and tactile integration with big muscle movement were no longer as compelling for him—he had reached a level of mastery that made practicing those tasks over and over again less interesting and rewarding. His inner drive, as Ayres called it, had switched to seat work: drawing, coloring, and writing. He spent hours each day with a pencil and sketch pad, drawing his favorite cartoon characters, the latest super-hero, or events from our own lives. To Rebecca, this shift signaled a plateau in his development that offered a logical ending place for therapy.

With some trepidation, immeasurable gratitude, and the reassurance that we could come back if we needed to, we said good-bye to Rebecca. I look back on the years that have passed since then and wonder if Evan would have made similar progress without occupational therapy. Of course, there is no way to know, but surely he would have eventually given up his training wheels, discovered his artistic talents, and surrendered to the necessity of daily hygiene. Surely at some point he would have settled into the routine at school. But at what cost? If I want to scare myself, I try to imagine where our family would be today if Rebecca hadn't taught us how to approach Evan's behavior from a sensory-based framework.

Would Evan's adjustment to kindergarten have been so smooth if we hadn't prepared him, his teacher, and ourselves for the sensory challenges of public school? In a student support team meeting that first month of school, I explained my concerns about Evan's sensory processing problems to a handful of teachers and the school counselor. They listened politely, but I got the feeling they were exercising patience with me. They hadn't noticed any problems with Evan. He hadn't been disruptive, except at naptime, which was not unusual for a kindergartener. He was settling in.

What they couldn't know, what they didn't see, was how much effort it took for him to stay on track. Every afternoon when I picked him up from school, he would announce his tally on the class behavior chart. Each student started the day with five "apples," but for each infraction of the rules, the teacher took away an apple. If a student lost all five apples by the end of the day, he would take home a behavior plan to be signed by his parents.

"I only lost three apples," Evan would solemnly report as he climbed into the car at the end of the school day. "I almost lost another one, but then I earned it back." No matter how I tried to shift the focus of our afternoon conversations to what happened on the playground, who he sat with at lunch, or what the art project was, he always wanted to discuss his behavior score.

Saying good-bye to him at the door of his classroom each morning, I felt like I was sending him off to battle. In a sense, I was. He lived in daily fear of bringing home a behavior plan, and it hurt me to think of him on edge throughout the day, constantly mindful of the possibility of making a mistake, losing an apple, using up his chances. I wanted his teacher to know that he was walking a sensory minefield. I wanted her to ease the pressure and help him avoid trouble.

Schoolwide gatherings were situations in which he had particular difficulty following directions. The volume and physical proximity of so many people in a confined space set him on edge, and he often got out of his place in search of a sensory respite. Evan came up with the idea of wearing a hooded vest to assemblies so that he could retreat under the hood, and his teacher and I agreed that this would be a good way for him to modulate his level of arousal.

On the morning of the next scheduled assembly, Evan and I reviewed his plan. I pulled his teacher aside and reminded her of our earlier discussion. We all understood what was to happen. That afternoon when I picked him up from school, I asked him how the assembly had gone.

"Oh, not too bad," he replied.

"Did your plan work?" I asked.

"Not really," he said. "A teacher made me take off my hood."

"Who was she?" I demanded.

"I don't know," he answered. "Just some teacher who said I shouldn't wear my hood when I'm inside."

All over again I was struck by the invisible nature of sensory processing problems and the nearly continuous possibility of misunderstanding that Evan faced in his attempts to cope with his body's reactions to the world around him. The most heartbreaking misinterpretation of Evan's behavior came at the end of that school year. The entire kindergarten and first grade—approximately 125 students—put on a musical play in the gymnasium. Evan was happy to be in the chorus, and he diligently memorized each word of every song. I worried about the challenges he would face during the performance: the vestibular demands of keeping his balance on the risers; the tactile demands of being touched and bumped by the children standing beside, behind, and in front of him; the proprioceptive demands of coordinating the dance movements with the song lyrics; the auditory demands of tuning out the din of the crowd; the emotional demands of high performance expectations. What if he couldn't handle it all?

My husband and I sat in the audience, enchanted by the performance. The children were well prepared, the costumes were adorable, and the music was catchy, but I couldn't take my eyes off of Evan. He smiled confidently from his position in the second row of the chorus. He watched attentively, waited for his teacher's cues, sang every word, and enthusiastically clapped, swayed, and moved in time to the music. For me, he was the show. While the parents sitting around me laughed and applauded, I fought back tears. *We've made it*, I thought. *We're going to be okay*.

The next day, Evan came home from school sad and confused. As a reward for their participation in the play, his class had gone on a field trip to a local ice cream store. But Evan had been left behind, because his music teacher had listed him as one of the children who had behaved inappropriately during the performance. I was shocked. Evan's triumphant accomplishment had suddenly turned into another encounter with shame and failure. I couldn't imagine why he had been punished.

His teacher's explanation was that at the very end of the show, during the rousing ovation from the audience, a few boys including Evan had gotten excited and jumped (fallen?) from the second row of the risers onto the floor and back up again. I had seen it—a momentary loss of control that had seemed understandable to me. They were kindergarteners, after all. But his music teacher found that behavior unacceptable. And so, rather than recognizing the pride, the joy, and the twenty-nine minutes of self-control that Evan had exhibited, she had penalized him for the split second during which he was out of bounds. His best effort hadn't been good enough.

Was I making excuses for him? This is a hard question for me to answer. I have a child with needs outside the ordinary, and it is difficult to differentiate between accommodating those needs and surrendering to them. I want Evan to develop to his fullest potential, to meet the standards that the world sets for him, and self-control is essential to his success. I don't want dysfunctional sensory integration to become a crutch. And yet his needs are real and they make it impossible for him to behave like everyone else in certain situations. How do I challenge him to conform without overwhelming him? How do I recognize his effort without lowering the bar?

Was Evan's momentary loss of control at the school play a sensory processing problem, or was it just a 6-year-old boy cutting up? Even now, three years later, I ask myself the same question in many different situations: Is this a sensory problem or something else?

When he talks too loud, despite repeated reminders, I think of him as having a sensory modulation problem. When he repeatedly calls his sister names, I think of him as a pest. When he refuses to clean up his room and insists that "somebody has to help me," I think of him as having a sensory discrimination and motor planning problem. When he argues about helping me set the table, I think of him as lazy. When his friend gets angry with him because he won't play catch, I think of the situation as a sensory-based social problem. When I get angry with him because he won't turn off the computer, I don't know what to think. He could be overstimulated, neurologically short-circuited, unable to use higher-order thinking to control his actions, or he could just be pushing the limits and testing my resolve.

Because, of course, a certain amount of defiance is to be expected from a 9-year-old boy. Developmentally, he still has a way to go before he'll be able to give up the immediate pleasure of a computer game just because the clock indicates that his time is up. (Some grown-ups still can't do this!) Children his age can't be relied on to use *what they know* to determine *what they do*, especially if they think they might be able to get away with ignoring or bending the rule. So, Evan's reluctance to turn off the computer is probably just normal, age-appropriate behavior.

What may not be normal is what happens next. He leaves the computer disoriented, whiny, and irritable. He complains that there is nothing to do. He flops onto the floor. He makes loud nyah-nyah-nyah noises that quickly get on my last nerve. He picks on his sister, then yells at her when she retaliates. If I remind him of our rules, he shrieks, "I know! I know! I know!" If I suggest that he take a chill-out, he refuses. If I walk out of the room, he hollers for me to come back. This extreme irritability, I think, is related to sensory dysregulation. As Evan once described it, he is "falling off a cliff." He is overaroused, completely unable to settle his system, organize his thoughts, or modulate his response to the world around him.

Even now, after all I've learned about sensory processing problems, it's difficult not to take offense when he lashes out. It's hard not to feel disrespected. Although it would be a mistake to discipline him at these times, it's what the angry part of me wants to do. A part of me wants to get loud and force him to do what I say. Another part of me—sometimes smaller, sometimes larger—knows not to take his out-of-bounds behavior personally. He is reacting on a primitive, brain stem level, and punishing him is like poking a stick at a riled-up rattlesnake.

I try to keep in mind the advice offered in a British snakebite kit my husband keeps as a souvenir of his days as a Peace Corps worker on the island of Borneo. For two years, he carried this pocket-size kit with him as protection against the two dozen types of poisonous snakes known to live in the Malaysian jungle. The directions inside the kit begin as follows: *If you are bitten by a viper, do not panic. Fix yourself a cup of tea and read these instructions carefully.*

It's good advice at home as well as in the jungle. When Evan is upset, I must remember not to panic or overreact, not to make demands that he can't meet. I have to remind myself that he is not thinking rationally at these times; instead, I am literally dealing with a person with the thinking capacity of a reptile. In his own words, he is "brainless"—his limbic system has seized control of his brain and locked his cortex in a closet. At those times, I need to stop talking, give him space, and let him chill out until the sensory, emotional, and thinking centers of his brain reconnect. That won't happen if I'm in his face, demanding that he get himself together on the count of three. He needs me to stay calm so that his internal alarm will stop ringing and his brain will switch from survival mode to problem-solving mode.

Once in the midst of a crisis, he said to me, "Someone has to calm me down, Mom. Someone has to *make me happy*." At the time, it seemed like he was asking me to give in to him in some way. This seemed like a big mistake, as if I would be rewarding him for being out-of-control—the very thing that I warn parents not to do when their children are misbehaving. But if the purpose of discipline is to teach (rather than to punish), then I must engage my pupil's attention before the lesson can begin. When Evan's reptilian brain is in charge, his body is preparing to fight or flee—not to learn. Therefore, I must wait, fix myself a cup of tea, and let him be.

Raising children—all children—requires creativity, a good sense of humor, and a healthy dose of empathy. For me, the most challenging aspect of parenting a child with sensory processing problems has been learning to control my emotional reactions to his emotional reactions. In order to teach Evan self-control, I must practice it. In *Emotional Intelligence*, Daniel Goleman points out that children are either helped or handicapped by their parents' own emotional capabilities. Some parents, as he puts it, are gifted emotional teachers; others are atrocious.

I recognize that I am both. Sometimes I manage to approach a crisis with Evan as an opportunity for growth and change. At other times, I'm sure that I pass on the frustration of not knowing how to handle him. I have to wonder what I am teaching him about himself and what I am teaching him about me. When I am calm and reasonable, what I want Evan to know deep down in his bones is how truly remarkable he is. Not just that he is intelligent and artistically talented and very, very funny—I'm pretty sure he knows these things. I want him to know that he is a hero in my eyes, because he fights a hidden battle and climbs an invisible mountain every day. Usually, he can count on his father or me for support, but sometimes when we just don't get it he struggles alone. He wouldn't like the word *hero*—it's too flashy, and he doesn't like to draw attention to himself. Call it what you will—I hope he recognizes and appreciates his own strength.

On a few occasions, my mother has told me that she considers Evan to be extremely fortunate to have been born into our family—as if my husband and I are paragons of patience and understanding. I don't see it that way. Too clearly, I see the problems that remain for Evan and I worry that I haven't done enough for him. Should I still be taking him to occupational therapy with Rebecca? Should we have tried biofeedback, craniosacral therapy, auditory integration training, nutritional counseling? Would medication help? Should I buy him a backyard trampoline, force him to keep taking tennis lessons, or insist that he learn yoga or tae kwon do?

Many parents ask me these same questions. It's certainly understandable that we would all be looking for a "cure," hoping that the next thing we try is going to solve all the problems and set everything right. And yet we know that life is not that way, not for any of us. As far as I can tell, life is about putting one foot in front of the other, day after day. It's about making the best of a less than perfect situation. It requires that we let go of our fantasies and learn to embrace the realities of life as we—and our children—experience them. We must believe that they are doing as well as they can, and so are we.

Giving up my notions of who Evan should be and learning to see him as he is has dramatically changed my relationship with him. Because I now empathize with his struggles, I no longer insist that he do things my way. In fact, I've learned to do many things his way. His frustrations have taught me patience. His complexity has humbled me. His humor has sustained me. His persistence has inspired me.

I am not the perfect mother, but in Evan's eyes I'm the perfect mother for him. And now I see, with absolute clarity, that he is the perfect boy for me. That is what I want him to know, deep down in his bones where his soul is anchored. He is the perfect boy for me.

—K.S.

ALMOST GROWN: A FINAL NOTE FROM BEN

Ben is 15 now, further along the developmental pathway than Evan. When I asked him how he felt about our writing this book, he replied, "I want you to do it. I want you to tell parents that it is going to get better." But as we talked, it became clear that his optimism was part of a more complicated story. Colorfully interwoven in the tapestry of his life are themes of success and failure, of gradual change and ongoing struggle, of joy and sorrow.

Ben is very much his own person. Passionate about movies, Japanese anime, sports, and world history, he writes film reviews for his school newspaper, plays on the intramural volleyball team, and is hoping to spend his junior year of high school in Japan. Despite his accomplishments, he is painfully aware that he is not always accepted outside his small group of friends. Managing the sensory demands of American teenage culture while meeting the emotional challenges of adolescence is more difficult for him than it is for others.

"I don't even talk much at lunch," he says. "Sometimes it's hard to keep up with conversations. Kids move from one topic to another and cut each other off. I can't follow that. I feel like saying to them, 'Having a conversation means not switching from one topic to another!'" Not being able to jump into the talk is very hard for a teen who reads the paper every day, absorbs tremendous amounts of information, and has an opinion about everything. What often happens in the world of teenagers is that those who cannot join in easily get shut out. All too often, Ben feels shut out.

Despite these challenges, Ben continues to reach out to others. For several months last year, he had a girlfriend. He surprised us by telling her about his struggles with sensory integration. We were curious about her response. "She wanted to know how I was ever going to get married," he said. "I told her my wife will just have to understand." And then he added, "It's important to communicate." Ben's self-awareness and willingness to share what he knows about himself with those he loves exceeds that of many adults—an unexpected benefit of his efforts to understand why he so often feels out of sorts.

At the same time, Ben insists that the sensory problems have lessened, to some degree, as he has grown. When I ask him what has made it better, he replies, "I don't know. It just gets better over time." Then he goes on to clarify, "Some parts get better than others. Sensory integration has many parts—some parts are very strong, other parts are weaker, some parts don't bother me at all."

He adds, "I've learned how to deal with the sound problems. At first, I could barely sit in the movies. But then, with a Walkman, I gradually started pushing the volume up a little louder to get used to people yelling at me. The clothing thing hasn't gotten any better, but that's because it was worse than the sound in the first place. But I've learned to cut my labels off. And if wearing something is important enough, I can force myself to do it. Like I remember I used to not wear socks—but today I'll just ignore them, even though sometimes they still bother me.

"The thing that bothers me the most now is people getting in my face. I let people in pretty close, but if they keep coming and get inside my personal space, it sets off that trigger."

"What do you do then?" I ask.

"I try to push my feelings down to a level I can deal with. It's like water pressure—I try to lower it. I try to ignore the feelings."

"Does it work?"

"Sometimes," he replies. "At other times it continues to bother me."

"I know I have this problem," he admits. "But when something really bothers me, it's not the first thing that comes to mind. Then I'll stop and think and realize, *Oh, it's that sensory thing.* It feels horrible, and sometimes I think, *Oh, why can't this be someone else's problem?*"

"People are different in every way," he goes on emphatically. "Some kids just have more problems than others." For Ben, the most frustrating aspect of his sensory processing difficulties has been the hidden nature of the problem. On numerous occasions he has said, "It's a problem, and people don't understand it. It's not something they can see. I wish someone would just give a talk about this to help people understand."

This book is our talk.

— K.G.

||||||||||||||||||||||||||||||||||||||||||||||||||||||||||||||||||||||||||||||||

Glossary

Adaptive behavior: a purposeful, well-organized, successful response to an environmental demand.

Arousal: a neurological state of alertness that readies a person to pay attention and respond appropriately to the immediate environment.

Asperger's syndrome: a psychiatric diagnosis characterized by impaired social skills, unusual repetitive patterns of behavior, mental preoccupations, and sensory sensitivities.

Attachment: the bond between an infant and caregiver, which is the blueprint for the development of healthy, satisfying connections with other people throughout the life span.

Attention deficit hyperactivity disorder: a psychiatric diagnosis characterized by inattention, impulsivity, and overactivity.

Bilateral coordination: the ability to use both sides of the body simultaneously in a coordinated manner.

Body map: the mental picture of one's own body, where its parts are, how they interrelate, and how they move.

Brain stem: the lowest area of the brain, emerging from the top of the spinal cord; sometimes called the "reptilian brain," it is the most ancient in evolutionary terms; takes in information from the senses and regulates states of arousal; responds to threatening sensations with fight, flight, or freeze reflexes.

Cerebral cortex: the most highly evolved part of the brain; the working site of language, perception, motor coordination, abstract reasoning, and memory; connected to the limbic structures and brain stem, allowing for flexible, well-integrated brain-body communication.

Defensive (or protective) system: a sensory feedback system that alerts one to real or potential danger and causes a self-protective response.

Discriminative system: a sensory feedback system that allows one to distinguish differences among separate sensory stimuli.

Dyspraxia: difficulty in planning and carrying out unfamiliar sequences of movement in a skillful manner.

Emotion regulation: the process of controlling and adjusting one's emotional arousal necessary for optimal attention, motivation, and adaptive behavior.

Facilitation: enhancement of or sensitization to particular sensory input.

Fight-flight-fright response: the instinctive reaction to defend oneself from real or perceived danger by becoming aggressive, running away, or freezing and playing dead.

Fine motor: referring to movement of the small muscles in the fingers, toes, eyes, and tongue.

Gravitational insecurity: abnormal distress or fear of falling in response to movement or a change in the position of one's head.

Gravitational security: the sense that one is well grounded and not threatened by body movements or changes in head position.

Gross motor: referring to movement of large muscles in the arms, legs, and trunk.

Habituation: automatic tuning out of irrelevant or routine sensory input.

Hypersensitivity: oversensitivity to input from any of the seven senses, characterized by a tendency to be fearful and cautious or negative and defiant.

Hyposensitivity: undersensitivity to input from any of the seven senses, characterized by a tendency to crave intense sensations or to be remote and difficult to engage.

Information processing: a cognitive model of the workings of the mind based on computer analogies; organizes mental processes into categories such as encoding, analysis, memory search, response search and selection, enactment, and evaluation.

Inhibition: reduction in sensitivity to particular sensory input.

Inner drive: Ayres's description of a person's motivation to participate in experiences that promote sensory integration.

Integration: the linking together of individual components of a complex, interrelated system; neural integration connects the activity of one region of the brain or body to other regions.

Learning disability: the inability to apply one's full intellectual capabilities to academic tasks; a marked discrepancy between a child's intellectual potential and his school performance, not due to emotional, behavioral, or motivational difficulties.

Limbic system: the middle region of the brain; regulates brain stem activity as well as internal bodily states, emotion, motivation, and social behavior. Connects and coordinates the activities of the lower and higher regions of the brain.

Modulation: the brain's automatic adjustment to the intensity with which sensory stimulation is received; this unconscious feedback process is continuous and self-correcting and is accomplished through inhibition, facilitation, and habituation to sensory input.

Motor planning (or praxis): the ability to conceive of, organize, and carry out an unfamiliar sequence of movements in a coordinated manner.

Myelination: the growth and development of myelin, a soft, white, fatty material that insulates nerve fibers and allows for more efficient conduction of nerve impulses.

Nonverbal learning disability: observed difficulties in tactile and visual-spatial processing, motor coordination, and social interactions; these difficulties can have a negative impact on academic achievement and emotional adjustment.

Occupational therapy: a health profession that facilitates an individual's play/leisure, personal, social, academic, and vocational functioning through sensory-based, physically based, and function-based activities/exercises.

Oppositional defiant disorder: a psychiatric diagnosis characterized by age-inappropriate levels of negative, uncooperative behavior.

Pervasive developmental disorder: a psychiatric diagnostic category that includes a spectrum of deficits in social interaction, communication, and goal-directed behavior; autism is the most severe manifestation of this range of difficulties.

Physical therapy: a health profession devoted to the improvement of an individual's physical abilities through activities that strengthen muscular control and motor coordination.

Plasticity: the potential for change, growth, and adaptation in the structure and function of the brain.

Postural stability: the feeling of security and self-confidence when moving through space based on one's body awareness.

Proprioceptive sense: sensations coming from one's joints, muscles, tendons, and ligaments; the "body position sense."

Pruning: a self-correcting neurological growth mechanism whereby the brain removes superfluous, underutilized synaptic connections in order to increase the strength and efficiency of essential, well-traveled neural pathways; this process is heavily influenced by experience and interaction with the environment.

Reactivity: responsiveness or sensitivity to arousing stimulation.

Receptors: specialized nerve cells that receive and send sensory information from inside and outside the body to the brain for analysis and response; the front line of sensory processing.

Regulatory disorder: observed difficulties in the modulation and regulation of emotion, sensation, motor coordination, and behavior.

Self-regulation: the ability to control one's activity level and state of alertness, as well as one's emotional, mental, or physical responses to sensations; self-organization.

Sensory defensiveness: the tendency to react negatively and emotionally to unexpected, unbidden sensory stimulation; especially common in the tactile and auditory systems.

Sensory diet: the multisensory experiences that one seeks on a daily basis to satisfy one's sensory appetite; planned and scheduled activities that an occupational therapist develops to help a person become better regulated.

Sensory integration: the continuous neurological process of taking in information from one's body and environment through the senses, organizing and analyzing this information, and using it to plan and execute adaptive responses that lead to successful functioning in daily life.

Sensory integration treatment: a set of occupational therapy techniques that encourage playful, meaningful full-body movements that stimulate the vestibular, proprioceptive, and tactile sensory systems. These activities theoretically improve the way the brain processes and organizes these sensations, thereby leading to more adaptive, integrated responses to daily tasks of living.

Speech and language pathologist: a specialist in the assessment, treatment, and prevention of communication disorders; may work in a hospital, school, rehabilitation center, health clinic, or private practice; sometimes specializes in work with particular populations or specific disorders.

Tactile sense: the sensory system that receives sensations of pressure, vibration, movement, temperature, and pain primarily through receptors in the skin.

Temperament: inborn differences in infants' emotional and behavioral responses to the world around them; influenced by genetics, maturity, and social experience.

Touch pressure: the tactile stimulus that causes receptors in the skin to respond. Deep pressure, such as a hug, activates receptors in the discriminative system. Light touch, such as a kiss, activates receptors in the protective system.

Vestibular sense: the sensory system that responds to body movement and changes in head position; coordinates movements of the eyes, head, and body through receptors in the inner ear.

APPENDIX B

||||||||||||||||||||||||||||||||||||||||||||||||||||||||||||||||||||||||||||||||||

Sensory Integration Resources

BOOKS ABOUT SENSORY PROCESSING

Anderson, E., and P. Emmons. 1996. *Unlocking the Mysteries of Sensory Dysfunction: A Resource for Anyone Who Works with or Lives with a Child with Sensory Issues.* Arlington, TX: Future Horizons.

Ayres, J. 1979. *Sensory Integration and the Child.* Los Angeles: Western Psychological Services.

Beninghof, A. 1998. *SenseAble Strategies: Including Diverse Learners Through Multisensory Strategies.* Longmont, CO: Sopris West.

Bundy, A. C., S. J. Lane, and E. A. Murray. 2002. *Sensory Integration: Theory and Practice.* 2nd ed. Philadelphia: F. A. Davis.

DeGangi, G. 2000. *Pediatric Disorders of Regulation in Affect and Behavior: A Therapist's Guide to Assessment and Treatment.* San Diego: Academic Press.

Ganz, J. 1998. *Including SI: A Guide to Using Sensory Integration Concepts in the School Environment.* Bohemia, NY: Kapable Kids.

Haldy, M., and L. Haack. 1995. *Making it Easy: Sensorimotor Activities at Home and School.* San Antonio: Therapy Skills Builders.

Heller, S. 2002. *Too Loud, Too Bright, Too Fast, Too Tight: What to Do If You Are Sensory Defensive in an Overstimulating World.* New York: HarperCollins.

Kranowitz, C. 1998. *The Out-of-Sync Child: Recognizing and Coping with Sensory Integration Dysfunction.* New York: Perigee.

———. 2003. *The Out-of-Sync Child Has Fun: Activities for Kids with Sensory Integration Dysfunction.* New York: Perigee.

Kranowitz, C., S. Szklut, L. Balzer-Martin, E. Haber, and D. Sava. 2000. *Answers to Questions Teachers Ask About Sensory Integration.* Las Vegas: Sensory Resources.

Liddle, T., and L. Yorke. 2003. *Why Motor Skills Matter.* New York: Contemporary Books.

Myles, B., K. Cook, N. Miller, L. Rinner, and L. Robbins. 2000. *Asperger Syndrome and Sensory Issues: Practical Solutions for Making Sense of the World.* Shawnee Mission, KS: Autism Asperger Publishing Co.

Quirk, N., and M. Dimatties. 1990. *Relationship of Learning Problems and Classroom Performance to Sensory Integration.* Norma Quirk and Marie Di Matties.

Trott, M. 1993. *SenseAbilities: Understanding Sensory Integration.* Tucson: Therapy Skill Builders.

Wilbarger, P., and J. Wilbarger. 1991. *Sensory Defensiveness in Children Aged 2–12.* Santa Barbara, CA: Avanti Educational Programs.

Williams, M., and S. Shellenberger. 1994. *How Does Your Engine Run?: Leader's Guide to the Alert Program™ for Self-Regulation.* Albuquerque: Therapy Works.

Williamson, G., and M. Anzalone. 2001. *Sensory Integration and Self-Regulation in Infants and Toddlers: Helping Very Young Children Interact with Their Environment.* Arlington, VA: Zero to Three.

AUDIOTAPES

Koomar, J., S. Szklut, and S. Cermak. 1998. *Making Sense of Sensory Integration.* Las Vegas: Sensory Resources/Belle Curve.

Kranowitz, C., and S. Szklut. 1999. *Teachers Ask About Sensory Integration.* Las Vegas: Sensory Resources/Belle Curve.

Lande, A., and B. Wiz. 2001. *Songames for Sensory Integration.* Las Vegas: Sensory Resources/Belle Curve.

CHILDREN'S BOOKS

Aliki. 2000. *My Five Senses.* New York: HarperTrophy.

Koomar, J., B. Friedman, and E. Woolf. 1992. *The Hidden Senses: Your Muscle Sense* and *The Hidden Senses: Your Balance Sense.* Rockville, MD: American Occupational Therapy Association.

O'Brien-Palmer, M. 1998. *Sense-Abilities: Fun Ways to Explore the Senses.* Chicago: Chicago Review Press.

Williams, M., and D. Burke. 1996. *Cool Cats, Calm Kids: Relaxation and Stress Management for Young People.* Atascadero, CA: Impact Publishers.

Ziefert, H., and A. Haley. 2002. *You Can't Taste a Pickle with Your Ear: A Book About Your 5 Senses.* Brooklyn, NY: Handprint Books.

RELATED READING

Ackerman, D. 1990. *A Natural History of the Senses.* New York: Random House.

Allen, J., and R. Klein. 1997. *Ready, Set, Relax: A Research-Based Program of Relaxation, Learning and Self-Esteem for Children.* Watertown, WI: Inner Coaching.

Brooks, R., and S. Goldstein. 2001. *Raising Resilient Children.* Chicago: Contemporary Books.

Campbell, D. 2000. *The Mozart Effect for Children: Awakening Your Child's Mind, Health, and Creativity with Music.* New York: William Morrow.

Chandler, B. E. 1997. *The Essence of Play: A Child's Occupation.* Bethesda, MD: American Occupational Therapy Association.

Duke, M., E. Martin, and S. Nowicki. 1996. *Teaching Your Child the Language of Social Success.* Atlanta: Peachtree Publishers.

Einon, D. 1985. *Play with a Purpose: Learning Games for Children Six Weeks to Ten Years.* New York: Pantheon.

Frankel, F., and B. Wetmore. 1996. *Good Friends Are Hard to Find: Help Your Child Find, Keep, and Make Friends*. London: Perspective Publishing.

Goleman, D. 1995. *Emotional Intelligence*. New York: Bantam Books.

Greene, R. 1998. *The Explosive Child*. New York: HarperCollins.

Greenspan, S. 1995. *The Challenging Child: Understanding, Raising, and Enjoying the Five "Difficult" Types of Children*. Reading, MA: Addison-Wesley.

Greenspan, S., and J. Salmon. 1993. *Playground Politics: Understanding the Emotional Life of Your School-Age Child*. Reading, MA: Addison-Wesley.

Hannaford, C. 1995. *Smart Moves: Why Learning Is Not All in Your Head*. Arlington, VA: Great Ocean Publishers.

Healy, J. 1990. *Endangered Minds: Why Children Don't Think—and What We Can Do About It*. New York: Touchstone.

———. 1994. *Your Child's Growing Mind: A Practical Guide to Brain Development and Learning from Birth to Adolescence*. New York: Doubleday.

Hickman, L., R. Hutchins, and J. Ellen. 2002. *Seeing Clearly: Fun Activities for Improving Visual Skills*. Las Vegas: Sensory Resources/Belle Curve.

Kurcinka, M. S. 1991. *Raising Your Spirited Child: A Guide for Parents Whose Child Is More Intense, Sensitive, Perceptive, Persistent, Energetic*. New York: HarperPerennial.

Levine, M. 2002. *A Mind at a Time*. New York: Simon & Schuster.

Nowicki, S., and M. Duke. 1992. *Helping the Child Who Doesn't Fit In*. Atlanta: Peachtree Publishers.

Schneider, C. 2001. *Sensory Secrets: How to Jump-Start Learning in Children*. Siloam Springs, AK: The Concerned Group.

Shure, M. 1994. *Raising a Thinking Child*. New York: Simon & Schuster.

Siegel, D. 1999. *The Developing Mind: How Relationships and the Brain Interact to Shape Who We Are*. New York: Guilford Press.

Siegel, D., and M. Hartzell. 2003. *Parenting from the Inside Out*. New York: Tarcher/Putnam.

Stewart, K. 2002. *Helping a Child with Nonverbal Learning Disability or Asperger's Syndrome: A Parent's Guide*. Oakland, CA: New Harbinger.

Thompson, M., C. Grace, and L. Cohen. 2001. *Best Friends, Worst Enemies: Understanding the Social Lives of Children*. New York: Ballantine Books.

Tomatis, A. 1996. *The Ear and Language*. Ontario, Canada: Moulin Publishing.

Turecki, S., and L. Tonner. 1989. *The Difficult Child*. New York: Bantam.

WEB SITES

These Web sites are useful resources for information, products, treatment programs, and links regarding dysfunctional sensory processing and related problems:

www.sinetwork.org
www.sensoryint.com
www.sensoryresources.com
www.sensorycomfort.com
www.out-of-sync-child.com
www.alertprogram.com
www.ateachabout.com
www.otawatertown.com
www.southpawenterprises.com
www.aota.org
www.devdelay.org
www.zerotothree.org

References

FOREWORD

Ayres, J. 1979. *Sensory Integration and the Child*. Los Angeles: Western Psychological Services.

Greene, R. 1998. *The Explosive Child*. New York: HarperCollins.

PROLOGUE

Anderson, L. 1984. *United States Live*. Warner Brothers.

Ayres, J. 1979. *Sensory Integration and the Child*. Los Angeles: Western Psychological Services.

Campbell, S. B. 1990. *Behavior Problems in Preschool Children: Clinical and Developmental Issues*. New York: Guilford Press.

———. 1995. Behavior problems in preschool children: A review of recent research. *Journal of Child Psychology and Psychiatry* 36: 113–149.

Diagnostic and Statistical Manual of Mental Disorders. 4th ed. 1994. Washington, DC: American Psychiatric Association.

Forehand, R., and N. Long. 2002. *Parenting the Strong-Willed Child*. 2nd ed. Lincolnwood, IL: McGraw-Hill/Contemporary Books.

Lavigne, J. V., C. Cicchetti, R. Gibbons, H. Binns, L. Larsen, and C. DeVito. 2001. Oppositional defiant disorder with onset in preschool years: Longitudinal stability and pathways to other disorders. *Journal of the American Academy of Child and Adolescent Psychiatry* 40: 1393–1400.

National Center for Clinical Infant Programs. 1994. *Diagnostic Classification: 0–3: Diagnostic Classification of Mental Health and Development Disorders of Infancy and Early Childhood.* Arlington, VA: Zero to Three.

Patterson, G. R. 1982. *Coercive Family Process.* Eugene, OR: Castalia.

Pepler, D., and K. H. Rubin, eds. 1990. *The Development and Treatment of Childhood Aggression.* Hillsdale, NJ: Erlbaum.

Robins, L. N., and M. Rutter, eds. 1990. *Straight and Devious Pathways from Childhood to Adulthood.* New York: Cambridge University Press.

Rourke, B. 1989. *Nonverbal Learning Disabilities: The Syndrome and the Model.* New York: Guilford Press.

Teeter, P. 1997. Neurocognitive interventions for childhood and adolescent disorders. In *Handbook of Clinical Child Neuropsychology* (2nd ed.): *Critical Issues in Neuropsychology,* ed. C. Reynolds and E. Fletcher-Janzen. New York: Kluwer/Plenum Publishers.

Webster-Stratton, C. 1990. Long-term follow-up of families with young conduct problem children: From preschool to grade school. *Journal of Clinical Child Psychology* 19: 144–149.

CHAPTER ONE

Ackerman, D. 1990. *A Natural History of the Senses.* New York: Random House.

Ayres, J. 1979. *Sensory Integration and the Child.* Los Angeles: Western Psychological Services.

Cermak, S., and V. Groza. 1998. Sensory processing problems in post-institutionalized children: Implications for social work. *Child and Adolescent Social Work Journal* 15 (1): 5–37.

Dodge, K. A. 1986. A social information processing model of social competence in children. In *Minnesota Symposium on Child Psychology*, vol. 18, ed. M. Perlmutter, 77–125. Hillsdale, NJ: Erlbaum.

Dodge, K. A., and C. L. Frame. 1982. Social cognitive biases and deficits in aggressive boys. *Child Development* 53: 620–635.

Emde, R. N., ed. 1984. *Rene A. Spitz: Dialogues from Infancy.* New York: International Universities Press.

Field, T. 2000. Infant massage treatment. In *Handbook of Infant Mental Health* (2nd ed.), ed. C. Zeanah, Jr. New York: Guilford Press.

Gouze, K. 1987. Attention and social problem solving as correlates of aggression in preschool males. *Journal of Abnormal Psychology* 15: 181–197.

Gunnar, M. R., and E. P. Davis. 2003. Stress and emotion in early childhood. In *Handbook of Psychology: Development Psychology*, vol. 6, eds. R. M. Lerner and A. M. Easterbrooks, 113–134. New York: John Wiley & Sons.

Gunnar, M. R., S. J. Morison, K. Chisholm, and M. Schuder. 2001. Salivary cortisol levels in children adopted from Romanian orphanages. *Development and Psychopathology* 13: 611–628.

Harlow, H. 1958. The nature of love. *American Psychologist* 13: 573–685.

———. 1976. Effects of maternal and peer separations on young monkeys. *Journal of Child Psychology and Psychiatry and Allied Disciplines* 17 (2): 101–112.

Healy, J. 1990. *Endangered Minds: Why Children Don't Think—and What We Can Do About It.* New York: Touchstone.

———. 1994. *Your Child's Growing Mind: A Practical Guide to Brain Development and Learning from Birth to Adolescence.* New York: Doubleday.

Hougas, A. 2001. *Psychological Death Row: Supermaximum Security Prisons, Sensory Deprivation and Effects of Solitary Confinement.* Available from the World Wide Web: http://danenet.danenet.org/amnesty/supermax.html.

Kramer, M., I. Chamorro, D. Green, and F. Knudtson. 1975. Extra tactile stimulation of the premature infant. *Nursing Research* 24: 324–334.

Lasagna, G., and M. Germoglio. 2002. Isolation and sensory deprivation—clinical observations following eight years of collaboration. In *Annals of Burns and Fire Disasters* (database online). Available from the World Wide Web: http://www.medbc.com/meditline/articles/vol=_3/num=_1/007/text/vol13n1p007.asp.

Montagu, A. 1985. *Touching: The Human Significance of the Skin.* New York: Harper and Row.

O'Connor, T., D. Bredenkamp, M. Rutter, and the English and Romanian Adoptees Study Team. 1999. Attachment disturbances and disorders in children exposed to early severe deprivation. *Infant Mental Health Journal* 20: 10–29.

Piaget, J. 1952. *The Origins of Intelligence in Children.* New York: W.W. Norton.

White, J.L., and R.C. Labarba. 1976. The effects of tactile and kinesthetic stimulation on neonatal development in the premature infant. *Developmental Psychobiology* 9: 569–577.

CHAPTER TWO

Ayres, J. 1979. *Sensory Integration and the Child*. Los Angeles: Western Psychological Services.

Bundy, A.C., S.J. Lane, and E.A. Murray. 2002. *Sensory Integration: Theory and Practice* (2nd ed.). Philadelphia: F.A. Davis.

Hanft, B.E., L.J. Miller, and S.J. Lane. 2000. Toward a consensus in terminology in sensory integration theory and practice: Part 3: Observable behaviors: Sensory integration dysfunction. *Sensory Integration: Special Interest Quarterly* 23.

Kranowitz, C. 1998. *The Out-of-Sync Child: Recognizing and Coping with Sensory Integration Dysfunction*. New York: Perigee.

Trott, M. 1993. *SenseAbilities: Understanding Sensory Integration*. Tucson: Therapy Skill Builders.

CHAPTER THREE

DeGangi, G. 2000. *Pediatric Disorders of Regulation in Affect and Behavior*. San Diego: Academic Press.

DeVito, C., and J. Hopkins. 2001. Attachment, parenting, and marital dissatisfaction as predictors of disruptive behavior in preschoolers. *Development and Psychopathology* 13: 215–233.

Diagnostic and Statistical Manual of Mental Disorders. 4th ed., 1994. Washington, DC: American Psychiatric Association.

Gopnik, A. 2002. The cooking game. *New Yorker*, August 19 and 26.

Greenberg, M.T., M.L. Speltz, M. DeKlynen, and K. Jones. 2001. Correlates of clinic referral for early conduct problems: Variable- and person-oriented approaches. *Development and Psychopathology* 13: 255–277.

Lavigne, J. V., R. Arend, D. Rosenbaum, H. Binns, K. K. Christoffel, A. Burns, and K. Smith. 1993. Mental health service use among young children receiving pediatric primary care. *Journal of the American Academy of Child and Adolescent Psychiatry* 37: 1175–1183.

Lavigne, J. V., H. J. Binns, K. K. Christoffel, D. Rosenbaum, R. Arend, K. Smith, J. R. Hayford, P. A. McGuire, and the Pediatric Research Group. 1993. Behavioral and emotional problems among preschool children in pediatric primary care: Prevalence and pediatrician's recognition. *Pediatrics* 91: 649–655.

Mangeot, S. D., L. J. Miller, D. N. McIntosh, J. McGrath-Clarke, J. Simon, R. J. Hagerman, and E. Goldson. 2001. Sensory modulation dysfunction in children with attention deficit hyperactivity disorder. *Developmental Medicine and Child Neurology* 43: 399–406.

Myles, B., K. Cook, N. Miller, L. Rinner, and L. Robbins. 2000. *Asperger Syndrome and Sensory Issues: Practical Solutions for Making Sense of the World.* Shawnee Mission, KS: Autism Asperger Publishing Co.

Patterson, G. R. 1982. *Coercive Family Process.* Eugene, OR: Castalia.

Rourke, B. 1995. The science of practice and the practice of science: The scientist–practitioner model in clinical neuropsychology. *Canadian Psychology* 36 (4): 260–277.

CHAPTER FOUR

Ainsworth, M., M. Blehar, E. Waters, and S. Wall. 1978. *Patterns of Attachment.* Hillsdale, NJ: Erlbaum.

Arend, R., F. Gove, and L. A. Sroufe. 1979. Continuity of individual adaptation from infancy to kindergarten: A predictive study of ego-resiliency and curiosity in preschoolers. *Child Development* 50: 950–959.

Ayres, J. 1979. *Sensory Integration and the Child.* Los Angeles: Western Psychological Services.

Bowlby, J. 1969. *Attachment and Loss,* vol. 1: *Attachment.* New York: Basic Books.

Dishion, T.J., G.R. Patterson, M. Stoolmiller, and M.L. Skinner. 1991. Family, school, and behavioral antecedents to early adolescent involvement with antisocial peers. *Developmental Psychology* 27: 172–180.

Easterbrooks, M.A., and W.A. Goldberg. 1993. Security of toddler–parent attachment: Relation to children's sociopersonality functioning during kindergarten. In *Attachment in the Preschool Years,* eds. M.T. Greenberg, D. Cicchetti, and M. Cummings. Chicago: University of Chicago Press.

Garmezy, N., and M. Rutter. 1983. *Stress, Coping and Development in Children.* New York: McGraw-Hill.

Greenspan, S., and J. Salman. 1993. *Playground Politics: Understanding the Emotional Life of Your School-Age Child.* Reading, MA: Addison-Wesley.

Hartup, W.W. 1992. Peer relations in early and middle childhood. In *Handbook of Social Psychology,* eds. V.B. Van Hasset and M. Hersen, 257–281. New York: Plenum Press.

Hinshaw, S. 1992. Academic underachievement, attention deficits, and aggression: Comorbidity and implications for intervention. *Journal of Consulting and Clinical Psychology* 60: 893–903.

Hodges, E., M. Boivin, F. Vitaro, and W. Bukowski. 1999. The power of friendship: Protection against an escalating cycle of peer victimization. *Developmental Psychology* 35: 94–101.

Kupersmidt, J.B., J.D. Coie, and K.A. Dodge. 1990. The role of poor peer relations in the development of disorder. In *Peer Rejection in*

Childhood, eds. S. R. Asher and J. D. Coie, 274–309. Cambridge, MA: Cambridge University Press.

Laird, R. D., K. Y. Jordan, K. Dodge, G. S. Petitt, and J. E. Bates. 2001. Peer rejection in childhood, involvement with antisocial peers in early adolescence, and the development of externalizing behavior problems. *Development and Psychopathology* 13: 337–355.

Maton, K. I., K. R. Gouze, and D. P. Keating. 1987. Towards an integrated strengths model of the person in community research: The relationship of providing and receiving support to well-being. Paper presented at the first biennial conference on Community Research and Action, South Carolina.

McClintock, M. 1971. Menstrual synchrony and suppression. *Nature* 229: 224–245.

Rubin, K. H., R. J. Coplin, N. A. Fox, and S. D. Calkins. 1995. Emotionality, emotion regulation, and preschoolers' social adaptation. *Development and Psychopathology* 7: 49–62.

Sroufe, L. A. 1983. Infant–caregiver attachment and patterns of adaptation in preschool: The roots of maladaptation and competence. In *Minnesota Symposium on Child Psychology,* vol. 16, 41–81. Hillsdale, NJ: Erlbaum.

CHAPTER FIVE

Ayres, J. 1979. *Sensory Integration and the Child.* Los Angeles: Western Psychological Services.

Chess, S., and A. Thomas. 1986. *Temperament in Clinical Practice.* New York: Guilford Press.

Cicchetti, D. 2002. How a child builds a brain: Insights from normality and psychopathology. In *Child Psychology in Retrospect and*

Prospect, eds. W. Hartup and R. Weinberg. The Minnesota Symposia on Child Psychology, vol. 32. Hillsdale, NJ: Erlbaum.

Cicchetti, D., J. Ganiban, and D. Garnett. 1991. Contributions from the study of high-risk populations to understanding the development of emotion regulation. In *The Development of Emotion Regulation and Dysregulation*, eds. J. Garber and K. Dodge. New York: Cambridge University Press.

DeGangi, G. 2000. *Pediatric Disorders of Regulation in Affect and Behavior*. San Diego: Academic Press.

Gregory, R., ed. 1987. *The Oxford Companion to the Mind*. Oxford: Oxford University Press.

Healy, J. 1994. *Your Child's Growing Mind*. New York: Doubleday.

Kagan, J., N. Smidman, and D. Arcus. 1995. The role of temperament in social development. *Annals of the New York Academy of Sciences* 771: 485–490.

MacLean, P. 1970. The triune brain, emotion and scientific bias. In F. Schmitt (Ed.), *The Neurosciences: Second Study Program*. New York: Rockefeller University Press.

Quartz, S., and T. Sejnowski. 2002. *Liars, Lovers, and Heroes*. New York: HarperCollins.

Schaaf, R. 1994. Neuroplasticity and sensory integration. *Sensory Integration Quarterly*, Spring/Summer. Sensory Integration International.

Siegel, D. 1999. *The Developing Mind: How Relationships and the Brain Interact to Shape Who We Are*. New York: Guilford Press.

Siegel, D., and M. Hartzell. 2003. *Parenting from the Inside Out*. New York: Tarcher/Putnam.

CHAPTER SIX

Ayres, J. 1972. *Sensory Integration and Learning Disorders*. Los Angeles: Western Psychological Services.

Barton, M., and D. Robins. 2000. Regulatory disorders. In *Handbook of Infant Mental Health* (2nd ed.), ed. C. Zeanah. New York: Guilford Press.

Bundy, A. C., S. J. Lane, and E. A. Murray. 2002. *Sensory Integration: Theory and Practice*, 2nd ed. Philadelphia: F. A. Davis.

Carrasco, R. 1993. Key components of sensory integration evaluation. *Sensory Integration Special Interest Section Newsletter* 16 (2), American Occupational Therapy Association.

Case-Smith, J. 1997. Clinical interpretation of "Factor Analysis on the Sensory Profile from a National Sample of Children Without Disabilities." *American Journal of Occupational Therapy* 51 (7).

Csikszentmihalyi, M., as quoted in Goleman, D. 1995. *Emotional Intelligence*. New York: Bantam Books.

DeGangi, G. 2000. *Pediatric Disorders of Regulation in Affect and Behavior*. San Diego: Academic Press.

DeGangi, G., R. Sickel, A. Wiener, and E. Kaplan. 1996. Fussy babies: To treat or not to treat? *British Journal of Occupational Therapy* 59 (10).

Dunn, W., and K. Westman. 1997. The sensory profile: The performance of a national sample of children without disabilities. *American Journal of Occupational Therapy* 51 (1).

Greene, R. 1998. *The Explosive Child*. New York: HarperCollins.

Heller, S. 2002. *Too Loud, Too Bright, Too Fast, Too Tight*. New York: HarperCollins.

Kranowitz, C. 1998. *The Out-of-Sync Child: Recognizing and Coping with Sensory Integration Dysfunction.* New York: Perigee.

———. 2003. *The Out-of-Sync Child Has Fun: Activities for Kids with Sensory Integration Dysfunction.* New York: Perigee.

Lai, J., A. Fisher, L. Magalhaes, and A. Bundy. 1996. Construct validity of the Sensory Integration and Praxis Tests. *Occupational Therapy Journal of Research* 16 (2).

Myles, B., K. Cook, N. Miller, L. Rinner, and L. Robbins. 2000. *Asperger Syndrome and Sensory Issues: Practical Solutions for Making Sense of the World.* Shawnee Mission, KS: Autism Asperger Publishing Co.

Ottenbacher, K., and M. Short. 1985. Sensory integrative dysfunction in children: A review of theory and treatment. *Advances in Developmental and Behavioral Pediatrics* 6: 287–329.

Shure, M. 1994. *Raising a Thinking Child.* New York: Simon & Schuster.

Trott, M. 1993. *SenseAbilities: Understanding Sensory Integration.* Tucson: Therapy Skill Builders.

CHAPTER SEVEN

Anderson, C. M. 1983. A psychoeducational program for families of patients with schizophrenia. In *Family Therapy in Schizophrenia,* ed. W. R. McFarlane, 99–116. New York: Guilford Press.

Beck, A. T. 1976. *Cognitive Therapy and Emotional Disorders.* New York: International Universities Press.

Cummings, E. M., E. M. Davies, P. T. Davies, and S. B. Campbell. 2000. *Developmental Psychopathology and Family Process: Theory, Research, and Clinical Implications.* New York: Guilford Press.

Dunbar, S. B. 1999. A child's occupational performance: Considerations of sensory processing and family context. *American Journal of Occupational Therapy* 53: 231–235.

Forehand, R., and N. Long. 2002. *Parenting the Strong-Willed Child.* 2nd ed. Lincolnwood, IL: McGraw-Hill/Contemporary Books.

Fristad, M. A., S. M. Gavazzi, and K. W. Soldano. 1998. Multi-family education groups for childhood mood disorders: A program description and preliminary efficacy data. *Contemporary Family Therapy* 20: 385–402.

Gottman, J. 2001. Meta-emotion, children's emotional intelligence and buffering children from marital conflict. In *Emotion, Social Relationships, and Health: Series in Affective Science,* eds. C. D. Ryff and B. H. Singer, 23–40. London: Oxford University Press.

Greene, R. 1998. *The Explosive Child.* New York: HarperCollins.

Greenspan, S. 1995. *The Challenging Child: Understanding, Raising and Enjoying the Five "Difficult" Types of Children.* Reading, MA: Addison-Wesley.

Ingoldsby, E. M., D. S. Shaw, and M. M. Garcia. 2001. Intrafamily conflict in relation to boys' adjustment at school. *Development and Psychopathology* 13: 35–53.

Jouriles, E. N., C. M. Murphy, and K. D. O'Leary. 1989. Interpersonal aggression, marital discord, and child problems. *Journal of Consulting and Clinical Psychology* 57: 453–455.

Seligman, M. P. 1995. *The Optimistic Child.* New York: Houghton-Mifflin.

Webster-Stratton, C. 1992. *The Incredible Years: A Trouble-Shooting Guide for Parents of Children Aged 3–8.* Toronto: Umbrella Press.

Webster-Stratton, C., and M. Hammond. 1999. Marital conflict, management skills, parenting style, and early-onset conduct problems: Processes and pathways. *Journal of Child Psychology and Psychiatry* 40: 917–927.

CHAPTER EIGHT

Brooks, R., and S. Goldstein. 2001. *Raising Resilient Children.* Chicago: Contemporary Books.

DeGangi, G. 2000. *Pediatric Disorders of Regulation in Affect and Behavior.* San Diego: Academic Press.

Greene, R. 1998. *The Explosive Child.* New York: HarperCollins.

Haldy, M., and L. Haack. 1995. *Making It Easy: Sensorimotor Activities at Home and School.* San Antonio: Therapy Skills Builders.

Healy, J. 1994. *Your Child's Growing Mind.* New York: Doubleday.

Kranowitz, C., and S. Szklut. 2001. *Answers to Questions Teachers Ask About Sensory Integration.* Las Vegas: Sensory Resources.

Kurcinka, M. S. 1991. *Raising Your Spirited Child: A Guide for Parents Whose Child Is More Intense, Sensitive, Perceptive, Persistent, Energetic.* New York: HarperPerennial.

Salls, J., and J. Bucey. 2003. Self-regulation strategies for middle school students. *OT Practice*, March.

Williams, M., and S. Shellenberger. 1994. *How Does Your Engine Run? Leader's Guide to the Alert Program™ for Self-Regulation.* Albuquerque: Therapy Works.

CHAPTER NINE

Asher, S. 1983. Social competence and peer status: Recent advances and future directions. *Child Development* 54: 1427–1434.

Bundy, A. C. 1989. A comparison of the play skills of normal boys and boys with sensory integration dysfunction. *Occupational Therapy Journal of Research* 9:84–100.

Coie, J. D., K. A. Dodge, and H. Coppotelli. 1982. Dimensions and types of social status: A cross-age perspective. *Developmental Psychology* 18: 557–570.

Crick, N., and K. Dodge. 1994. A review and reformulation of social information-processing mechanisms in children's social adjustment. *Psychological Bulletin* 115 (1): 74–101.

Einon, D. 1985. *Play with a Purpose: Learning Games for Children Six Weeks to Ten Years.* New York: Pantheon Books.

Frankel, F., and B. Wetmore. 1996. *Good Friends Are Hard to Find: Help Your Child Find, Keep, and Make Friends.* London: Perspective Publishing.

Greenspan, S., and J. Salman. 1993. *Playground Politics: Understanding the Emotional Life of Your School-Age Child.* Reading, MA: Addison-Wesley.

Gresham, F. M. 1990. Best practices in social skills training. In *Best Practices in School Psychology*, vol. 2, eds. A. Thomas and J. Grimes, 695–709. Washington, DC: National Association of School Psychologists.

Hartup, W. W. 1992. Peer relations in early and middle childhood. In *Handbook of Social Psychology*, eds. V. B. Van Hasset and M. Hersen, 257–281. New York: Plenum Press.

Hodges, E., M. Boivin, F. Vitero, and W. M. Bukowski. 1999. The power of friendship: Protection against an escalating cycle of peer victimization. *Developmental Psychology* 35: 94–101.

Little, S. 1993. Nonverbal learning disabilities and socioemotional functioning: A review of recent literature. *Journal of Learning Disabilities* 26: 653–675.

Masters, J. C., and W. Furman. 1981. Popularity, individual friendship selection, and specific peer interaction among children. *Developmental Psychology* 17: 344–350.

Nowicki, S., and M. Duke. 1992. *Helping the Child Who Doesn't Fit In.* Atlanta: Peachtree Publishers.

Parfenoff, S. H., and K. R. Gouze. 1992. A look at self-generated adolescent coping strategies in response to major and minor events. Paper presented at the biennial meeting of the Society for Research in Adolescence, Washington, DC.

Thompson, M., C. Grace, and L. Cohen. 2001. *Best Friends, Worst Enemies: Understanding the Social Lives of Children.* New York: Ballantine Books.

CHAPTER TEN

Ayres, J. 1979. *Sensory Integration and the Child.* Los Angeles: Western Psychological Services.

Bundy, A. C., S. J. Lane, and E. A. Murray. 2002. *Sensory Integration: Theory and Practice.* 2nd ed. Philadelphia, PA: F. A. Davis.

Cohn, E. 2001. Parent perspectives of occupational therapy using a sensory integration approach. *American Journal of Occupational Therapy* 55: 285–293.

Cohn, E., and S. A. Cermak. 1998. Including the family perspective in sensory integration outcomes research. *American Journal of Occupational Therapy* 52: 540–546.

Cohn, E., L. J. Miller, and L. Tickle-Degan. 2000. Parental hopes for therapy outcomes: Children with sensory modulation disorders. *American Journal of Occupational Therapy* 54: 36–43.

Coster, W. 1997. Occupation-centered assessment of children. *American Journal of Occupational Therapy* 52: 337–344.

Cummins, R. 1991. Sensory integration and learning disabilities: Ayres' factor analysis reappraised. *Journal of Learning Disabilities* 24: 160–68.

DeGangi, G., R. Sickle, A. Wiener, and E. Kaplan. 1996. Fussy babies: To treat or not to treat? *British Journal of Occupational Therapy* 59: 457–464.

Dunn, W. 2001. The sensations of everyday life: Empirical, theoretical, and pragmatic considerations. *American Journal of Occupational Therapy* 55: 608–620.

Dunn, W., and K. Westman. 1997. The sensory profile: The performance of a national sample of children without disabilities. *American Journal of Occupational Therapy* 51: 25–34.

Ermer, J., and W. Dunn. 1997. The sensory profile: A discriminant analysis of children with and without disabilities. *American Journal of Occupational Therapy* 52: 283–290.

Foodman, A. 1996. ADD and soft signs. *Journal of the American Academy of Child and Adolescent Psychiatry* 35: 841–842.

Frick, S. 2000. An overview of auditory interventions. *Sensory Integration Quarterly*, Spring/Summer: 1–3.

Hanft, B. C., L. J. Miller, and S. J. Lane. 2000. Toward a consensus in terminology in sensory integration theory and practice: Part 3: Observable behaviors: Sensory integration dysfunction. *Sensory Integration Special Interest Section Quarterly* 23 (3).

Hoehn, T. P., and A. A. Baumeister. 1994. A critique of the application of sensory integration therapy to children with learning disabilities. *Journal of Learning Disabilities* 27: 338–350.

Huang, Y., B. Liu, and Y. Wang. 2001. A cross-sectional study of sensory integrative dysfunction among children aged 3–6 in urban Beijing. *Chinese Mental Health Journal* 15:44–46 (English abstract).

Humphries, T., L. Snider, and B. McDougall. 1993. Clinical evaluation of the effectiveness of sensory integrative and perceptual motor therapy in improving sensory integration function in children with learning disabilities. *Occupational Therapy Journal of Research* 13: 163–182.

Humphries, T., M. Wright, B. McDougall, and J. Vertes. 1991. The efficacy of sensory integration therapy for children with learning disability. *Physical and Occupational Therapy in Pediatrics* 10: 1–17.

Humphries, T., M. Wright, L. Snider, and B. McDougall. 1992. A comparison of the effectiveness of sensory integrative therapy and perceptual-motor training in treating children with learning disabilities. *Journal of Developmental and Behavioral Pediatrics* 13: 31–40.

Kaplan, B. J., H. J. Polatajiko, B. N. Wilson, and P. D. Faris. 1993. Reexamination of sensory integration treatment: A combination of two efficacy studies. *Journal of Learning Disabilities* 26: 342–347.

Lane, S. J., L. J. Miller, and B. E. Hanft. 2000. Toward a consensus in terminology in sensory integration theory and practice: Part 2: Sensory integration patterns of function and dysfunction. *Sensory Integration Special Interest Section Quarterly* 23 (2).

Mangeot, S. D., L. J. Miller, D. N. McIntosh, J. McGrath-Clarke, J. Simon, R. J. Hagerman, and E. Goldson. 2001. Sensory modulation dysfunction in children with attention deficit hyperactivity disorder. *Developmental Medicine and Child Neurology* 43: 399–406.

May-Benson, T. A. 1997. Sensory processing in children with ADD and sensory integrative dysfunction: A comparison with typical peers on a sensory history. Unpublished paper. Occupational Therapy Associates, Watertown, MA.

McIntosh, D. N., L. J. Miller, V. Shyu, and R. Hagerman, 1999. Sensory modulation disruption, electrodermal responses, and functional behaviors. *Developmental Medicine and Child Neurology* 41: 608–615.

Miller, L. J. 2003. Empirical evidence related to therapies for sensory processing impairments. *Communique* 31 (5): 34–37.

Miller, L. J., and S. J. Lane, 2000. Toward a consensus in terminology in sensory integration theory and practice: Part 1: Taxonomy of neurophysiological processes. *Sensory Integration Special Interest Section Quarterly* 23 (1).

Mulligan, S. 1996. An analysis of score patterns of children with attention disorders on the Sensory Integration and Praxis Tests. *American Journal of Occupational Therapy* 50: 647–654.

Ottenbacher, K. 1982. Sensory integration therapy: Affect or effect. *American Journal of Occupational Therapy* 36: 571–578.

Ottenbacher, K., and M. A. Short. 1985. Sensory integration dysfunction: A review of theory and treatment. *Developmental and Behavioral Pediatrics* 6: 287–329.

Parham, D. L. 1998. The relationship of sensory integration development to achievement in elementary students: Four-year longitudinal patterns. *Occupational Therapy Journal of Research* 18: 105–127.

Polatajiko, H. J., B. J. Kaplan, and B. N. Wilson, 1992. Sensory integration treatment for children with learning disabilities: Its status 20 years later. *Occupational Therapy Journal of Research* 12: 323–341.

Polatajiko, H. J., M. Law, L. J. Miller, R. Schaffer, and J. Macnah. 1991. The effect of a sensory integration program on academic achievement, motor performance, and self-esteem in children identified as learning disabled: Results of a clinical trial. *Occupational Therapy Journal of Research* 11: 155–176.

Ren, G., Y. Wang, and B. Gu, 1999. Clinical effect of sensory integrative therapy on 481 children. *Chinese Mental Health Journal* 13: 353–355 (English abstract).

Ren, G., Y. Wang, B. Gu, and Y. Shen. 1995. Investigation of the prevalence of sensory integrative dysfunction in 1994 school children in a Beijing urban area. *Chinese Mental Health Journal* 9: 70–73 (English abstract).

Ren, G., Y. Wang, B. Gu, and R. Zhu. 1995. Clinical efficacy of sensory integrative therapy. *Chinese Mental Health Journal* 9: 74–76 (English abstract).

Stepp-Gilbert, E. 1988. Sensory integration dysfunction. *Issues in Comprehensive Pediatric Nursing* 11: 313–318.

Vargas, S., and G. Camilli. 1999. A meta-analysis of research on sensory integration treatment. *American Journal of Occupational Therapy* 53: 189–198.

Werry, J. S., R. Scaletti, and F. Mills. 1990. Sensory integration and teacher-judged learning problems: A controlled intervention trial. *Journal of Pediatrics and Child Health* 26 (1): 31–35.

Wilson, B. N., B. J. Kaplan, S. Fellowes, C. Gruchy, and P. Faris. 1992. The efficacy of sensory integration treatment compared to tutoring. *Physical and Occupational Therapy in Pediatrics* 12: 1–36.

EPILOGUE

Goleman, D. 1995. *Emotional Intelligence*. New York: Bantam Books.

Kranowitz, C. 1998. *The Out-of-Sync Child: Recognizing and Coping with Sensory Integration Dysfunction*. New York: Perigee.

Index

changing attitudes toward
children, 145–146
changing behavioral problems,
with rewards and
punishments, 11
Chess, Stella, 107
child development
connections with brain-
behavior relationship theory,
xv, 97–111
psychological research on, xiv
child rearing, empathic,
respectful approach to, xvii
childhood, 81
the children
Ben, xiii, xvi, 16–18, 44,
62–63, 109, 128, 130, 136,
143–144, 146–147, 150,
155–156, 160, 162, 182,
190, 197, 202–204,
209–211, 224, 233–235
Britanny, 97
building strong relationships
with, 139–140
celebrating the strengths of
each, 223
Cody, 188–189
David, 75–80, 144, 183–187
desire for approval, xiv, 20
Ella, 151–152
Evan, xiii, xvi, 1–24, 27, 38,
45, 113, 127–128, 134, 136,
137–139, 149, 156, 162,
190, 205–206, 224–233
helping them help themselves,
112–135
increasing satisfaction in,
120–122

James, 206–207
Jessica, 65
John, 142–143, 145, 190,
200–201
Jorge, 71–75, 80, 170–171,
187–188
learning from, 21–22
Marcus, 166–167
Mike, 21, 112, 115–116,
132–134
numbers affected by sensory
processing problems, 215
outgrowing sensory processing
problems, 218–219
Patty, 91–93
providing a stable home
environment for, 136–161
rebuilding the brains of,
122–124
Sally, 44
Sarah, 31
Stephen, 193–194
Thomas, 167–168, 194–195
Tony, 65–66, 68–71, 80
unhappiness of, 3–4, 7, 11–12,
23
vulnerabilities of, 23
whose senses have failed them,
xiii
chilling-out, 147–148, 158
Cicchetti, Dante, 110
classroom, sensory solutions in,
170–172
clinical psychology, xiii–xv
and blaming, xiii–xiv
early detection of phenomena
by, 12
traditional teachings of, xiii